The Revised

LATIN PRIMER

By

Benjamin Hall Kennedy, DD

Revised & Updated
Simon Wallenberg Press

© 2007 Simon Wallenberg ISBN 1-84356-029-1
The Revised Latin Primer
Benjamin Hall Kennedy

This is an updated version of The Revised Latin Primer
With Chapters from the Public School Latin Primer and
Public School Latin Grammar. Rearranged, Revised and
improved by the Simon Wallenburg Press.

Revised Latin Primer - Eight Edition Published London
1911 -This Edition Revised Improved & Enlarged 2007

A Wallenberg Grammar Book

Published by the Simon Wallenberg Press
wallenberg.press@gmail.com

Printed on acid-free paper.

Benjamin Hall Kennedy
(November 6, 1804 – April 6, 1880)

Was an English scholar. He was born at Summer Hill, near
Birmingham, the eldest son of Rann Kennedy (1772–1851),
of a branch of the Ayrshire family which had settled in Staf-
fordshire.

Rann was a scholar and man of letters, several of whose sons
rose to distinction. Benjamin was educated at Shrewsbury
School, and St John's College, Cambridge. After a brilliant
university career he was elected fellow and classical lecturer
of St John's College in 1828. Two years later he became an
assistant master at Harrow, whence he went to Shrewsbury
as headmaster in 1836. He retained this post until 1866, the
thirty years being marked by a long series of successes for
his pupils, chiefly in classics.

When he retired from Shrewsbury a large collection was
made, and was used partly on new school buildings and
partly on the founding of a Latin professorship at Cambridge. The first holders were both Kennedy's old pupils,
HAJ Munro and JEB Mayor. In 1867, Kennedy was elected
Regius Professor of Greek at Cambridge and canon of Ely
Cathedral.

From 1870 to 1880 he was a member of the committee for
the revision of the New Testament. He supported the admission of women to university, and took a prominent part in the
establishment of Newnham and Girton colleges.

In politics, he had liberal sympathies. Among a number of
classical school-books published by him are two, a Public
School Latin Primer and Public School Latin Grammar,

which were for long in use in nearly all English schools. He died near Torquay.

His other chief works are: Sophocles, Oedipus Tyrannus (2nd ed., 1885), Aristophanes, Birds (1874); Aeschylus, Agamemnon (2nd ed1882), with introduction, metrical translation and notes; a commentary on Virgil (3rd ed., 1881); and a translation of Plato, Theaetetus (1881).

He contributed largely to the collection known as Sabrinae Corolla, and published a collection of verse in Greek, Latin and English under the title of Between Whiles (2nd ed., 1882), with many autobiographical details.

Kennedy's Books remain popular right up to the present day for students of the Latin Language.

All of Benjamin hall Kennedy's language Books in their Revised and updated editions are published by the Simon Wallenberg Press.

PREFACE

THIS BOOK is a complete revision of the Public School Latin Primer.

The report of the Public School Commission of 1862 having recommended the use of a common Latin Grammar in Public Schools, the Head Masters of the Schools included in that Commission resolved to adopt my Elementary Latin Grammar, which had for some years been widely used, as the basis of such a common Grammar, and the Public School Latin Primer, prepared in accordance with that resolution, was published with their sanction in the year 1866.

During the period which has since elapsed, various improvements have from time to time occurred to me or been suggested by others. But, looking at the joint authority under which the Primer was issued, I did not feel myself free to introduce into it the alterations which under other circumstances I should have made. When, however, I found that a revision of the Primer was generally desired, and when, after communication with the Conference of Head Masters, I found myself in a position to act in the matter of revision upon my own responsibility, I gladly entered upon the work of which the present Revised Primer is the result. My first step was to collect as widely as possible from Masters of Public and Private Schools opinions with regard to the objections to the Primer as it stood, and the nature and extent of the changes which teachers of experience deemed to be desirable. With the kind and generous aid of my old pupils and friends Mr. Hallam, of Harrow, and Mr. Page, of Charterhouse, and by the courtesy of many teachers who have communicated with me either directly or through them, I have been enabled to obtain a number of valuable suggestions on these points.

The aim which I have kept steadily in view in this revision of the Primer has been that the book should be suitable both for beginners and for all boys up to the Fifth Form in Public Schools.

The greatest care has been taken to make the arrangement in respect of form as clear and plain as possible. For this purpose I have (1) brought into the text under the appropriate headings the matter which in the original Primer is contained in Appendix I.; (2) omitted such technical terms as seemed to be reasonably open to objection.

The Declension of Substantives and Adjectives has been arranged upon the 'Stem' principle, and the words are classed as far as possible in accordance with the latest results of the comparative study of Latin and the related languages, especially the ancient Italian dialects. The old order of the Declensions has, after careful consideration, been retained. In a text-book of this kind there is an obvious advantage in keeping, wherever it is possible, a popular and well-understood system, and I believe that the old order of Declension is, from a purely philological point of view, wholly unobjectionable. With regard to Verbs, I have adhered in the Paradigms to the arrangement of the four Conjugations, as I am satisfied that an alteration would involve such inconvenience to teacher and learner as would far outweigh any possible gain in scientific accuracy.

To meet a general wish, I have prefixed to the Accidence a chapter on Letters and Laws of Sound. I desire it to be understood that this chapter is placed at the beginning of the book because that seemed to me to .be the most natural and, for purposes of reference, the most convenient position for it—and not from any intention that it should necessarily be learnt as a whole at the outset.

I have purposely refrained from any attempt to give fixed rules for the pronunciation of Latin, because in the present stage of the investigation of that subject, such rules could be only of a provisional kind. For the results which have so far been reached I would refer to the small pamphlet lately issued by the Cambridge Philological Society.

In order to simplify as far as possible the marking of quantity, I have marked the quantity as a rule only on the long vowels. In this book vowels which have no mark of quantity are generally to be taken as short, and the short quantity is marked only where it seems especially necessary to guard against mistake.

The memorial lines on Gender are placed in an appendix instead of being, as in the original Primer, included in the text.

Throughout the book—except in a few cases in the chapter on Letters and Laws of Sound, where Word-formation, not Grammar or meaning, is being dealt with—Latin words are immediately followed by their translation in English.

Some of these improvements of course involve additional printed matter, but the addition is rather in the apparent size of the book than in the actual matter to be learnt.

In conclusion I offer my cordial thanks to many teachers, Head Masters and Assistant Masters in Public Schools, and also Masters of Private Schools (among whom I must mention especially the Rev. E. D. Stone and Mr. C. S. Jerram) for the assistance which they have directly and indirectly rendered to me by communication and correspondence.

Of the special co-operation which has been given throughout by Mr. Page and Mr. Hallam I have already spoken. For many reasons their constant help has been to me invaluable.

During the progress of the work I have received criticisms on many points of philology and grammar from my friends Dr. Peile, Master of Christ's College, and Professor J. E. B. Mayor, which, last, but not least, I desire gratefully to acknowledge.

B. H. KENNEDY.

The Elms, Cambridge:
  May 1888.

PREFACE TO THE SEVENTH EDITION.

In bringing out the present edition the Editors have taken the opportunity to make some improvements in points of detail which have been suggested to them by various Teachers. They desire in particular to thank Mr. Frank Ritchie for several criticisms and suggestions.

CONTENTS

LATIN PRIMER.

—•◇•—

1   THE LATIN LANGUAGE.

LATIN was the dialect of the Latini, or people of Latium in Italy.
It was spoken by the ancient Romans, and, as their poets and
prose-writers all used this dialect, the language was called Latin,
not Roman.

Latin belongs to the family of languages known as Indo-
European, or Aryan; the other languages of this family are, in
Asia, the Indian, which includes Sanskrit, and the Iranian; in
Europe, the Keltic, the Teutonic, the Greek, the Slavonic, and
the Lettic. The imperial power of Rome made Latin the general
speech of Western Europe, and from it are derived the modern
Italian, French, Spanish, Portuguese, and Wallachian, hence
called Romance languages.

> *Note.*—In England, after its conquest by the Angles and Saxons,
> a branch of the Teutonic language, called Anglo-Saxon, or old
> English, was spoken. From about the tenth century, and especially
> after the Norman Conquest (1066 A.D.), this became mixed with
> Norman French, a Romance dialect, an offshoot of Latin. After the
> revival of learning in the sixteenth century, a large number of words
> were brought into English direct from Latin, and more have been
> added since, so that to understand the English language thoroughly
> it is necessary to have a knowledge of Latin.

The influence of Greek civilisation on Latin was very great;
it was chiefly exerted at two distinct eras. The first of these
began about 550 B.C., through the commerce of the Romans
with the Greek colonies in Southern Italy. The second may be

dated from the third century B.C., when literary activity began at Rome. This influence was further developed through the conquest of Greece by Rome, which was completed 146 B.C.

All Latin literature, except the satiric writings of Horace, Persius, and Juvenal, is formed on Greek models. The earliest specimens of Latin we possess are inscriptions, laws, annals, and fragments of songs.

The credit of authorship is first ascribed to Livius Andronicus, who is said to have exhibited plays at Rome 240 B.C. The works of the poets who followed soon after this date have mostly perished, except the comedies of Plautus and Terence, about 200 to 140 B.C., and a prose fragment of the elder Cato.

The ages regarded as classical may be said to begin about 80 B.C., lasting about 200 years.

The so-called Golden Age ended with the death of Augustus, A.D. 14, when the Silver Age began, ending about 120 A.D. The authors most studied are—in prose, Cicero, Caesar, Livy, Tacitus; in poetry, Lucretius, Vergil, Horace, Ovid, and Juvenal.

LETTERS AND LAWS OF SOUND.

2   **The Latin Alphabet.**—The Latin Alphabet contains twenty-three letters, with the following signs :—

A B C D E F G H I (J) K L M N O P Q R S T U (V) X Y Z
a b c d e f g h i (j) k l m n o p q r s t u (v) x y z

> *Note.*—In early times C was written to represent the sounds of both C and G, which were probably not clearly distinguished in speaking. Afterwards G was made out of C, and K becoming superfluous went out of use. Y and Z were added in Cicero's time, being borrowed direct from the Greek alphabet, but they are only found in words taken from the Greek.

The letters are divided into :

1. **Vowels** or **Sonants** (sounding by themselves) ;
2. **Consonants** (sounding with a vowel).

Vowels.

3 The pure vowels are **a**, **e**, **o**; **i** and **u** are classed as vowels and also as semi-consonants, because they have both vowel and consonant sound.

The most open sound is **a**; the closest sharp sound is **i**; and the closest flat sound is **u**; **e** is intermediate between **a** and **i**, and **o** is intermediate between **a** and **u**.

a
e **o**
i **u**

y is always a vowel, as in lyra, and was sounded as French *u*.

4 **Quantity of Vowels.**—Each of the five vowels can be either short or long: short when pronounced quickly, like English **a** in *man*; long when the voice dwells on the sound, as in *far*. A short vowel is distinguished by the sign ˘, a long one by the sign ¯: ămō. Thus the five vowels stand for ten different sounds:

ă, ā, ĕ, ē, ĭ, ī, ŏ, ō, ŭ, ū.

There were no doubt many finer shades of sound for each vowel, which cannot be exactly ascertained, but the following five words may give an approximate idea of their pronunciation.

quĭnīne, dĕmēsne, păpā, prŏpōse, Zŭlū.

Note.—A vowel before two consonants is said to be long 'by position.' A vowel before another vowel, or before h followed by a vowel, is nearly always short.

5 **Diphthongs.**—A Diphthong (double sound) is formed by two vowels meeting in one syllable. The diphthongs commonly found in Latin are **ae**, **oe**, **au**; more rarely **eu**: Caesar, moenia, laus, heu.

In the oldest Latin there were six diphthongs: ai, au, ei, eu, oi, ou. Of these, ai passes in classical Latin into ae, mensae for mensai; au remains unchanged; ei is found in old inscriptions, but in the literary language its place is taken by ē or by ī, as in dīco, except in the exclamation ei; eu is found in ceu, heu, neu, seu, and in many words of Greek origin; oi passes into oe, and sometimes into later u; poena, punio; ou becomes ū, as in dūco.

The diphthongs are always long.

CONSONANTS.

6   I. MUTES (closed sounds), formed by complete closure of the mouth passage; the sound being the explosion heard when the stoppage is removed.   They are:

(i.) **Gutturals** (throat sounds)   {Hard, c, (k), qu. Soft, g.

(ii.) **Dentals** (teeth sounds)   {Hard, t. Soft, d.

(iii.) **Labials** (lip sounds)   {Hard, p. Soft, b.

II. SPIRANTS (open sounds), formed by the friction of the breath in the mouth passage when partially closed:

(i.) **The Palatal Spirant, j** (sounded as y).

(ii.) **The Dental Spirant or Sibilant, s.**

(iii.) **The Labio-Dental Spirant, f.**

(iv.) **The Labial Spirant, v** (sounded as w).

(v.) **The Spirant, h.**

III. SEMI-CONSONANTS:

(i.) **Consonant i** (written **j**), **consonant u** (written **v**).

(ii.) **Nasals, n, m.**

(iii.) **Liquids, l, r.**

x is really a double letter, standing for **cs, gs.**

y, z and the three Greek aspirates, **ch, ph, th,** are only found in Greek words, as zōna, chlamys, phalanx, theātrum.

Note.—The spirants j and v, though distinct in the parent language, cannot be separated in Latin from consonant i and u.

7 Pronunciation of Consonants.—The guttural mutes, c, g, are sounded before all vowels, as in English, *can, go*; never as in *cease, gem*; **k** is only found in a few words, and is sounded as in English : kalendae.

The dental mutes, **t, d,** are sounded nearly as in English, but **t** must never be pronounced as *sh*; natio is not like English *nation* (nashun).

The labial mutes, **p, b,** as in English.

s always hard, as in English *sing*, but in the oldest Latin, **s** between two vowels was soft as in *rise*. This soft **s** or **z** afterwards became **r**, as in arbores for arboses.

Consonant **i** and **u** have the sound of *y, w,* in *ye, we*.

h is a strong breathing at the beginning of a word, but between two vowels very faintly sounded.

l as in English ; **r** more strongly trilled than English *r*.

n and **m** as in English ; the guttural nasal **ng**, though written **n**, was sounded like *ng* in *sing* or *n* in *sink* : inquam was sounded ing-quam.

Table of Consonants.

	Mutes.		Spirants.		Semi-Consonants.	
	Hard (tenues).	Soft (mediae).	Hard (tenues).	Soft (mediae).	Nasal.	Liquid.
Guttural	c, (k), qu	g	h		ng	
Palatal				j (y)		
Lingual						r, l
Dental	t	d	s		n	
Labio-dental			f			
Labial	p	b		v (w)	m	

8 **Syllables.**—A syllable consists of one or more letters which can be sounded with a single accent or tone of the voice : ī-lex.

When a consonant comes between two vowels, it belongs to the same syllable as the vowel which follows it : pă-ter.

When two or more consonants come between two vowels, they belong to the vowel which follows them if they are letters which can come together at the beginning of a word : pa-tres, a-stra. In an-nus one n belongs to each syllable, because double n cannot begin a word. So men-sa, vic-trix.

A syllable ending in a vowel is an open syllable.

A syllable ending in a consonant is a closed syllable.

A syllable is long or short according as its vowel is long or short, either by nature or position.

> *Note.*—The last syllable of a word is called ultimate ; the last but one penultimate ; the last but two ante-penultimate.

9 **Accent.**—The accent or tone falls on some one syllable in every word. The accented syllable was pronounced with greater force and also in a higher key than the other syllables. In Latin the rule is to throw the accent back ; therefore in words of two or more syllables, the last syllable is never accented.

In words of more than two syllables the accent always falls on the last but one (penultimate), if it is long.

If the penultimate is short, the accent falls on the last but two (ante-penultimate).

The accents are not usually printed in Latin.

10   Vowel Change.

I. Change in Accented Syllables.

 1. Original e may become i: simul (cf. semel), venia (cf. vindex).

 2. e becomes o before l : soluo (se-luo) ; or in connexion with u : nouos (for neuos), douco (later duco).

 3. i becomes e before r : sero (for siso).

 4. o sometimes becomes u : huc (for ho-ce).

11 II. **Change in Unaccented Syllables.**

(A) In final syllables :

1. o becomes u : corpus (stem corpos-).
2. i becomes e : mare (stem mari-), or is lost altogether :
animal (for animale, stem animali-).

(B) In medial syllables the vowel is commonly affected by the
next consonant :

1. e appears before r : cineres (cinis), caperis (capio).
2. u appears before l or a labial : as in cultus (colo),
epistula (earlier epistola). But when i or e precedes,
the vowel remains o : as filiolus, alveolus.
3. i appears before any other single consonant : as in
meritus, monitus (moneo). (For exception see **13**.)

12 (C) **In Compounds :**

Here the principle is the same, and generally the rules are
the same as in (B), but the examples are much more numerous.

a to e in closed syllables and before r : consecro from sacer ;
descendo from scando ; tradere from dare.

a to i in most open syllables and before **ng** : difficilis from
facilis ; attingo from tango.

a to u or i before labials : occŭpo and accipio from capio ;
and before l : insulto, insilio, from salto, salio.

e to i often in open syllables, but never before r : diligo from
lego ; but fero, aufero.

ae to ī : collīdo from laedo.

au to ū or ō : inclūdo from claudo ; explōdo from plaudo.

o and u are generally unchanged in compounds.

Note.—There is a vowel variation often seen in Latin flexion
which is not due to change in the Latin language itself, but came
down to it from the Indo-European language. Thus the same noun
can have two or more Stems, as homo; older stem **homon-**, later
weak stem, **homin-** ; **agmen-, agmin-** ; **pater, patr-** ; **genus-**
(orig. **genos**), **gener-.**

In these words the vowel of the strong stem is preserved in the
Nom. Sing., while the weak stem appears in the other cases.

13 Vowel Assimilation and Dissimilation.—The vowels of two following syllables tend to become alike in sound : vegeo, vegetus (vigeo), pupugi (for pepugi), nihil (for ne-hil), mihi, tibi.

On the other hand, two vowels coming together are sometimes dissimilated : ii becomes ie in pietas, societas, abietis.

14 Vowel Contraction.—When two similar vowels are separated by consonant i or u, or by h, they commonly throw out the letter between them, and unite in a long vowel : rēs is contracted from re-i-es, nēmo from ne-h-emo, nīl from ni-h-il, audisse from audivisse.

Two dissimilar vowels sometimes unite in the same manner : amāre from ama-i-ere ; amō from ama-i-o ; amāsti from ama-v-isti.

Two vowels placed next each other often contract : dēgo from de-ago ; nullus from ne-ullus ; prōmo from pro-emo.

15 Syncope.—Dropping of an unaccented vowel between two consonants : dextra for dextera ; valde for valide.   It often takes place in compounds : calfacio for calefacio.   The vowel of the reduplicating syllable sometimes drops ; reppuli for repepuli.

> *Note.*—Sometimes when any one of the letters l, r, m, or n follows a consonant, a vowel not found in the stem springs up before it because of the semi-vocalic character of the sound ; ager, stem agro- ; populus, original stem poplo- ; asinus (asno-) ; volumus (contrast vul-tis).

16

Apocope.—Dropping of a final vowel : e is dropped in hic for hi-ce ; quin for qui-ne ; dic for dice ; i falls off in ut for uti, quot, tot (totidem).

17 Changes of Quantity.—A vowel generally shortens before another vowel : thus rēi became rĕi.   A long vowel often becomes short through effect of the accent on the preceding or following syllable : jūro becomes pérjŭro, afterwards weakening to pējĕro ; lūcerna from lūceo.   In flexional endings, a vowel originally final is sometimes shortened.   But when a final consonant is lost (as final d in the ablative), the length of the vowel seems to be preserved : Gnaeō (earlier Gnaivōd).

Vowel lengthening is often due to Compensation.   When two consonants follow an accented vowel the first of the two is often dropped, and the vowel lengthened, so that the syllable keeps its length ; hōc for hod-ce ; nīdus for nisdus (English *nest*).

18

Consonant Change.

Consonants at the beginning of a word.—Two mute consonants at the beginning of a word were avoided. Thus we find locus for original stlocus, tilia for ptilia. Sometimes a spirant preceding a mute is dropped : caveo for scaveo, but generally it is retained : scando, sterno, spēro. A mute followed by a liquid is generally unchanged : as cresco, tres, plaudo ; but g before n is lost in nōtus for gnotus (cf. ignōtus), and in nōdus, *knot*. Two spirants remain : flos, frons ; but **sm** becomes **m**, as in mīrus, memor ; **sn** becomes **n** in nix (*snow*), nŭrus (Old English snoru), *daughter-in-law* ; **sv** sometimes remains : suādeo ; sometimes **v** is lost : salum (*swell*), sibi (cf. su-us).

19 Consonants in the middle of a word.—In the middle of a word if two consonants come next each other which cannot be easily sounded together, either one drops out, quālus for quas-lus, *basket*, or one is assimilated to the other, as in sella for sedla, *a seat*. A mute often drops out before a nasal or liquid, with lengthening of the preceding vowel, as in exāmen for exagmen.

Other cases in which a letter is dropped are quintus for older quinctus ; ascribo for ad-scribo ; asporto for abs-porto ; bimestris from stem bi-menstri- ; jūdex from jus-dic-.

20 Consonant Assimilation is of two kinds :

(*a*) Complete Assimilation, when the first letter becomes the same as the following one :

Assimilation of mute to semi-vowel : alloquor for ad-loquor ; arrogo for ad-rogo ; summus for supmus (supremus).

Mute to spirant : assentio for ad-sentio, offero for ob-fero.

Mute to mute : suggero for sub-gero ; accido for ad-cado ; succumbo for sub-cumbo.

Spirant to spirant : differo for dis-fero.

(*b*) Partial assimilation, when the first letter changes to one which combines more easily with the following one.

A soft mute becomes hard before another hard sound : rexi (rec-si), rectum from rego ; scripsi, scriptum, from scribo.

m becomes **n** (**ng**) before a guttural and **n** before a dental :

congruo (sounded cong-gruo), condūco, consto. n becomes m before a labial : impotens, imbibo. A hard mute becomes soft between vowels or between a vowel and a semi-vowel : trīginta for tricenta ; publĭcus, stem poplico-.

> *Note.*—tt and dt change to ss : hence the supines in -sum and past participles in -sus are formed : defend-to- becomes defensso-, defensum ; claudto-, clausso-, clausum, pat-to- becomes passo-, passus.
>
> Occasionally a following consonant is assimilated to the preceding one : collum for colsum ; ferre for ferse.

Dissimilation is seen in caeruleus from caelum, meridies for medidies ; and in Adjectives in -aris and -alis, familiāris, naturālis.

s (when soft) between two vowels always changes to r : flōres, honōres, from flōs, hŏnōs ; quaeso becomes quaero.

21   Metathesis.—Interchange of position between a vowel and semi-vowel in the same syllable. This is chiefly seen in the case of r : ter, trēs ; sperno, sprēvi ; tĕro, trīvi.

> *Note.*—When the vowel becomes the last letter of the stem by this change of position, it is always lengthened.

22   Consonants at the end of a word.—A Latin word never ends in a double consonant : mell-, farr-, become mel, far.

A dental drops off after a guttural : lac, from stem lact-.

The only exceptions are a labial mute or nasal followed by s : urbs, stirps, dens, hiems (usually written hiemps).

c or g followed by s becomes x : dux, rex.

d falls off in cor, stem cord-, and in the ablative singular extra(d), intra(d).

n regularly falls off in the nominative of the n-stems : leo.

> *Note.*—Both m and n were very lightly sounded at the end of a word, and a syllable ending in m is sometimes elided before a vowel : ' animum advertere.' This elision takes place regularly in poetry. Final d and t were also lightly sounded and are sometimes interchanged :. haud, haut.

23   Dropping of Syllables.—When two syllables beginning with the same letter come together in the middle of a word, the first one is sometimes dropped. Thus veneni-ficium becomes veneficium, consuetitudo consuetudo.

FLEXION.

24 FLEXION is a change made in the form of a word to show differences of meaning and use.

The **Stem** is the simplest form of a word in any language before it undergoes changes of Flexion.

The **Character** is the final letter of the Stem.

The **Root** is the primitive element which the word has in common with kindred words in the same or in other languages. Every word has a Stem and a Root. They may be the same, but more often the Stem is formed from the Root. Thus in agitāre, **agita-** is the Stem and **a** the Stem-Character, but **ag-** is the Root, as shown by other words, **ag**ere, **ag**men, **ag**ilis.

> *Note 1.*—A language which expresses changes of meaning chiefly by Flexion, and makes little use of help-words, is called synthetic. Latin is a synthetic language. A language which has little Flexion and uses many help-words is called analytic. English as now spoken is an analytic language. In analytic languages the place of the flexional endings is often supplied by prepositions used with nouns: Caesăris, *of Caesar*; by auxiliaries used with verbs: agitur, *it is being done*. Analytic languages also use the article: rex, *a king*, or *the king*; and they use pronouns with verbs: ăgo, *I do*.

> *Note 2.*—Flexion sometimes takes place by letter-change in the Root-syllable, **ag**ĭ-mus, **ēg**ĭ-mus, or by an addition before it, which is called a Prefix, as **ce**-cĭn-i from căno. Most frequently, however, it consists in an addition made after the Stem, which is called a Suffix. In agita**re**, **-re** is a Suffix, and is also the ending; in agitarē**mus**, a second Suffix, **-mus**, is added and becomes the ending.

25

PARTS OF SPEECH.

Words are divided into :

I. Nouns : which are of three kinds :

Substantives,* names of persons, places, or things :
Caesar, *Caesar* ; **Rōma,** *Rome* ; **sōl,** *sun* ; **virtūs,** *virtue.*

Adjectives, which express the qualities of Substantives :
Roma **antīqua,** *ancient Rome* ; sol **clārus,** *the bright sun.*

Pronouns, which stand for a Substantive or Adjective :
ego, *I* ; **ille,** *that, he* ; **meus,** *my, mine.*

II. Verbs : which express an action or state :
Sol **dat** lūcem, *the sun gives light* ; Roma **manet,** *Rome remains.*

III. Particles : which are of four kinds :

Adverbs, which qualify and limit Verbs, Adjectives, and sometimes other Adverbs :
Roma **diu** flōruit ; nunc **minus** potens est.
Rome flourished long ; now it is less powerful.

Prepositions, which denote the relation of a Noun to other words in the sentence :
Per Romam erro, *I wander through Rome.*

Conjunctions, which connect words, phrases, and sentences :
Caelum suspicio **ut** lūnam **et** sīdera videam.
I look up to the sky that I may see the moon and stars.

Interjections : words of exclamation : **heu, ēheu,** *alas !*

---

* In this book the word Noun is often used for Noun Substantive,

The Parts of Speech are therefore eight :

(1) **Substantives**	(5) **Adverbs**
(2) **Adjectives**	(6) **Prepositions**
(3) **Pronouns**	(7) **Conjunctions**
(4) **Verbs**	(8) **Interjections**
Which have Flexion.	Which are without Flexion except the comparison of Adverbs.

26 The flexion of Nouns is called Declension ; that of Verbs, Conjugation.

There is no Article in Latin. Lux may stand for *a light, the light,* or simply *light.*

27 Substantives are (*a*) Concrete : vir, *man* ; mensa, *table.* (*b*) Abstract : virtūs, *virtue.* Proper names are names of persons or places : Caesar, Roma. A Collective Substantive includes many persons or things of the same kind : turba, *crowd.*

Numerals are words which express Number. They are Adjectives, as unus, *one* ; duo, *two* ; or Adverbs, as semel, *once* ; bis, *twice.*

DECLENSION.

28 Declension is the change of form which Nouns undergo to show changes of **Number** and **Case.**

29 The NUMBERS are two :

Singular for one person or thing : mensa, *a table* ; gens, *a nation.*

Plural for more than one : mensae, *tables* ; gentēs, *nations.*

30 **Case** is the form which a Noun takes to show its relation to other words in the sentence.

The CASES are six :

Nominative, the Subject Case, answering the question Who ? or What ?

Vocative, the Case of one addressed.

Accusative, the Object Case, answering the question Whom ? or What ?

Genitive, answering the question Of whom ? or Of what ?

Dative, answering the question To whom ? or To what ?

Ablative, answering the question From whom ? or From what ?

Examples of the cases :

Nominative.	Sol lūcet,	*the sun shines.*
Vocative.	Sol *or* o sol,	*o sun.*
Accusative.	Sōlem lucēre video,	*I see the sun shine.*
Genitive.	Solis lux,	*the sun's light,* or *the light of the sun.*
Dative.	Solī lux addĭtur,	*light is added to the sun.*
Ablative.	Solĕ lux ēdĭtur,	*light issues from the sun.*

Note 1.—The dative is also rendered *for* in English : Senātus urbi consulit, *the Senate consults for the city.*

Note 2.—The ablative is rendered by many English prepositions besides *from* : *in, by, with.* To express the person by whom an action is done, the ablative is used with the preposition a, ab : Remus a Rōmulo interfectus est, *Remus was slain by Romulus.* To express the instrument with which an action is done, the ablative is used alone : Remus gladiō interfectus est, *Remus was slain with* (or *by*) *a sword.*

Note 8.—In ancient Latin there were two more cases, the Instrumental answering the question With what ? and the Locative answering the question Where ? The use of the Instrumental passed entirely to the ablative. But the Locative is often found in classical literature : humĭ, *on the ground* ; Romae, *at Rome* ; Athēnĭs, *at Athens.*

RULES OF GENDER.

31 The Genders are three :

1, Masculine ; 2, Feminine ; 8, Neuter (neutrum, *neither of the two*).

Gender is shown by the form of a word and by its meaning.

(A) Form :

(*a*) Masculine are most Substantives in -us of the Second and Fourth Declensions, and those in -er of the Second Declension.

(*b*) Feminine are nearly all Substantives in -a of the First Declension and in -es of the Fifth Declension.

(*c*) Neuter are Substantives in **-um** of the Second Declension, in **-u** of the Fourth Declension, and indeclinable nouns, including the infinitive verb-noun.

For the third declension no general rule can be given.

(B) Meaning :

(*a*) Masculine are all names of men, gods, months, and winds; also of most rivers and mountains: Rōmulus, Mars, Octōber, Boreās, *north wind*, Tiberis, Olympus. ·

> Exceptions : Some mountains and a few rivers ending in **-a** or **-e** are feminine : Allia, Lēthē, Aetna, Rhodopē, Alpēs (plur.); neuter, Pēlion, Soractĕ.

(*b*) Feminine are all names of women, goddesses, islands; and of most countries, cities, and trees : Cornēlia, Jūno, Lesbos, Asia, Roma, pīnus, *pine*.

> Exceptions : Countries ending in **-um**, neuter; Latium ; Pontus, masculine. Cities with plur. form in **-i** are masc. : Coriŏli, Delphi; those in **-um, -on, -a** (plur.) are neuter : Tarentum, Ilion, Arbēla.
>
> *Note 1.*—In the early ages people imagined natural objects as living beings, and made them masculine or feminine, according to their notions of their qualities : ventus, *wind*, fluvius, *river*, mons, *mountain*, masculine ;—regio, *country*, urbs, *city*, arbor, *tree*, feminine ; and words belonging to these classes took the same genders.
>
> *Note 2.*—Many **o-** Stems masc. (called Mobilia) have a corresponding form in **-a** feminine :

> filius, *son.*   deus, *god.*   arbĭter ⎫ *umpire.*
> filia, *daughter.*   dea, *goddess.*   arbitra ⎭

Other corresponding forms are used : rex, *king*, rēgīna, *queen* ; victor, victrix, *conqueror* ; nepōs, *grandson*, neptis, *granddaughter* ; socer, socrus, *father-, mother-in-law*.

> *Note 3.*—Nouns which include both masculine and feminine are said to be of common gender : sacerdōs, *priest* or *priestess*, vātēs, *seer*, parens, *parent*, dux, *leader*, comes, *companion*, cīvis, *citizen*, custōs, *guardian*, jūdex, *judge*, hēres, *heir*, āles, *bird*, canis, *dog*, serpens, *serpent*, tĭgris, *tiger*.

Many names of animals, though used of both sexes, have (in grammar) only one gender; they are called Epicene : aquĭla, *eagle*, fem.; lepus, *hare*, masc.; passer, *sparrow*, masc.

(For Memorial Lines on Gender, see Appendix IV.)

32   DECLENSION OF SUBSTANTIVES.

Substantives are grouped in Declensions according to the Character or final letter of the Stem as follows:

(1) FIRST DECLENSION: A- Stems.
(2) SECOND DECLENSION: O- Stems.
(3) THIRD DECLENSION: Consonant Stems and I- Stems.
(4) FOURTH DECLENSION: U- Stems.
(5) FIFTH DECLENSION: E- Stems.

TABLE OF CASE-ENDINGS.

Decl.	I.	II.	III.		IV.	V.
Stem Char.	ă-	ŏ-	consonant	I-	ŭ-	ĕ-
			SINGULAR			
	f. (m.)	m. (f.) n.	m. f. n.	f. m. n. ĕ	m. (f.) n.	f.
Nom.	ă	ŭs um	various	ĭs es l r	ŭs ū	ēs
Voc.	—	ĕ —	— —	— —	— —	—
Acc.	am	um —	em —	im em —	um —	em
Gen.	ae	ī	ĭs	ĭs	ūs	eī
Dat.	ae	ō	ī	ī	ŭī (ū)	eī
Abl.	ā	ō	ĕ	ī or ĕ	ū	ē
			PLURAL			
Nom. Voc.	ae	ī ă	ēs ă	ēs iă	ūs uă	ēs
	—	— —	— —	— —	— —	—
Acc.	ās	ōs —	ēs —	īs ēs	ūs —	ēs
Gen.	ārum	ōrum	um	ĭum	uum	ērum
Dat. Abl.	īs	īs	ĭbŭs	ĭbŭs	ĭbŭs	ēbŭs

33 The Character of the Stem is most clearly seen before the ending **-um** or **-rum** of the Genitive Plural.

The Nominative, masculine and feminine, takes **s**, except in **a-** Stems, some Stems in **ro-** of the Second Declension, and Stems in **s, l, r, n,** of the Third.   The Vocative (which is not a true case) is like the Nominative, except in the singular of Nouns in **-us** of the Second Declension.

Neuters have the Accusative like the Nominative in both singular and plural; the plural always ends in **a.**

34 FIRST DECLENSION.

A- Stems.

The Nominative Singular is the same as the Stem.

Stem mensă-
table, f.

	SING.		PLUR.	
Nom.	**mensă,**	*a table.*	**mensae,**	*tables.*
Voc.	**mensa,**	*o table.*	**mensae,**	*o tables.*
Acc.	**mensam,**	*a table.*	**mensās,**	*tables.*
Gen.	**mensae,**	*of a table.*	**mensārum,**	*of tables.*
Dat.	**mensae,**	*to a table.*	**mensīs,**	*to tables.*
Abl.	**mensā,**	*from a table.*	**mensīs,**	*from tables.*

Decline like **mensa**: aquila, *eagle*; lūna, *moon*; rēgĭna, *queen*; stella, *star*.

Stems in **a** are mostly feminine.   A few are masculine, as scrība, *a notary*; Hadria, *the Adriatic sea.*

Note 1.—An old form of the gen. sing. **-āī** for **-ae** is sometimes used by poets, as aulāī. Also an old genitive of familia remains in compounds : pater- (māter-) familias, *father (mother) of a family.*

Note 2.—The locative sing. ends in **-ae**; the plur. in **-īs**; Romae, *at Rome*; mīlitiae, *at the war*; Athēnīs, *at Athens.*

Note 3.—The gen. plur. is sometimes formed in **-um** instead of **-arum,** by compounds with -cŏla, -gĕna: such as agricola, *a farmer.*

Note 4.—Dea and filia have dat. and abl. plural -ăbŭs, in order to distinguish them from the dat. and abl. plural of deus and filius.

C

35   Second Declension.

O- Stems.

The Nominative is formed from the Stem by adding **s**; in neuter nouns, **m**; the Character ŏ being weakened to ŭ.

In the greater number of nouns whose Stem ends in **ero**, or in **ro** preceded by a mute, the **o** is dropped, and the Nom. ends in -er.

Stem	annŏ- *year*, m.		puĕrŏ- *boy*, m.	măgistrŏ- *master*, m.	bellŏ- *war*, n.
SING.					
Nom.	annŭs,	*a year*	puĕr	magistĕr	bellum
Voc.	annĕ,	*o year*	puĕr	magistĕr	bellum
Acc.	annum,	*a year*	puerum	magistrum	bellum
Gen.	annī,	*of a year*	puerī	magistrī	bellī
Dat.	annō,	*to a year*	puerō	magistrō	bellō
Abl.	annō,	*from a year*	puerō	magistrō	bellō
PLUR.					
Nom.	annī,	*years*	puerī	magistrī	bellă
Voc.	annī,	*o years*	puerī	magistrī	bellă
Acc.	annōs,	*years*	puerōs	magistrōs	bellă
Gen.	annōrum,	*of years*	puerōrum	magistrōrum	bellōrum
Dat.	annīs,	*to years*	puerīs	magistrīs	bellīs
Abl.	annīs,	*from years*	puerīs	magistrīs	bellīs

Decline like **annus**: amīcus, *friend*; dominus, *lord*; servus, *slave*.

Decline like **puer**: gener, *son-in-law*; socer, *father-in-law*; līberī (plur.), *children*; lūcifer, *light-bringer*; armiger, *armour-bearer*.

Decline like **magister**: ager, *field*; cancer, *crab*; līber, *book*.

Decline like **bellum**: regnum, *kingdom*; verbum, *word*.

Nouns in **us**, **er**, are masculine; in **um** neuter.

The following in **ŭs** are feminine besides words feminine by meaning: alvus, *paunch*; colus, *distaff*: humus, *ground*; vannus, *winnowing-fan*; also several from the Greek: arctus, *the bear constellation*; carbasus, *linen*; plur. carbasa, n., *sails*. Neuter in **us** (and used in the sing. only) are pelagus, *sea*; vīrus, *venom*.

Note.—Vulgus, *crowd*, is generally neuter, rarely masculine.

The following have some exceptional forms :—

Stem	fīliŏ-son, m.	vĭrŏ-man, m.	deŏ-god, m.
SING.			
Nom.	fīliŭs	vĭr	deŭs
Voc.	fīlī	vĭr	deŭs
Acc.	filium	virum	deum
Gen.	filii *or* filī	virī	deī
D. Abl.	filiō	virō	deō
PLUR.			
N. V.	filiī	virī	di (dei)
Acc.	filiōs	virōs	deōs
Gen.	filiōrum	virōrum *or* virum	deōrum *or* deum
D. Abl.	filiīs	virīs	dīs (deis)

Note 1.—Like filius are declined gĕnius, *guardian spirit*, and many proper names in -**ius** : Claudius, Vergilius ; like vir, its compounds, decemvir, triumvir, &c. The contracted gen. sing. in -**i**, as filī, ingenī, is used by writers of the best age, especially poets.

Note 2.—The locative singular ends in ī ; the plural in īs : humī, *on the ground* ; belli, *at the war* ; Milēti, *at Milētus* ; Philippis, *at Philippi*.

Note 3.—The genitive plural in -**um** is often found ; especially in words denoting coins, sums, weights, and measures : nummus, *coin* ; talentum, *talent*. Some nouns have genitive plural in -**um** *or* -**orum** : socius, *ally* ; faber, *smith* ; līberi, *children*.

36

THIRD DECLENSION.

Consonant and I- Stems.

The Third Declension contains—

A. Consonant Stems.

MUTES—

    (1) Gutturals, c, g.
    (2) Dentals, t, d.
    (3) Labials, p, b.

SPIRANT s.
NASALS, n, m.
LIQUIDS, l, r.

B. I- Stems.

37   *Syllabus of Consonant Substantives, showing Stem-ending*
with Nominative and Genitive Singular.

Stem-ending	Nominative Sing.	Genitive Sing.	English
Stems in Gutturals with x in Nom. for cs or gs.			
ăc-	fax, f.	făcĭs	torch
āc-	pax, f.	pācis	peace
ĕc-	nex, f.	nĕcis	death
ĕc- ĭc-	apex, m.	apĭcis	peak
ēc-	vervex, m.	vervēcis	wether
ĭc-	fornix, m.	fornĭcis	arch
ĭc-	jūdex, c.	judĭcis	judge
īc-	rādix, f.	radīcis	root
ōc-	vox, f.	vōcis	voice
ŭc-	dux, c.	dŭcis	leader
ūc-	lux, f.	lūcis	light
ĕg-	grex, m.	grĕgis	flock
ēg-	rex, m.	rēgis	king
ĕg- ĭg-	rēmex, m.	remĭgis	rower
ĭg-	strix, f.	strĭgis	screech-owl
ŭg-	conjunx, c.	conjŭgis	wife or husband
ūg-	wanting	frūgis, f.	fruit
ĭv-	nix, f.	nĭvis	snow

Stems in Dentals drop t, d, before s in the Nom.

ăt-	ănăs, f.	anătĭs	duck
āt-	aetās, f.	aetātis	age
ĕt-	sĕgĕs, f.	segĕtis	corn-crop
ĕt-	pariēs, m.	pariĕtis	room-wall
ēt-	quiēs, f.	quiētis	rest
ĕt- ĭt-	mīlĕs, c.	mīlĭtis	soldier
ĭt-	căpŭt, n.	capĭtis	head
ōt-	nĕpōs, m.	nepōtis	grandson
ūt-	virtūs, f.	virtūtis	virtue
ct-	lac, n.	lactis	milk
ăd-	vās, m.	vădis	surety
ĕd-	pēs, m.	pĕdis	foot
ēd-	mercēs, f.	mercēdis	hire
aed-	praes, m.	praedis	bondsman
ĕd- ĭd-	obsĕs, c.	obsĭdis	hostage
ĭd-	lăpĭs, m.	lapĭdis	stone
ōd-	custōs, c.	custōdis	guardian
ŭd-	pĕcus, f.	pecŭdis	beast
ūd-	incūs, f.	incūdis	anvil
aud-	laus, f.	laudis	praise
rd-	cŏr, n.	cordis	heart

Stems in Labials form Nom. regularly with s.

ăp-		wanting	dăpĭs, f.	banquet
ĕp- ĭp-		princeps, c.	princĭpis	chief
ĭp-		wanting	stĭpis, f.	dole (a small coin)
ŏp-		wanting	ŏpis, f.	help
ĕn- ŭp-		auceps, m.	aucŭpis	fowler

Stems in the Spirant s, which, except in vās, becomes r.

âs-	vās, n.	vāsis	vessel
aes- aer-	aes, n.	aeris	copper, bronze
ēs- ĕr-	Cerēs, f.	Cĕrĕris	Ceres
ĭs- ĕr-	cinis, m.	cĭnĕris	cinder
ōs- ōr-	honōs, m.	honōris	honour
ŏs- ŏr-	tempŭs, n.	tempŏris	time
ŭs- ĕr-	opŭs, n.	opĕris	work
ûs- ūr-	crūs, n.	crūris	leg

Stems in Liquids.

ăl-	sal, m.	sălĭs	salt
ell-	mel, n.	mellis	honey
ĭl-	mūgil, m.	mūgĭlis	mullet
ōl-	sōl, m.	sōlis	sun
ŭl-	consŭl, m.	consŭlis	consul
ăr-	jubăr, n.	jubăris	sunbeam
arr-	far, n.	farris	flour
ĕr-	ansĕr, m.	ansĕris	goose
ēr-	vēr, n.	vēris	spring
ter- tr-	māter, f.	mātris	mother
ŏr-	aequŏr, n.	aequŏris	sea
ŏr-	ĕbŭr, n.	ebŏris	ivory
ōr-	sorŏr, f.	sorōris	sister
ŭr-	vultŭr, m.	vultŭris	vulture
ūr-	fūr, m.	fūris	thief

Stems in Nasals.

ĕn- ĭn-	nōmĕn, n.	nomĭnis	name
ŏn- ĭn-	hŏmo, m.	homĭnis	man
ōn-	leo, m.	leōnis	lion
iōn-	rătio, f.	ratiōnis	reason
ĭn-	caro, f.	carnis	flesh
ăn-	cănĭs, c.	canis	dog
ĕn-	juvenĭs, c.	juvenis	young person
ĕm-	hiemps, f.	hiĕmis	winter

A. Consonant Stems.

38   (1) Stems in **Gutturals** : c, g.

Stem	jūdĭc- *judge*,		rādĭc- *root*, f.	rēg- *king*, m.
Sing.				
N. V.	jūdex,	*a judge*	rādix	rex
Acc.	jūdĭcem,	*a judge*	radīcem	rēgem
Gen.	judicĭs,	*of a judge*	radicĭs	regĭs
Dat.	judicī,	*to a judge*	radicī	regī
Abl.	judicĕ,	*from a judge*	radicĕ	regĕ
Plur.				
N. V.	judicēs,	*judges*	radicēs	regēs
Acc.	judicēs,	*judges*	radicēs	regēs
Gen.	judicum,	*of judges*	radicum	regum
Dat.	judicĭbŭs,	*to judges*	radicĭbŭs	regĭbŭs
Abl.	judicĭbŭs,	*from judges*	radicĭbŭs	regĭbŭs

Decline also : f. vox, **vōc-**, *voice* ; c. dux, **dŭc-**, *leader* ; m. grex, **grĕg-**, *flock*.

39   (2) Stems in **Dentals** : t, d.

Stem	aetāt- *age*, f.	pĕd- *foot*, m.	căpĭt- *head*, n.
Sing.			
N. V.	aetās	pēs	căpŭt
Acc.	aetātem	pĕdem	capŭt
Gen.	aetatĭs	pedĭs	capĭtĭs
Dat.	aetatī	pedī	capitī
Abl.	aetatĕ	pedĕ	capitĕ
Plur.			
N. V.	aetatēs	pedēs	capită
Acc.	aetatēs	pedēs	capită
Gen.	aetatum	pedum	capitum
Dat.	aetatĭbŭs	pedĭbŭs	capitĭbŭs
Abl.	aetatĭbŭs	pedĭbŭs	capitĭbŭs

Decline also : f. virtūs, **virtūt-**, *virtue* ; c. mīlĕs, **milĭt-**, *soldier* ; m. lapĭs, **lapĭd-**, *stone* ; f. laus, **laud-**, *praise*.

    Note.—nox, **noct-**, *night*, līs, **lit-**, *strife*, dōs, **dōt-**, *dower*, all f., have gen. plur. in **-ium** ; sometimes also stems in āt-, as **aetāt-**, **civitāt-**. Alĕs, **alit-**, *bird*, has in poetry gen. plur. alituum.

40

(8) Stems in Labials: p, b.

Stem princĕp-
princĭp-
chief, c.

Sing.		Plur.	
N. V.	princeps		principēs
Acc.	princĭpem		principēs
Gen.	principĭs		principum
Dat.	principī		principĭbŭs
Abl.	principĕ		principĭbŭs

Decline also: c. forceps, **forcĭp-**, *tongs*; m. auceps, **aucŭp-**, *fowler.*

41

Stems in the Spirant s.

Stems in **s** do not add **s** in the Nominative Singular, and generally they change **s** into **r** in the other cases.

Stem	flōs- flōr- *flower,* m.	ŏpŭs- ŏpĕr- *work,* n.	crūs- crūr- *leg,* n.
Sing.			
N. V.	flōs	opŭs	crūs
Acc.	flōrem	opŭs	crūs
Gen.	florĭs	opĕrĭs	crūrĭs
Dat.	florī	operī	crurī
Abl.	florĕ	operĕ	crurĕ
Plur.			
N. V.	florēs	operă	crură
Acc.	florēs	operă	crură
Gen.	florum	operum	crurum
Dat.	florĭbŭs	operĭbŭs	crurĭbŭs
Abl.	florĭbŭs	operĭbŭs	crurĭbŭs

Decline also: m. honōs, **honōr-**, *honour*; n. tempus, **tempŏr-**, *time*; corpus, **corpŏr-**, *body*; genus, **genĕr-**, *race*; jūs, **jūr-**, *law.*

Note 1.—Vās, vas-, *a vessel*, keeps **s** in all the cases, and has plural vāsa, vasōrum, vasīs. Os, oss-, n., *bone*, as, ass-, m., *a coin*, keep **s** in all the cases, and have gen. plur. ossium, assium. Mūs, *mouse*, glīs, *dormouse*, m., make gen. plur. mūrium, glīrium.

Note 2.—Honōs, colōs, *colour*, and other stems changed in later Latin to honŏr, colŏr, &c., in the nom. sing., with gen. -ōris. Arbōs, f., changed to arbŏr, arbŏris, *tree*.

42　　　　　　　Stems in **Liquids** : **l, r.**

Stems in **l, r,** do not take **s** in the Nominative Singular.

Stem	consŭl-	ămōr-	păter- patr-	aequŏr-
	consul, m.	*love,* m.	*father.*	*sea,* n.
Sing.				
N. V.	consŭl	ămŏr	pătĕr	aequŏr
Acc.	consŭlem	amōrem	patrem	aequŏr
Gen.	consŭlĭs	amorĭs	patrĭs	aequŏris
Dat.	consulī	amorī	patrī	aequorī
Abl.	consŭlĕ	amorĕ	patrĕ	aequorĕ
Plur.				
N. V.	consulēs	amorēs	patrēs	aequoră
Acc.	consulēs	amorēs	patrēs	aequoră
Gen.	consulum	amorum	patrum	aequorum
Dat.	consulĭbŭs	amorĭbŭs	patrĭbŭs	aequorĭbŭs
Abl.	consulĭbŭs	amorĭbŭs	patrĭbŭs	aequorĭbŭs

Decline also : m. sōl, **sōl-,** *sun*; orātŏr, **oratōr-,** *speaker*; carcĕr, **carcĕr-,** *prison*; frāter, **fratr-,** *brother*; n. ebŭr, **ebŏr-,** *ivory.*

43　　　　　　　Stems in **Nasals** : **n, m.**

Stems ending in **n** do not take **s** in the Nominative Singular.
Stems in **ōn, ŏn,** drop the **n.**

Stem	lĕōn-	virgōn- virgĭn-	nōmĕn- nomĭn-
	lion, m.	*virgin,* f.	*name,* n.
Sing.			
N. V.	leō	virgō	nōmĕn
Acc.	leōnem	virgĭnem	nomĕn
Gen.	leonĭs	virginĭs	nōmĭnĭs
Dat.	leonī	virginī	nominī
Abl.	leonĕ	virginĕ	nominĕ
Plur.			
N. V.	leonēs	virginēs	nomină
Acc.	leonēs	virginēs	nomină
Gen.	leonum	virginum	nominum
Dat.	leonĭbŭs	virginĭbŭs	nominĭbŭs
Abl.	leonĭbŭs	virginĭbŭs	nominĭbŭs

Decline also : m. latrō, **latrōn-,** *robber* ; f. ratiō, **ratiōn-,** *reason* ; m. ordō, **ordĭn-,** *order* ; homō, **homĭn-,** *man* ; n. carmĕn, **carmĭn-,** *song.*

There is only one Stem in **m** : hiemps, *winter* ; Gen. hiĕmis, f.

44 B. **I- Stems.**

Stems ending in i may be divided into four groups :
  (1) Nouns with Nom. Sing. in -is, and in -er.
  (2) Nouns with Nom. Sing. in -es.
  (3) Nouns which have two consonants before the i of the
      stem and drop the i before s in the Nom. Sing.
  (4) Neuter stems in -ĕ, -ăl, -ăr.

(1) Stems with Nom. Sing. in -is, and in -er from stem ri- :

45

Stem	cīvĭ-	imbrĭ-
	citizen, c.	*shower,* m.
SING.		
N. V.	cīvĭs	imbĕr
Acc.	civem	imbrem
Gen.	civĭs	imbrĭs
Dat.	civī	imbrī
Abl.	civĕ	imbrĕ
PLUR.		
N. V.	civēs	imbrēs
Acc.	civēs	imbrēs
Gen.	civium	imbrium
Dat.	civĭbŭs	imbrĭbŭs
Abl.	civĭbŭs	imbrĭbŭs

Decline like **civis**: m. amnis, *river*; collis, *hill*; canalis, *canal*; f. ovis, *sheep*; avis, *bird*.

Decline like **-imber**: f. linter, *boat*; m. ūter, *leathern bottle*.

Note 1.—A few words keep always acc. -**im**, abl. ī : f. tussis, *cough*; sitis, *thirst* (sing. only), and most rivers and towns, m. Tiberis, *Tiber*; f. Neāpolis, *Naples*. So usually, f. febris, *fever*; puppis, *stern*; restis, *rope*; sēcūris, *axe*; turris, *tower*. Often also, f. clavis, *key*; navis, *ship*. Ignis, m. *fire*, has usually abl. ignī. Amussis, f. *a carpenter's rule*, is used chiefly in the phrase ad amussim, *accurately*.

Note 2.—The acc. plur. of **I**-stems is often written -**īs**, which is the older form.

Note 3.—f. Apis, *bee*; volucris, *bird*; m. pānis, *bread*, have usually gen. plur. in -**um**.

Note 4.—f. Vīs, *force*, is the only long i -stem. It has acc. sing. vim, abl. sing. vī, plur. vīres, vīrium, vīribus.

(2) Stems with Nom. Sing. in -es :

46

Stem	nūbĭ- *cloud*, f.	
	Sing.	Plur.
N. V.	nūbēs	nubēs
Acc.	nubem	nubēs
Gen.	nubĭs	nubium
Dat.	nubī	nubĭbŭs
Abl.	nubĕ	nubĭbŭs

Decline also: cautēs, *rock*; mōlēs, *pile*; rūpēs, *crag*.

> Note 1.—Several stems have nom. sing. -is or -es : vallēs, *valley*, vulpēs, *fox*. Trabs, *beam*, and plebs, *the common people*, are generally found for trabēs, plēbēs.

> Note 2.—Vātēs, *seer*, c., has gen. plur. **-um**. Famēs, *hunger*, has abl. sing. famē.

(3) Stems which have two consonants (a liquid or nasal and a mute) before i, and drop i before the s in the Nom. Sing. :

47

Stem	montĭ- *mountain*, m,	urbĭ- *city*, f.
Sing.		
N. V.	mons	urbs
Acc.	montem	urbem
Gen.	montĭs	urbĭs
Dat.	montī	urbī
Abl.	montĕ	urbĕ
Plur.		
N. V.	montēs	urbēs
Acc.	montēs	urbēs
Gen.	montium	urbium
Dat.	montĭbŭs	urbĭbŭs
Abl.	montĭbŭs	urbĭbŭs

Decline also : m. dens, **denti-**, *tooth*; f. arx, **arci-**, *citadel*; ars, **arti-**, *art*; stirps, **stirpi-**, *stem*; frons, **fronti-**, *forehead*; frons, **frondi-**, *leaf*; bidens **bidenti-**, *sheep*, but m. *fork*; c. parens, **parenti-**, *parent*.

> Note.—Words of one syllable in this group have gen. plur. **-ium**. Words of two or more syllables vary between **-um** and **-ium**. Compounds of dens, as bidens, *a pitchfork*, have abl. sing. ĕ.

48 (4) Neuter stems with Nom. Sing. in -ĕ, -ăl, -ăr :

These either change ĭ into ĕ in the Nom. Sing. or drop the vowel and shorten the final syllable.

Stem	mărĭ- *sea*	ănĭmălĭ- *animal*	calcārĭ- *spur*
SING.			
N. V. Acc.	mărĕ	animăl	calcăr
Gen.	marĭs	animālĭs	calcārĭs
Dat. Abl.	marī	animalī	calcarī
PLUR.			
N. V. Acc.	mariă	animaliă	calcariă
Gen.	marium	animalium	calcarium
Dat. Abl.	marĭbŭs	animalĭbŭs	calcarĭbŭs

Decline also : conclāvĕ, *room* ; cubīlĕ, *couch* ; rētĕ, *net* (abl. sing. ĕ) ; tribūnal, *tribunal* ; exemplar, *pattern*.

49   *Note* 1.—Consonant stems and I- stems are grouped in one leclension, because of the difficulty in distinguishing their forms.

I- stems are very rare in the earliest known specimens of Latin ; they were a later formation, and were being developed in the Classical period ; therefore the forms were liable to uncertainty. The gen. plur. (by which in other declensions the stem is determined) often varies in the third declension between **-um** and **-ium**, especially after **t**. Horace writes in one place parentium virtus ; in another, aetas parentum. Livy writes always civitatium ; Cicero, chiefly civitatum.

In classing words as Consonant stems or I- stems, the gen. plur. **-um** or **-ium** must be considered, together with the acc. sing. **-em** or **-im**, abl. sing. **-ĕ** or **-ī**; acc. plur. **-es** or **-īs**, and in neuters the nom. plur. **-ia**; but often the classification remains doubtful. Of many words, as cor, rus, sal, no genitive plural is found, and the classification rests chiefly on analogy with other Latin words, or on comparison with cognate words in other languages. (See Appendix IV. p. 225.)

Note 2.—The locative sing. of the third declension ends in -ī or -ĕ; the plural in -ĭbus : rūrī or rūrĕ, *in the country* ; vesperī or vesperĕ, *in the evening* ; Carthāginī or Carthāginĕ, *at Carthage* ; Gādibus, *at Gades (Cadiz)*.

50 The following have exceptional forms :—

(1) Juppiter (for Dieus-piter) and bos (for bous), *ox.*

		Sing.	Plur.
N. V.	Juppiter	bos	bŏvēs
Acc.	Jŏvem	bŏvem	boves
Gen.	Jovĭs	bovĭs	boum
Dat.	Jovī	bovī	bōbŭs *or* būbŭs
Abl.	Jovĕ	bovĕ	bōbŭs *or* būbŭs

(2) Two stems in **-u,** declined like consonant nouns : grūs, *crane,* sūs, *pig.* These are the only uncontracted **u**- nouns.

	Sing.	Plur.
N. V.	grus	gruēs
Acc.	gruem	gruēs
Gen.	gruĭs	gruum
Dat.	gruī	gruibŭs
Abl.	gruĕ	gruibŭs.

Sus has dat. abl. plur. suibus or sūbus.

Itĕr, *journey,* has gen. sing. itinĕris (and rarely iteris).

Jĕcŭr, *liver,* jecŏris, and jecinŏris.

Sĕnex, *old man,* has Sing. Acc. senem, Gen. senis, Dat. seni, Abl. sene ; Plur. N. Acc. senes, Gen. senum, Dat. Abl. senibus.

Supellex, *furniture,* forms the other cases from stem supellectili-.

Jusjurandum, *oath,* is declined in both parts : N. V. Acc. jusjurandum ; Gen. jurisjurandi ; Dat. jurijurando ; Abl. jurejurando. No plural.

Paterfamiliās, māterfamiliās, *father, mother of a family,* have pater, māter fully declined in the sing. cases, but familiās remains unaltered. The plur. patresfamiliarum is sometimes found.

GENDER IN THIRD DECLENSION.

51 *Consonant Stems.*

Masculine are nouns which end in **-os, -o** (except **-do, -go, -io**), **-or, -er,** and nouns in **-is** or **-es** which have more syllables in the other Cases than in the Nominative.

Exceptions :

cōs, *whetstone,* dōs, *dowry,* f.; ŏs, ossis, *bone,* ōs, oris, *mouth,* n.

ēcho, *echo,* căro, *flesh,* f.

arbŏr, *tree,* f.; aequor, *sea,* marmor, *marble,* cor, *heart,* n.

vēr, *spring,* cadāver, *corpse,* iter, *journey,* tūber, *hump,* über, *udder,* verber, *lash,* n.; also some names of plants, as păpāver, *poppy.*

compēs, *fetter,* mercēs, *hire,* mergĕs, *sheaf,* quiēs, *rest,* requiēs, *rest,* sĕgĕs, *corn,* tĕgĕs, *mat,* f.

52   Feminine are nouns which end in **-x, -as, -ps, -do, -go, -io,** and nouns in **-ūs** of more than one syllable.

Exceptions :

Nouns in **-ex** are masculine or common, but lex, *law,* nex, *death,* forfex, *shears,* supellex, *furniture,* ilex, *oak,* f.

calix, *cup,* fornix, *arch,* m. ; dux, *leader,* c.

as, *coin,* vas, *surety,* m.; fas, *right,* nefas, *wrong,* vas, *vessel,* n.

manceps, *buyer,* m.; municeps, *burgess,* c.; princeps, *chief,* c.

cardo, *hinge* ; ordo, *order,* m.

ligo, *hoe,* m. ; margo, *brink,* c.

Concrete nouns in **-io** are masculine : pūgio, *dagger* ; pāpilio, *butterfly.* The numerous Abstract nouns in **-io** are feminine ; ratio, *reason.*

53   Neuter are nouns in **-ŭs, -ūs** (in words of one syllable), **-en, -l, -ar, -ur.**

Exceptions :

lepus, *hare,* m.; pecus, pecŭdis, *single head of cattle,* f.

mūs, *mouse,* m. ; grūs, *crane,* sūs, *pig,* c.

pectĕn, *comb,* rēn, *kidney,* splēn, *spleen,* m.

mūgil, *mullet,* sal, *salt,* sol, *sun,* m.

lar, *god of the hearth,* m.

furfŭr, *bran,* lemŭr, *goblin,* turtŭr, *turtle dove,* vultŭr, *vulture,* m.

Praes, *bondsman,* is masc.; laus, *praise,* fraus, *deceit,* are fem.; lac, *milk,* caput, *head,* aes, *copper,* are neuter.

54   *I- Stems.*

Most nouns in **-is** and **-es** which have the same number of syllables in the Nominative and the other sing. cases are feminine.

Exceptions : the following nouns in **-is** are masculine :

amnis, *river*	crīnis, *hair*	mensis, *month*	unguis, *nail*
axis, *axle*	ensis, *sword*	orbis, *circle*	vectis, *lever*
canālis, *canal*	fascis, *bundle*	pānis, *bread*	vermis, *worm*
caulis, *cabbage*	follis, *bag*	piscis, *fish*	cassēs, *nets*
clunis, *haunch*	fustis, *cudgel*	postis, *post*	mānēs, *shades* } plur.
collis, *hill*	ignis, *fire*	torris, *firebrand*	

Generally masculine are callis, *path* ; finis, *end* ; fūnis, *rope* ; sentis, *thorn* ; torquis, *necklace.*

Acīnaces, *scimitar,* and verres, *boar,* are masculine.

Nouns in **-al, -ar,** and **-e** are neuter.

Nouns in **-x, -bs, -ls, -ns, -rs** are feminine ; but fons, *fountain,* mons, *mountain,* dens, *tooth,* bidens, *fork,* rudens, *rope,* torrens, *torrent,* oriens, *east,* occidens, *west,* masculine ; infans, *infant,* parens, *parent,* c.

55

FOURTH DECLENSION.

U- Stems (contracted).

The Nominative of masculine and feminine nouns is formed by adding **s** ; neuters have the plain stem with ū (long).

Stem	grădŭ- *step*, m.		gĕnū *knee*, n.
SINGULAR.			
Nom.	grădŭs	*a step*	gĕnū
Voc.	gradŭs	*o step*	genū
Acc.	gradum	*a step*	genū
Gen.	gradūs	*of a step*	genūs
Dat.	graduī	*to a step*	genū
Abl.	gradū	*from a step*	genū
PLURAL.			
Nom.	gradūs	*steps*	genŭă
Voc.	gradūs	*o steps*	genuă
Acc.	gradūs	*steps*	genuă
Gen.	graduum	*of steps*	genuum
Dat.	gradĭbŭs	*to steps*	genĭbŭs
Abl.	gradĭbŭs	*from steps*	genĭbŭs

Decline like **gradus** : m. fructus, *fruit* ; senātus, *senate* ; f. manus, *hand.*

Decline like **genu** : cornu, *horn* ; veru, *spit* (dat. abl. plur., ŭbus).

Feminine nouns of this declension, besides manus, are : acus, *needle* ; porticus, *porch* ; tribus, *tribe* ; Idūs, *Ides*, and words feminine by meaning. Neuters are only three : genu, cornu, veru.

Note 1.—The dat. sing. **-uī** is sometimes contracted into **-ū.** The dat. and abl. plur. **-ŭbŭs** is generally changed into **-ĭbŭs** ; but acus, tribus, arcus, *bow*, lacus, *lake*, partus, *birth*, portus, *harbour*, and artūs (plur.), *limbs*, have always **-ŭbus.**

Note 2.—Some nouns have forms of both **u-** and **o-** Stems, especially names of trees : cupressus, *cypress* ; ficus, *fig* ; laurus, *bay* ; myrtus, *myrtle* ; also, colus, *distaff*, domus, *house.*

56 Domus, f., is thus declined :

	SINGULAR.	PLURAL.
N. V.	dŏmŭs	domūs
Acc.	domum	domūs *or* domōs
Gen.	domūs	domōrum *or* domuum
Dat.	domuī *or* domō	domĭbŭs
Abl.	domō	domĭbŭs

The locative domĭ, *at home*, is often used.

57

FIFTH DECLENSION.

E- Stems.

The Nom. Sing. is formed by adding **s** to the Stem.

Stem rē-, *thing.*

	SINGULAR.			PLURAL.	
Nom.	rēs	*a thing*	rēs	*things*
Voc.	rēs	*o thing*	rēs	*o things*
Acc.	rem	*a thing*	rēs	*things*
Gen.	rĕī	*of a thing*	rērum	*of things*
Dat.	rĕī	*to a thing*	rēbŭs	*to things*
Abl.	rē	*from a thing*	rēbŭs	*from things*

Decline like **res**: diēs, *day* (gen. dat., diēī); aciēs, *line of battle*; faciēs, *face*; seriēs, *series*; speciēs, *form*; spēs, *hope*; fidēs, *faith*; glaciēs, *ice*; meridiēs, *noon*.

Res and dies are the only nouns used in the Gen., Dat., and Abl. Plural. Fides, glacies, meridies, are Singular only.

All nouns of this declension are feminine except dies and meridies. Dies also is feminine when it means 'an appointed day' *or* 'a period of time.'

Note 1.—The greater number of nouns of this declension were originally **ia-** Stems, and have forms both of **e-** and **a-** Stems. They are declined like materiēs, *matter*, singular only.

Stem,	materia-,	and materie-.
N. V.	materia	materiēs
Acc.	materiam	materiem
Gen. Dat.	materiae	(materieī)
Abl.	materia	materiē

Note 2.—The contracted gen. and dat. sing. in **-ē**, as fidē for fidei, is found in Virgil and Horace. An old gen. in -ī occurs in tribunus plebi, *tribune of the people*. The locative ends in **-ē**.

58   *Note* 3.—**Respublica**, *the public interest, the republic, the State*, is declined in both its parts:

Sing. Acc. rempublicam, Gen. reipublicae, Dat. reipublicae, Abl. rēpublicā.

Plur. Nom. respublicae, Acc. respublicas, Gen. rerumpublicarum, D. Abl. rebuspublicis.

59   DEFECTIVE AND VARIABLE SUBSTANTIVES.

Many nouns are found only in the Singular ; these are chiefly proper names and words of general meaning : as

humus,	*ground.*	ævum,	*an age.*
justitia,	*justice.*	aurum,	*gold.*
lætitia,	*joy.*	argentum,	*silver.*
ver,	*spring.*	cælum,	*heaven.*
vesper,	*evening.*	lētum,	*death.*

Note.—In poetry some words take plural form with singular meaning : mella, *honey*, nives, *snow*, silentia, *silence*, rura, *country*.

60   Many nouns are used only in the Plural :

arma,	*arms.*	insidiae,	*ambush.*
artūs,	*limbs.*	līberi,	*children.*
cūnae,	*cradle.*	mānes,	*departed spirits.*
dīyitiae,	*riches.*	moenia,	*town walls.*
fasti,	*annals.*	nūgae,	*trifles.*
fēriae,	*holidays.*	penates,	*household gods.*
indūtiae,	*truce.*	tenebrae,	*darkness.*

And names of towns, days, festivals : Athēnae, Delphi, Kalendae, *Calends* ; Bacchanālia, *festival of Bacchus.*

61   Some words have a different meaning in Singular and Plural :

SINGULAR.		PLURAL.	
aedes,	*temple.*	aedes,	*house.*
auxilium,	*help.*	auxilia,	*allied forces.*
castrum,	*fort.*	castra,	*camp.*
cēra,	*wax.*	cērae,	*waxen tablet.*
cōpia,	*plenty.*	cōpiae,	*forces.*
fīnis,	*end.*	fines,	*boundaries.*
grātia,	*favour.*	gratiae,	*thanks.*
impedīmentum,	*hindrance.*	impedimenta,	*baggage.*
littera,	*letter of the alphabet.*	litterae,	*epistle, literature.*
lūdus,	*play.*	ludi,	*public games.*
opem (acc.),	*help.*	opes,	*wealth.*
opera,	*labour.*	operae,	*work-people.*
sal.	*salt.*	sales.	*wit.*

62 Some nouns have two or more forms of Declension :

Nom.	Gen.		Nom.	Gen.	
tergum,	-i, n.	} back.	pecŭs,	-ŏrĭs, n.	} cattle.
tergus,	-ŏris, n.		pecŭs,	-ŭdis, f.	} a single head of cattle.
ēventum,	-i, n.	} event.	plebs,	-is, f.	} the common
ēventus,	-ūs, m.		plebes,	-ei, f.	people.

			Nom.	Gen.	Abl.	
jugerum,	-i, n.	} acre.	vespera,	-ae	-a, f.	} evening.
[juger],	-ĭs, n.		vesper,	-i	-o, m.	
			vesper,	—	-e, -i, m.	

Quiēs, f., *rest*, -ētis, is a t- Stem only ; but its compound requiēs takes also the e- forms : requiem, requiē.

63 Some o- Stems vary between masc. and neut. in Sing. or Plur. : baculus, m., baculum, n., *a stick* ; pīleus, m., pileum, n., *a hat*.

locus, m., *place*, pl. { loci. loca.   frēnum, n., *bit*, pl. { freni. frena.

jocus, m., *jest*, pl. { joci. joca.   rastrum, n., *harrow*, pl. { rastri. rastra.

64 In many nouns some of the cases are wanting ; thus :

	feast, f.,	*fruit*, f.,	*help*, f.,	*prayer*, f.,	*change*, f.
N. V.	—	—	—	—	—
Acc.	dăpem	frūgem	ŏpem	prĕcem	vĭcem
Gen.	dapĭs	frugĭs	opĭs	—	vicĭs
Dat.	dapī	frugī	—	precī	—
Aől.	dapĕ	frugĕ	opĕ	precĕ	vicĕ

These have full plural -es, -um, -ibus, except Gen. vicium.

65 Many are used in the Abl. Sing. only.

coactu,	*by force.*	natu,	*by birth.*
concessu,	*by permission.*	noctu,	*by night.*
(diu) interdiu,	*by day.*	rogātu,	*by request.*
jussu,	*by command.*	sponte,	*by choice.*
injussu,	*without command.*		

66 Some have only Nom. Acc. S. : fās, *right*, nefās, *wrong*, instar, *likeness*, *size*, opus, *need*, nihil, *nothing*.

D

DECLENSION OF GREEK NOUNS.

67

FIRST DECLENSION, a- STEMS.

At an early time many Greek nouns were used in Latin, in an almost or entirely Latin form. Masc. nouns ending in -ās, -ēs, and fem. nouns in -ā, -ē, all alike took the ending -ă in the nom., and were declined throughout like mensa. Such words are nauta, *sailor*, poēta, *poet*.

Afterwards the Greek forms, especially of proper names, were brought in by the poets, and thus in many instances both Greek and Latin forms of the same words are found, while of some words, used chiefly in poetry, the Greek forms alone occur.

Patronymics (*race-names*) are usually in the Greek form, as Atrīdēs (*son of Atreus*), Pēlīdēs (*son of Peleus*); and though they sometimes have -ă for ēs in the nom. they always retain the Greek acc. in -ēn.

Names of people ending in -ātēs, -ītēs, or -ōtēs, as Eleātēs (inhabitant of Elea), generally have -em or -am in acc., being nearer to Latin words.

All these usually follow the Latin declension in the plural, even when they have the Greek form in the singular.

MASCULINE NOUNS IN -ās, -ēs, AND FEMININE NOUNS IN -ē.

SINGULAR.

N.	Aenēās	Atrīdēs, -ă	Cȳbělē, ă
V.	Aeneā	Atridē, -ā, -ă	Cȳbělē, -ă
A.	Aeneān	Atridēn	Cybelēn
G.	Aeneae	Atridae	Cybelēs, -ae
D.	Aeneae	Atridae	Cybelae
Abl.	Aeneā	Atridē, -ā	Cybelē, -ă

Plural in all cases like that of mensa.

Decline also: Boreās, *the north wind*, Persă (-ēs), *a Persian*, Ēpirōtēs -ōtă), *native of Epirus*, Hělěnē, f.

68 SECOND DECLENSION, O- STEMS.

Greek nouns of the Second Declension, especially names of persons and places, often keep their Greek forms in the nom. and acc., but the other cases generally take the Latin forms.

SINGULAR.

Nom.	Dēlŏs, f.	Athōs, m.	Pēliŏn, n.
Voc.	(Delĕ)	(Athōs)	(Peliŏn)
Acc.	Delŏn, -um	Athōn	Peliŏn
Gen.	Delī	Athō	Peliī
D., Abl.	Delō	Athō	Peliō

The fem. words of this Declension are chiefly names of towns, islands, plants, and precious stones.

Nouns ending in -ros sometimes take the Latin ending -er in the nom., as Evander (-dros).

Decline also : scorpiŏs, m., *scorpion* ; lotŏs, f., *lotus* ; Samŏs, Īliŏn.

The Greek plural forms are rare, but plural nom. in -oe, as Cānēphŏroe, and plur. gen. in -ōn, as Būcolicōn, are sometimes found.

69 THIRD DECLENSION.

Consonant Stems and Stems in e, i, o, eu, y.

These nouns are very numerous, having many different endings in the Nom. Sing.

SINGULAR.		PLURAL.	SINGULAR.		PLURAL.
N., V.	hērōs, m., *hero*	herōĕs	lynx, c., *lynx*		lynces
Acc.	herŏ-ă, -ém	herōăs	lync-em, -ă		lync-ăs, -ēs
Gen.	herōïs	herōum	lyncīs		lyncum
Dat.	herōi	herōïbŭs	lynci		lyncĭbŭs
Abl.	herōĕ	herōïbŭs	lyncĕ		lyncĭbŭs

Decline also : f. lampăs, gen. lampadis, *torch* ; m. gigās, gigantis, *giant*; āēr, āĕris, *air* ; aethēr, aethĕris, *the upper air.*

Names of this class are found in different forms, from the tendency to latinise Greek words. Thus Persēūs is called Persĕus by Livy, but by Cicero latinised to Perses in the nom., with the other cases like Greek names of the First Declension, as Atrides.

Greek nouns in **-ōn** often drop the **n** in the nom., as Plato, Platonis; but sometimes it is kept, as in Cimon. Some nouns have a second form, as elephas, *elephant,* which is usually declined like gigas, but sometimes latinised to elephantus, elephanti.

Dīdo also has two forms of declension, (1) as an **-ōn** stem, gen. Didōnis, (2) as a **u-** Stem, gen. Didūs.

Pŏēma, poemătis, n., *poem,* is regularly declined, but Cicero has dat. and abl. plur. poematis. Poēsis, f., *poetry,* is an I- noun, acc. poes-in or poes-im, abl. poesi.

The accusative singular endings in **-em** and in **-a** are both frequent. Gen. sing. usually in **-is,** but the Greek ending **-os** is often found in poetry. The abl. sing. is always in **-ĕ,** and dat. sing. in **-ī,** but the latter is often short (**ĭ**) as in Greek. The nom. plur. is always in **-es,** often short. In acc. plur. the Greek **-ăs** is usual. The Greek ending of the abl. plur. in -si (-sin) is occasionally used by the poets.

Many names in **-es, -eus,** and in **-is** have cases from two forms. I- forms and Consonant forms appear in

Nom.	V.	Acc.	Gen.	Dat.	Abl.	
Thal-es	-es -e	-em, ĕn, ētă	-is, -ētĭs	-ī, ētĭ	-ē, ētĕ	m.
Par-is Iris	-ĭ	{ -idem, ĭdă { -in, -im	-ĭdĭs, -ĭdŏs	-ĭdi	-ĭdĕ	f. m.

Forms of both the Second and Third Declension appear in

Nom.	V.	Acc.	Gen.	Dat.	Abl.	
Orpheus	-eu	-ĕum, -ĕă	-ĕī, -ĕŏs	-ĕī	-ĕō, -ĕō	
Achilleus	-eu	-ĕă	-ĕī, -ĕŏs	-ī		m.
Achilles	-ē	-em, -ēn	-is, -ī	-ī	-ĕ	m.

Note.—Tigris, *tiger,* is declined throughout as an I- noun, like clavis; but also as a Consonant Stem in d, like Paris; forming plur. tigridĕs, tigridum, tigridăs, without dat. and abl.

Decline Ulixeus (Ulixes) like Achilleus (Achilles).

70   DECLENSION OF ADJECTIVES.

Adjectives are declined by Gender, Number and Case.

71   A. Adjectives of three endings in -us, -a, -um or -er, -a, -um
are declined like Substantives of the Second and First Declension, O- and A- Stems.

Stem	bŏnŏ-	bŏnă	bŏnŏ-

good.

Sing.	M.	F.	N.
Nom.	bonŭs	bonă	bonum
Voc.	bonĕ	bonă	bonum
Acc.	bonum	bonam	bonum
Gen.	bonī	bonae	bonī
Dat.	bonō	bonae	bonō
Abl.	bonō	bonă	bonō

Plural.			
Nom.	bonī	bonae	bonă
Voc.	bonī	bonae	bonă
Acc.	bonōs	bonās	bonă
Gen.	bonōrum	bonārum	bonōrum
Dat.	bonīs	bonīs	bonīs
Abl.	bonīs	bonīs	bonīs

Decline also: cārus, *dear*; dūrus, *hard*; malus, *bad*; magnus, *great*;
parvus, *small*; dubius, *doubtful.*

Stem	tĕnĕrŏ-	tĕnĕrā-	tĕnĕrŏ-
		tender.	

SING.	M.	F.	N.
Nom.	tenĕr	tenĕrā	tenĕrum
Voc.	tener	tenerā	tenerum
Acc.	tenerum	teneram	tenerum
Gen.	tenerī	tenerae	tenerī
Dat.	tenerō	tenerae	tenerō
Abl.	tenerō	tenerā	tenerō

PLURAL.			
N. V.	tenerī	tenerae	teneră
Acc.	tenerōs	tenerās	teneră
Gen.	tenerōrum	tenerārum	tenerōrum
D., Abl.	tenerīs	tenerīs	tenerīs

Decline also: asper, *rough*; lacer, *torn*; līber, *free*; miser, *wretched*; prosper, *prosperous*; frugifer, *fruit-bearing*, plumiger, *feathered*, and other compounds of fero and gero; also satur, *full*, satŭra, satŭrum.

Stem	nĭgrŏ-	nĭgră-	nĭgrŏ-
		black.	

SING.	M.	F.	N.
Nom.	nĭgĕr	nĭgră	nĭgrum
Voc.	nigĕr	nigră	nigrum
Acc.	nigrum	nigram	nigrum
Gen.	nigrī	nigrae	nigrī
Dat.	nigrō	nigrae	nigrō
Abl.	nigrō	nigrā	nigrō

PLURAL.			
N. V.	nigrī	nigrae	nigră
Acc.	nigrōs	nigrās	nigră
Gen.	nigrōrum	nigrārum	nigrōrum
D., Abl.	nigrīs	nigrīs	nigrīs

Decline also: aeger, *sick*; āter, *jet-black*; pulcher, *beautiful*; ruber, *red*; sacer, *sacred*.

Note.—Dexter, *on the right hand*, may be declined like tener or like niger.

72 B. Adjectives of two endings and of one ending in the Nominative Singular are declined like Substantives of the Third Declension.

73 (1) Adjectives with Nominative Singular in **-is**, Masc. and Fem.; in **-e** Neuter: I- Stems.

Stem   tristĭ-, *sad.*

	SINGULAR.		PLURAL.	
	M. F.	N.	M. F.	N.
N. V.	tristĭs	tristĕ	tristēs	tristiă
Acc.	tristem	tristĕ	tristēs, -īs	tristiă
Gen.	tristĭs	tristĭs	tristium	tristium
D., Abl.	tristī	tristī	tristĭbŭs	tristĭbŭs

Decline also: brĕvis, *short*; omnis, *all*; aequālis, *equal*; hostīlis, *hostile*; facilis, *easy*; illustris, *illustrious*; lūgubris, *mournful.*

Some stems in **ri-** form the Masc. Nom. Sing. in **-er** :

Stem   ăcrĭ-, *keen.*

SING.	M.	F.	N.
N. V.	ācĕr	ăcrĭs	ācrĕ
Acc.	acrem	acrem	acrĕ
Gen.	acrĭs	acrĭs	acrĭs
Dat.	acrī	acrī	acrī
Abl.	acrī	acrī	acrī

PLUR.			
N. V.	acrēs	acrēs	acriă
Acc.	acrēs, -īs	acrēs, -īs	acriă
Gen.	acrium	acrium	acrium
D., Abl.	acrĭbŭs	acrĭbŭs	acrĭbŭs

Decline like acer the following: celĕber, *famous*; salūber, *healthy*; alăcer, *brisk*; volŭcer, *winged*; campester, *level*; equester, *equestrian*; pedester, *pedestrian*; paluster, *marshy*; puter, *crumbling*; with September, October, November, December, masculine only.

Note.—In celer, celĕris, celĕrĕ, *swift*, the Stem ends in **-ĕrĭ-** and the e is kept throughout.

74   (2) Adjectives with Nom. Sing. the same for all genders :.

(a) *I- Stems.*

Stem   fēlīcĭ-, *happy.*

	M. F. SING.	N.	M. F. PLUR.	N.
N. V.	felix	felix	felicēs	feliciă
Acc.	felĭcem	felix ·	felicēs, -īs	feliciă
Gen.	felicĭs	felicĭs	felicium	felicium
Dat.	felicī	felicī	felicĭbŭs	felicĭbŭs
Abl. ·	felicī, -ĕ	felicī, -ĕ	felicĭbŭs	felicĭbŭs

Stem   ingentĭ-, *huge.*

	M. F. SING.	N.	M. F. PLUR.	N.
N. V.	ingens	ingens	ingentēs	ingentia
Acc.	ingentem	ingens	ingentēs, -īs	ingentiă
Gen.	ingentĭs		ingentium	
Dat.	ingentī		ingentĭbŭs	
Abl.	ingentī, -ĕ		ingentĭbŭs	

Decline also: audax, audāci-, *bold* ; simplex, simplici-, *simple* ; duplex, duplici-, *double* ; vēlox, velōci-, *swift* ; amans, amanti-, *loving* ; sapiens, sapienti-, *wise* ; concors, concordi-, *agreeing* ; par, pari-, *like.*

Note 1.—The genitive plural of Participles is almost always in **-ium.** Of some adjectives it is in **-um**: dēgener, *degenerate* ; inops, *destitute* ; memor, *mindful* ; supplex, *suppliant* ; vigil, *wakeful.* Many adjectives with Stems in **tĭ-** have gen. plur. **-ium** or **-um.***

Note 2.—The abl. sing. generally ends in **ī** when an adjective is used with a substantive : a mīlite vigili, *by a watchful soldier* ; and in **e** when an adjective stands for a substantive : a vigile, *by a watchman.* The same rule applies to present participles ; and in the ablative absolute construction the ablative always ends in **e** : viridanti quercu cinctus, *wreathed with green oak* ; viridante quercu, *when the oak is green.*

* It is to be remarked that when either in a Substantive or an Adjective a long syllable comes before the Stem Character, the genitive plural generally ends in **-ium** ; when a short vowel comes before the Stem Character, it ends in **-um** ; but this cannot be laid down as an invariable rule.

75   (b) *Consonant Stems.*

Consonant Stems, except pauper, form the Nom. Sing. in **s**.

Stem   divet-,   divit-, *rich.*

SING. *N. V.*	**divĕs**	PLUR. **divitēs**
Acc.	**divĭtem**	**divitēs**
Gen.	**divitĭs**	**divitum**
Dat.	**divitī**	**divitĭbŭs**
Abl.	**divitĕ**	**divitĭbŭs**

Decline like **dives**: pauper, pauper-, *poor*; sospes, sospit-, *safe*; superstes, superstit-, *surviving*; deses, desid-, *slothful*; reses, resid-, *reposing*; compos, compot-, *possessing*; caelebs, caelib-, *unmarried*; pubes, puber-, *full grown*; vetus, veter-, *old.*

Note.—Dives has a contracted form dīs, acc. ditem, &c.; with abl. sing. diti and neut. plur. dītia; gen. plur. ditium. Dives and vetus are used as neut. acc. sing. Vetus has neut. plur. vetera. The rest have no neuter forms.

COMPARISON OF ADJECTIVES.

76   Adjectives are compared in three degrees.

(1) Positive :   **dūrus,** *hard.*   **tristis,** *sad.*
(2) Comparative : **duriŏr,** *harder.* **tristiŏr,** *sadder.*
(3) Superlative : **durissimus,** *hardest.* **tristissimus,** *saddest.*

The Positive is the adjective itself expressing the quality; the Comparative expresses a greater degree; the Superlative expresses a very great, or the greatest, degree of the quality.

The Comparative is formed from the Positive by adding the suffix **-ior** to the last consonant of the Stem; the Superlative generally by adding **-issimus** to the last consonant of the Stem.

Stem	Positive	Comparative	Superlative
dur-o-	durus	dur-iŏr	dur-issimus
trist-i-	tristis	trist-iŏr	trist-issimus
audāc-i-	audax, *bold*	audac-iŏr	audac-issimus

77   The Comparative is declined as follows :

	M. F. SING.	N.	M. F. PLUR.	N.
N. V.	**tristior**	**tristius**	**tristiōrēs**	**tristiŏră**
Acc.	**tristiōrem**	**tristius**	**tristior-es**	**tristiŏră**
Gen.	**tristiōrĭs**		**tristiorum**	
Dat.	**tristiorī**		**tristiorĭbŭs**	
Abl.	**tristior-ĕ, -ī***		**tristiorĭbŭs**	

* The Ablative in -i of the Comparative is rare, and only used by late writers.

78.   The Superlative is declined from o- and a- Stems, like bonus.

Adjectives with Stems in **ro-**, **ri-**, form the Superlative by doubling the last consonant of the Stem and adding **-imus**. Words like niger insert **e** before **r** in the Superlative.

Stem	Positive	Comparative	Superlative
tenero-	tener	tenerior	tenerrimus
nigro-	niger	nigrior	nigerrimus
celeri-	celer	celerior	celerrimus
veteri-	vetus (veter)	vetustior (veterior)	veterrimus

Six adjectives with Stems in **ili-** also form the Superlative by doubling the last consonant of the Stem and adding -imus :

facilis, *easy.*	similis, *like.*	gracilis, *slender.*
difficilis, *difficult.*	dissimilis, *unlike.*	humilis, *lowly.*

facili-	facilis	facilior	facillimus

79   Many Participles are compared like adjectives :

amans, *loving*	amantior	amantissimus
parātus, *ready*	paratior	paratissimus

IRREGULAR COMPARISON.

80   (1) Some Comparatives and Superlatives are formed from Stems distinct from that of the Positive :

Positive	Comparative	Superlative
bonus, *good.*	melior, *better.*	optimus, *best.*
malus, *bad.*	pējor, *worse.*	pessimus, *worst.*
parvus, *small.*	minor, *less.*	minimus, *least.*
multus, *much.*	plūs, *more.*	plūrimus, *most.*
magnus, *great.*	mājor	maximus
nēquam (indecl.), *wicked.*	nequior	nequissimus
frūgi (indecl.), *honest.*	frugalior	frugalissimus
senex, *old.*	{ senior { nātu mājor	natu maximus
juvenis, *young.*	{ jūnior { nātu minor	natu minimus

Note 1.—Senior, junior are not used as true comparatives of senex, juvenis, but with the meaning *old rather than young,* and *young rather than old.*

Note 2.—Dives has both uncontracted and contracted forms :

dives } (dis) } , *rich.*	{ dīvitior { dītior	dīvitissimus dītissimus

Plus in the Sing. is neuter only :

SING.		M. F. PLUR.	N.
N. V. Acc.	plus	plures	plura
Gen.	pluris	plurium	
Dat. Abl.	pluri	pluribus	

81 (2) Adjectives compounded with -dĭcus, -fĭcus, -vŏlus (from dico, facio, volo), form the Comparative and Superlative as if from participles in -ens.

Positive	Comparative	Superlative
malĕdĭcus, *evil-speaking.*	maledīcentior	maledīcentissimus
benĕfĭcus, *beneficent.*	beneficentior	beneficentissimus.
benĕvŏlus, *well-wishing.*	benevolentior	benevolentissimus
Also: egēnus, *needy.*	egentior	egentĭssimus
prōvĭdus, *provident.*	providentior	providentissimus

82 (3) Adjectives in -eus, -ius, -uus are generally compared with the adverbs magis, maxime; as dubius, *doubtful,* magis dubius, *more doubtful,* maxime dubius, *most doubtful.*

Note.—Some adjectives in **-uus** are compared regularly: aequus, *level,* aequior, aequissimus; antiquus, *ancient*; and more rarely, strēnuus, *vigorous,* strenuior. Egregius has comp. egregior.

83 (4) Some adjectives have no Comparative forms; some no Superlative; of some the Comparative and Superlative are found without the Positive: ōcior, *swifter,* ocissimus, *swiftest.*

84 Some Comparatives denoting relations of place have no Positive, but correspond to Adverbs from the same Stem.

Adverb.	Comparative Adj.	Superlative Adj.
*extrā, *outside.*	extĕrior	extrēmus, extĭmus
intrā, *within.*	intĕrior	intĭmus
*suprā, *above.*	supĕrior	suprēmus, summus
*infrā, *below.*	infĕrior	infĭmus, ĭmus
citrā, *on this side.*	citĕrior	citĭmus
ultrā, *beyond.*	ultĕrior	ultĭmus
prae, *before.*	prior	prīmus, *first.*
*post, *after.*	postĕrior	postrēmus, *last.*
prŏpĕ, *near.*	propior	proximus

*Note.—The adjectives exterus, superus, inferus, posterus, are, however, sometimes found. Also :

dexter (adj.), *on the right.*	dexterior	dexterrimus, dextimus
sinister (adj.), *on the left.*	sinisterior	
[deter-]	detĕrior, *worse.*	deterrimus, *worst.*

COMPARISON OF ADVERBS.

85   Adverbs derived from adjectives and ending in -ē, -ō, -ter, and rarely -ĕ, form Comparative in -ius, Superlative in -issimē.

Note.—These forms are the neut. acc. sing. of the Comp. adjective and an old neut. abl. sing. of the Superl. adjective.

Adjective	Adverb	Comparative	Superlative
dignus, *worthy.*	dignē, *worthily.*	dignius	dignissimē
tutus, *safe.*	tūtō, *safely.*	tutius	tutissimē
fortis, *brave.*	fortiter, *bravely.*	fortius	fortissimē
constans, *firm.*	constanter, *firmly.*	constantius	constantissimē
audax, *bold.*	audacter, *boldly.*	audācius	audacissimē
facilis, *easy.*	facile, *easily.*	facilius	facillimē

86   Irregular comparison has corresponding forms in Adverbs.

Adverb	Comparative	Superlative
benĕ, *well.*	melius	optimē
malĕ, *ill.*	pējus	pessimē
paullum, *little.*	mĭnus	mĭnimē
multum, *much.*	plus	plurimum
magnŏpĕre, *greatly.*	măgis	maximē
	ocius, *more quickly.*	ocissimē

Magis, *more* (in degree) ; plus, *more* (in quantity).

87   In like manner are compared :

diū, *long.*	diūtius	diūtissimē
intus, *within.*	intĕrius	intimē
(prae, *before*).	prius	primo
post, *after.*	postĕrius	postrēmō
prŏpĕ, *near.*	propius	proximē
saepĕ, *often.*	saepius	saepissimē
nūper, *lately.*		nuperrimē

88 NUMERALS.

Numeral Adjectives are of three kinds :
1. Cardinals ; answering the question, *How many ?*
2. Ordinals; answering the question, *Which in order of number ?*
3. Distributives ; answering the question, *How many each ?*

Numeral Adverbs answer the question, *How many times ?*

89 Unus, from **o-** and **a-** Stems, is declined as follows :

	SING.				PLUR.	
Nom.	ūnus	ūna	ūnum	unī	unae	ună
Acc.	unum	unam	unum	unōs	unās	una
Gen.	unius	unius	unius	unorum	unarum	unorum
Dat.	unī	unī	unī	unīs	unīs	unīs
Abl.	unō	unā	unō	unīs	unīs	unīs

Dŭŏ is an **o-** Stem, and trēs an **i-** Stem.

	M.	F.	N.	M. and F.	N.
Nom.	dŭŏ	duae	dŭŏ	trēs	tria
Acc.	duōs, dŭō	duās	duo	trēs	tria
Gen.	duōrum	duārum	duōrum	trium	trium
D., Abl.	duōbŭs	duābŭs	duōbŭs	trĭbŭs	trĭbŭs

Decline like **duo** : ambō, *both*.

Note.—Duum is sometimes used for duorum.

The Cardinals from quattuor to centum are indeclinable. Hundreds from *two* to *nine hundred* are **o-** and **a-** Stems, ducentī, ducentae, ducenta. Mille (*a thousand*) is an indeclinable adjective ; but mīlia (*thousands*) is a neuter substantive declined like animalia. Mille passus, *a mile*.

In Compound Numbers above twenty, the order is the same as in English. Either the smaller number with **et** comes first, or the larger without **et** : septem et trīginta, *seven and thirty* ; or trīginta septem, *thirty-seven*. Unus usually stands first : unus et vīgintī, *twenty-one*. In numbers above a hundred the larger comes first, with or without **et**.

Thousands are expressed by putting (1) the numeral adverbs bis, ter, &c., before mille : bis mille ; or (2) cardinal numbers before milia : duo milia. Milia is followed by a genitive : duo milia hominum, *two thousand men*.

Arabic Numerals	Roman Numerals	Cardinals; answering the question Quŏt? how many?	Ordinals; answering the question Quŏtus? which in order of number? m. -ŭs, f. -ă, n. -um.	Distributives; answering the question Quŏtēnī? how many each? m. -ī, f. -ae, n. -ă	Numeral Adverbs; answering the question Quŏtiens? how many times?
1	I	ūnus	primus (prior), first	singŭlī, one each	sēmĕl, once
2	II	duo	secundus (alter), second	bīnī, two each	bĭs, twice
3	III	trēs	tertius, third, &c.	ternī, or trinī, three each, &c.	tĕr, three times, &c.
4	IIII or IV	quattuor	quartus	quăternī	quătĕr
5	V	quīnque	quintus	quīnī	quinquiens
6	VI	sex	sextus	sēnī	sexiens
7	VII	septem	septimus	septēnī	septiens
8	VIII or IIX	octo	octāvus	octōnī	octiens
9	VIIII or IX	nŏvem	nōnus	nŏvēnī	noviens
10	X	dĕcem	decimus	dēnī	deciens
11	XI	undĕcim	undecimus	undenī	undĕciens
12	XII	duodecim	duodecimus	duodenī	duodeciens
13	XIII	tredecim	tertius decimus	ternī denī	tredeciens
14	XIIII or XIV	quattuordecim	quartus decimus	quaternī denī	quattuordeciens
15	XV	quindecim	quintus decimus	quīnī denī	quindeciens
16	XVI	sēdecim	sextus decimus	sēnī denī	sēdeciens
17	XVII	septemdecim	septimus decimus	septeni denī	septiesdeciens
18	XVIII or XIIX	{duodēvigintī / octodecim}	duodēvicensimus	duodēvicenī	duodeviciens
19	XVIIII or XIX	{undēvigintī / novendecim}	undēvicensimus	undēvicenī	undeviciens
20	XX	vigintī	vicensimus	vicēnī	viciens
21	XXI	unus et vigintī	unus et vicensimus	viceni singulī	semel et viciens
22	XXII	duo et vigintī	alter et vicensimus	viceni bīnī	bis et viciens
28	XXVIII or XXIIX	duodetrigintā	duodetrigensimus	duodetricenī	duodētriciens
29	XXVIIII or XXIX	undetrigintā	undetrigensimus	undetricenī	undetriciens

30	XXX trīginta	trīgensimus	trīcēni	trīciens
40	XXXX or XL quādrāginta	quādrāgensimus	quādrāgēni	quādrāgiens
50	L quinquāginta	quinquāgensimus	quinquāgēni	quinquāgiens
60	LX sexāginta	sexāgensimus	sexāgēni	sexāgiens
70	LXX septuāginta	septuāgensimus	septuāgēni	septuāgiens
80	LXXX or XXC octōginta	octōgensimus	octōgēni	octōgiens
90	LXXXX or XC nōnāginta	nōnāgensimus	nōnāgēni	nōnāgiens
98	XCIIX or IIC octo et nōnāginta	duodēcentensimus	duodēcentēni	duodēcentiens
99	XCIX or IC undēcentum	undēcentensimus	undēcentēni	undēcentiens
100	C centum	centensimus	centēni	centiens
101	CI centum et unus	centensimus primus	centēni singuli	centiens semel
126	CXXVI centum vīginti sex	centensimus vicensimus sextus	centēni vicēni sēni	centiens viciens sexiens
200	CC dūcenti, ae, a	ducentensimus	duceni	ducentiens
300	CCC trēcenti	trecentensimus	trecēni	trecentiens
400	CCCC quadringenti	quadringentensimus	quadringēni	quadringentiens
500	Io or D quingenti	quingentensimus	quingēni	quingentiens
600	Ioc sexcenti	sexcentensimus	sēcēni	sexcentiens
700	Iocc septingenti	septingentensimus	septingēni	septingentiens
800	Ioccc octingenti	octingentensimus	octingēni	octingentiens
900	Iocccc nongenti, noning-	nongentensimus	nongēni	nongentiens
1,000	cIo or M millē	millensimus	singula milia	miliens
2,000	cIocIo or MM duo milia	bis-millensimus	bīna milia	bis miliens
5,000	Ioo quinque milia	quinquiens millensimus	quīna milia	quinquiens miliens
10,000	ccIoo decem milia	deciens millensimus	dēna milia	deciens miliens
50,000	Iooo quinquāginta milia	quinquāgiens millensimus	quinquāgēna milia	quinquāgiens miliens
100,000	ccIooo centum milia	centiens millensimus	centēna milia	centiens miliens
500,000	Ioooo quingenta milia	quingentiens millensimus	quingēna milia	quingentiens miliens
1,000,000	ccIoooo deciens centum milia	deciens centiens millensimus	deciens centēna milia	deciens centiens miliens

Note 1.—MULTIPLICATIVES, answering the question, *how many fold?* (formed with Stem **plic—,** *fold*). are: simplex, duplex, triplex, &c., centuplex, *a hundredfold*.

Note 2.—PROPORTIONALS, answering the question, *how many times as great?* are: simplus; duplus, *double*; triplus, *treble*; quadruplus, *quadruple*.

PRONOUNS.

91 Pronouns either stand in the place of Substantives, or stand in the place of Adjectives, to define or point out Substantives.

There are three Persons :

First : The person speaking : *I* or *we.*
Second : The person spoken to : *thou* or *ye* (*you*).
Third : The person or thing spoken of : *he, she, it, they.*

Personal Pronouns stand only in place of Substantives. Possessive Pronouns, as meus, *my*, stand only for Adjectives. Most of the others can stand for Substantives or Adjectives.

92 PERSONAL AND REFLEXIVE.

SINGULAR.

	1st Person.		2nd Person.	
Nom.	**ĕgŏ,**	*I.*	**tū,**	*thou* (so also Voc.)
Acc.	**mē,**	*me.*	**tē,**	*thee.*
Gen.	**meī,**	*of me.*	**tuī,**	*of thee.*
Dat.	**mĭhĭ,**	*to me.*	**tĭbĭ,**	*to thee.*
Abl.	**mē,**	*from me.*	**tē,**	*from thee.*

PLURAL.

	1st Person.		2nd Person.	
Nom.	**nōs,**	*we.*	**vōs,**	*ye* (so also Voc.)
Acc.	**nōs,**	*us.*	**vōs,**	*you.*
Gen.	{**nostrī** / **nostrum**},	*of us.*	{**vestrī** / **vestrum**},	*of you.*
Dat.	**nōbīs,**	*to us.*	**vōbīs,**	*to you.*
Abl.	**nōbīs,**	*from us.*	**vōbīs,**	*from you.*

Reflexive Pronoun.

Nom.	—	
Acc.	**sē** or **sēsē,**	*himself, herself, itself,* or *themselves.*
Gen.	**suī,**	*of himself, &c.*
Dat.	**sĭbĭ,**	*to himself, &c.*
Abl.	**sē** or **sēsē,**	*from himself, &c.*

For the Personal Pronoun of the 3rd Person, *he, she, it*, the Demonstrative **is, ea, id,** is used.

Note.—Nostri, vestri, are called Objective Genitives : memor nostri, *mindful of us* (264). Nostrum, vestrum, are called Partitive Genitives, because they are used after words which express a part : unus nostrum, *one of us* (259).

93 POSSESSIVE.

SING.
1st Person : **meŭs, meă, meum,** *my.*
2nd Person : **tuŭs, tuă, tuum,** *thy.*

PLUR.
1st Person : **nostĕr, nostră, nostrum,** *our.*
2nd Person : **vestĕr, vestră, vestrum,** *your.*

Suus, sua, suum, *his, her, its, their,* is the Possessive Pronoun of the Reflexive.

Note.—Meus, tuus, suus are declined like bonus : noster, vester, like niger. Meus has voc. sing. masc. **mī.** The other possessives, except noster, have no vocative.

94 DEMONSTRATIVE.

Is, *that,* or *he, she, it.*

	SINGULAR.			PLURAL.		
	M.	**F.**	**N.**	**M.**	**F.**	**N.**
Nom.	ĭs	eă	ĭd	iī *or* eī	eae	eă
Acc.	eum	eam	id	eōs	eās	eă
Gen.	ējŭs	ējŭs	ējŭs	eōrum	eārum	eōrum
Dat.	eī	eī	eī	iīs (eīs)	iīs (eīs)	iīs (eīs)
Abl.	eō	eā	eō	iīs (eīs)	iīs (eīs)	iīs (eīs)

Hic, *this (near me),* or *he, she, it.*

	SINGULAR.			PLURAL.		
	M.	**F.**	**N.**	**M.**	**F.**	**N.**
Nom.	hĭc	haec	hōc	hī	hae	haec
Acc.	hunc	hanc	hoc	hōs	hās	haec
Gen.	hūjus	hūjus	hūjus	hōrum	hārum	hōrum
Dat.	huic	huic	huic	hīs	hīs	hīs
Abl.	hōc	hāc	hōc	hīs	hīs	hīs

Ille, *that (yonder),* or *he, she, it.*

	SINGULAR.			PLURAL.		
	M.	**F.**	**N.**	**M.**	**F.**	**N.**
Nom.	illĕ	illă	illŭd	illī	illae	illă
Acc.	illum	illam	illud	illōs	illās	illă
Gen.	illĭus	illĭus	illĭus	illōrum	illārum	illōrum
Dat.	illī	illī	illī	illīs	illīs	illīs
Abl.	illō	illă	illō	illīs	illīs	illīs

Istĕ, *that (near you),* is declined like ille.

95

DEFINITIVE.

Idem, *same.*

SINGULAR.

	M.	F.	N.
Nom.	īdem	eădem	īdem
Acc.	eundem	eandem	idem
Gen.	ējusdem	ējusdem	ējusdem
Dat.	eīdem	eīdem	eīdem
Abl.	eōdem	eādem	eōdem

PLURAL.

	M.	F.	N.
Nom.	eīdem *or* īdem	eaedem	eădem
Acc.	eosdem	easdem	eadem
Gen.	eōrundem	eārundem	eōrundem
Dat.	eīsdem *or* īsdem		
Abl.	eīsdem *or* īsdem		

Ipsĕ, *self.*

	SINGULAR.			PLURAL.		
	M.	F.	N.	M.	F.	N.
Nom.	ipsĕ	ipsă	ipsum	ipsī	ipsae	ipsă
Acc.	ipsum	ipsam	ipsum	ipsōs	ipsas	ipsă
Gen.	ipsĭus	ipsĭus	ipsĭus	ipsōrum	ipsārum	ipsōrum
Dat.	ipsī	ipsī	ipsī	ipsīs	ipsīs	ipsīs
Abl.	ipsō	ipsā	ipsō	ipsīs	ipsīs	ipsīs

96

Note.—The suffixes -met, -te, -pte *or* -pse, -ce are added to some cases of pronouns for emphasis:

(*a*) met may be joined (1) to ego and its cases, except gen. plur.: egomet, *I myself*; (2) to the cases of tu, except nom. sing.: vosmet, *ye yourselves*; (3) to se and its cases, except sui: sibimet; (4) to the cases of suus: suamet facta.

(*b*) te is joined to tu: tute; also tutemet, *thou thyself.*

(*c*) pte is joined especially to the abl. sing. of the possessive pronouns: meopte consilio, *by my advice.*

(*d*) ce is joined to the demonstrative: hunce, hujusce.

For istece, illece, are written istic, illic:

SING.	M.	F.	N.
Nom.	istic	istaec	istuc
Acc.	istunc	istanc	istuc
Gen.	istiusce	istiusce	istiusce
Abl.	istoc	istac	istoc

Idem (for is-dem), and ipse (for is-pse), are emphatic forms of is.

97

RELATIVE.

Qui, *who, which.*

	SINGULAR.			PLURAL.		
	M.	F.	N.	M.	F.	N.
Nom.	quī	quae	quŏd	quī	quae	quae
Acc.	quem	quam	quod	quōs	quās	quae
Gen.	cūjŭs	cūjŭs	cūjŭs	quōrum	quārum	quōrum
Dat.	cuī	cuī	cuī	quĭbŭs *or* quīs		
Abl.	quō	quā	quō	quĭbŭs *or* quīs		

98

INTERROGATIVE.

Quis, *who ? what ?*

	M.	F.	N.		M.	F.	N.
Nom.	{ quĭs	(quĭs)	quĭd	*Acc.*	{ quem	quam	quĭd
	{ quī	quae	quŏd		{ quem	quam	quŏd

In all other Cases singular and plural qui Interrogative is
like the Relative.

99

INDEFINITE.

Quis, *anyone* or *anything.*

	M.	F.	N.		M.	F.	N.
Nom.	{ quĭs	quă	quĭd	*Acc.*	{ quem	quam	quĭd
	{ quī	quae	quŏd		{ quem	quam	quŏd

In the other Cases singular and plural the Indefinite is like
the Relative, except that quă or quae may be used in neut. nom.
and acc. plural.

Quis, both Interrogative and Indefinite, and its compounds,
are used **chiefly** as Substantives; **qui** and its compounds **chiefly**
as Adjectives.

Quid and its compounds are used **only** as Substantives;
quod and its compounds **only** as Adjectives.

EXAMPLES :

Homo qui venit,	*The man who comes.*	(qui, relative.)
Quis venit ?	*Who comes ?*	(quis, interrogative.)
Qui homo venit ?	*What man comes ?*	(qui, interrogative.)
Aliquid amari,	*Some bitterness.*	
Aliquod verbum,	*Some word*	

100

COMPOUND PRONOUNS.

MASC.	FÉM.	NEUT.	
quīcŭmquĕ,	quaecumquĕ,	quodcumquĕ,	} whosoever, or
quisquĭs,	quisquĭs,	quidquĭd or quicquĭd,	} whatsoever.
quīdam,	quaedam,	quiddam (quoddam),	{ a certain person or thing.
ălĭquĭs,	ălĭquă,	ălĭquid,	} someone or
aliquī,	aliquă,	aliquod,	} something.
quispiam,	quaepiam,	quippiam (quodpiam),	someone.
quīvīs,	quaevīs,	quidvīs (quodvīs),	} anyone you
quīlĭbĕt,	quaelĭbĕt,	quidlĭbĕt (quodlĭbĕt),	} like.
quisquam	——	quidquam or quicquam,	{ anyone at all.
quisquĕ,	quaequĕ,	quidquĕ (quodque),	{ each one severally.
ŭterquĕ,	utraquĕ,	utrumquĕ,	each of two.
ūnusquisquĕ,	ūnăquaequĕ,	ūnumquiquĕ (unumquodquĕ),	} each single one.
ecquis,	ecquă,	ecquid (ecquod),	{ Is there any who ?
quisnam,	quaenam,	quidnam (quodnam)	Who, pray ?

Note 1.—Quisquis is found only in nom. acc. and abl.

Note 2.—Quisquam is used as a substantive, sing. only, chiefly in negative sentences and the adjective which corresponds to it is ullus : haud quisquam, *not anyone.*

Note 3.—In the Compound Pronouns qui, quis, and uter follow their own declension in the oblique cases; the prefix or suffix is unaltered : alicujus, cujusque, cuivis, utroque, quamlibet. In unus-quisque both unus and quisque are declined.

The following Pronominal Adjectives form the Gen. Sing. in -ius and the Dat. Sing. in -ī like ille : alius, *other, another* ; ullus, *any* ; nullus, *none* ; sōlus, *sole* ; tōtus, *whole* ; ŭter, *which of two* ; alter, *one of two, the other* ; neuter, *neither.*

101

	SINGULAR.			PLURAL.		
	M.	**F.**	**N.**	**M.**	**F.**	**N.**
Nom.	ălĭŭs	ălĭă	ălĭŭd	ălĭī	ălĭae	ălĭă
Acc.	alium	aliam	alĭŭd	aliōs	aliās	alia
Gen.	alīŭs	alīŭs	alīŭs	aliōrum	aliārum	aliōrum
Dat.	alĭī	alĭī	alĭī	aliīs	aliīs	aliīs
Abl.	aliō	aliā	aliō	aliīs	aliīs	aliīs

> *Note.*—In alius the i of the Gen. Sing. is always long. In the Gen. of words declined like it the quantity of the i is doubtful; also in the Gen. of uter, neuter.

Like alius, but with Neuter Singular in -um, are declined ullus, nullus, sōlus, tōtus.

SINGULAR.

	M.	**F.**	**N.**
Nom.	altĕr	altĕră	altĕrum
Acc.	altĕrum	altĕram	altĕrum
Gen.	alterĭŭs	alterĭŭs	alterĭŭs
Dat.	alterī	alterī	alterī
Abl.	alterō	alteră	alterō

PLURAL.

	M.	**F.**	**N.**
Nom.	altĕrī	altĕrae	altĕră
Acc.	alterōs	alterās	altĕră
Gen.	alterōrum	alterārum	alterōrum
Dat.	alterīs	alterīs	alterīs
Abl.	alterīs	alterīs	alterīs

Like alter, but casting out e before r in all cases except the Nom. Sing. Masculine, are declined,—

ŭter, utra, utrum, *which (of two)* ; neuter, neutra, neutrum, *neither.* These are seldom used in the plural.

> *Note 1.*—Uter forms compounds by taking nearly all the same suffixes as quis and qui: utercumque, *whichever of two* ; ŭtervĭs, ŭterlĭbĕt. Alterŭter, *one or the other*, is usually declined only as uter, but sometimes both parts are declined.
>
> *Note 2.*—The genitive and ablative singular of nullus are used for the genitive and ablative of the substantive nemo, *nobody*, which are very rarely found.

102

Interrogative.	*Demonstrative.*	*Relative.*	*Indefinite* (1).
quis, qui, *who? which?*	is, *that.*	qui, *who, which.*	(si) quis, *if any one.*
uter, *which of two?*	alter, *one of two, other of two.*		
quālis, *of what kind?*	tālis, *of such kind.*	qualis, *as.*	
quantus, *how great?*	tantus, *so great.*	quantus, *as (great).*	
quot, *how many?*	tot, *so many.*	quot, *as (many).*	
ubi, *where?*	ibi, *there.*	ubi, *where.*	si(cubi), *if anywhere.*
unde, *whence?*	inde, *thence.*	unde, *whence.*	si(cunde), *if from any quarter.*
quo, *whither?*	eo, *thither.*	quo, *whither.*	(si) quo, *if anywhither.*
quā, *by what way?*	eā, *by that way.*	quā, *by what way.*	(si) quā, *if by any way.*
quam, *how?*	tam, *so.*	quam, *as.*	
quando, *when?*	tum, *then.*	quando, *when.* ubi, *when.* cum, *when.*	(si) quando, *if ever.*
quotiens, *how often?*	totiens, *so often.*	quotiens, *as (often).*	

Pronouns and Adverbs.

Indefinite (2).	Distributive.	Universal Relative.
aliquis, *some one.*	quisque, *each.*	quicumque, *whoever whatever.*
alteruter, *one or other of two.*	uterque, *each of two.*	utercumque, *whichever of two.*
		qualiscumque, *of what kind soever.*
aliquantus, *some (in quantity).*		quantuscumque, *however great.*
aliquot, *some (in number).*		quotcumque, *however many.*
alicubi, *somewhere.*	ubique, *everywhere.*	ubicumque, *wheresoever.*
alicunde, *from some quarter.*	undique, *from every side.*	undecumque, *whencesoever.*
aliquo, *somewhither.*		quocumque, *whithersoever.*
aliquā, *by some way.*		quācumque, *by whatsoever way.*
aliquando, *at some time.*		quandocumque, *whensoever.*
aliquotiens, *at some (various) times.*		quotienscumque, *however often.*

103

VERBS.

The **Verb** has:

The **Three Persons**—First, Second, Third.
The **Two Numbers**—Singular and Plural.
Six Tenses:
    (1) Present, (2) Future Simple, (3) Past
        Imperfect, (4) Perfect or Aorist,
        (5) Future Perfect, (6) Pluperfect.
Three Moods:
    (1) Indicative, (2) Imperative, (3) Conjunctive.

⎱ The Verb Finite.

The **Infinitive** (Verbal Substantive).
Three Participles (Verbal Adjectives).
The **Gerund** and **Gerundive** (Verbal Substantive
    and Adjective).
Two Supines (Verbal Substantives).

⎱ The Verb Infinite.

Two Voices:

    (1) Active, (2) Passive.

The Verb Finite is so called because it is limited by Mood
and Persons; while the Verb Infinite is not so limited.

104   PERSON AND NUMBER.

In English, Pronouns are used with Verbs to express the
three Persons Singular and Plural: *I am, We are.* But in
Latin the Pronouns are expressed by the personal suffixes.

su-**m**,	*I am,* am-o, *I love.*	su-**mus**,	*we are.*
e-**s**,	*thou art (you are).*	es-**tis**,	*ye are.*
es-**t**,	*he (she, it) is.*	su-**nt**,	*they are.*

TABLE OF PERSONAL ENDINGS IN THE INDICATIVE AND CONJUNCTIVE MOODS.

		ACTIVE VOICE.	PASSIVE VOICE.
Singular	1	-m *or* -ō	-r
	2	-s	-rĭs *or* -rĕ
	3	-t	-tŭr
Plural	1	-mŭs	-mŭr
	2	-tĭs	-mĭnī
	3	-nt	-ntŭr

The Imperative Mood has only the Second and Third Person Singular and Plural, not the First.

105   TENSES.

Tenses express the time of the action or state denoted by the Verb, as being:

    (1) Present, Past, or Future ;

    (2) Complete or Incomplete ;

    (3) Momentary or Continuous.

In English, by means of auxiliary Verbs, differences of time can be more accurately expressed than in Latin; so that one tense in Latin may correspond to two tenses in English, of which one is momentary, the other continuous. Thus, rogo, *I ask*, has the following tenses :

Present	Present	*incomplete*	rogo	{ *I ask* { *I am asking*
	Perfect	*complete*	rogavi	{ *I have asked* { *I have been asking*
Future	Fut. Simple	*incomplete*	rogabo	{ *I shall ask* { *I shall be asking*
	Fut. Perf.	*complete*	rogavero	{ *I shall have asked* { *I shall have been asking*
Past	Perfect } Imperf. }	*incomplete*	{ rogavi { rogabam	{ *I asked* { *I was asking*
	Pluperf.	*complete*	rogaveram	{ *I had asked* { *I had been asking*

Note.—Latin has no separate tenses corresponding to the Greek Aorist and Perfect; therefore the Perfect has to fill the place of two Tenses: the Aorist, *I loved*, and the Perfect, *I have loved.*

The Present, the Future Simple, and the Future Perfect are called **Primary** Tenses.

The Imperfect and the Pluperfect are called **Historic** Tenses.

The Perfect in the sense of *I have loved* is **Primary**; in the sense of *I loved* it is **Historic**.

106

Mood.

Moods are the forms in which the idea contained in the Verb is presented.

The **Indicative** is the mood which states a fact: amo, *I love.*

The **Imperative** is the mood of command: amā, *love thou.*

> *Note.*—The forms of the Imperative in **-to, -tote,** are emphatic, and were used anciently in laws.

The **Conjunctive** is the mood which represents something as thought of or as dependent: ut amem, *that I may love*; si amarem, *if I were to love.*

It has no Future tense-forms, but its other tenses can be used with future meaning.

> *Note.*—In the Paradigms the tenses of the Conjunctive are given without any English translation, because their meaning varies so much according to the context that it is impossible to convey it by any one rendering.

107
THE VERB INFINITE.

The **Infinitive** is a Verb Noun expressing action or state in general, without limit of person or number : amāre, *to love.*

The **Gerund** is a Verbal Substantive declined like neuters of the Second Declension. It supplies Cases to the Infinitive : as amandi, *of loving.*

The **Gerundive** is a Participle, or Verbal Adjective : amandus, a, um, *meet to be loved.*

The **Supines** are Cases of a Verbal Substantive : amātum, *in order to love*; amātu, *for* or *in loving.*

The **Participles** are so called because they have partly the properties of Verbs and partly those of Adjectives ; there are three besides the Gerundive :

(*a*) Act. Pres. amans, *loving* (declined like ingens).
(*b*) Act. Fut. amatūrus, *about to love*⎱ (declined like
(*c*) Pass. Perf. amātus, *loved* ⎰ bonus).

Note.—The three Participles wanting are : (*a*) Active Perfect, (*b*) Passive Present, (*c*) Passive Future.

108
VOICE.

The **Active Voice** expresses what the Subject of a Verb is or does :
sum, *I am*; valeo, *I am well*; amō, *I love*; regō, *I rule.*

The **Passive Voice** expresses what is done to the Subject of the Verb :

109
amor, *I am loved*; regor, *I am ruled.*

Deponent Verbs are Verbs which have chiefly the forms of the Passive Voice with the meaning of the Active Voice.

Verbs in the Active Voice and Deponent Verbs are,

110
(*a*) Transitive (transire, *pass over*), acting on an object : amo eum, *I love him*; hortor vōs, *I exhort you.*

(*b*) Intransitive, not acting on an object : stō, *I stand*; loquor, *I speak.*

Only Transitive Verbs have the full Passive Voice.

111

The Conjugations.

Verbs are generally arranged according to the Character of the Present Stem in four Conjugations.

The Character is most clearly seen before the suffix -re (or -ĕre) of the Infinitive Present Active. It is either one of the vowels a, e, i, u, or a Consonant.

> First Conjugation,   **A- Stems.**
> Second Conjugation, **E- Stems.**
> Third Conjugation, **Consonant and U- Stems.**
> Fourth Conjugation, **I- Stems.**

Deponent Verbs are also divided into four Conjugations with the same Stem endings.

The following forms must be known in order to give the full Conjugation.

112	A- Stems.	E- Stems.	Consonant and U- Stems.	I- Stems.

Active Voice.

	A- Stems.	E- Stems.	Consonant and U- Stems.	I- Stems.
1 Pers. Pres. Indic.	ămo	mŏneo	rĕgo	audio
Infin. Pres.	amārĕ	monērĕ	regĕrĕ	audīrĕ
Perfect.	amāvī	monuī	rexī	audīvī
Supine in -um.	amātum	monĭtum	rectum	audītum

Passive Voice.

	A- Stems.	E- Stems.	Consonant and U- Stems.	I- Stems.
1 Pers. Pres. Indic.	amor	moneor	regor	audior
Infin. Pres.	amārī	monērī	regī	audīrī
Partic. Perf.	amātus	monĭtus	rectus	audītus
Gerundive	amandus	monendus	regendus	audiendus

113

In the Perfects -āvi, -ēvi, -ōvi, v sometimes drops out before -is or -er, and contraction follows : amāvisti becomes amasti, amāvērunt amārunt, amavissem amassem. In I- Stems there is no contraction : audīvi becomes audii, audīvērunt audiērunt. (See **14**.)

For -ērunt (3rd pers. pl. Perf. Act.), -ēre is often written ; amavēre, implēvēre, audīvēre ; but these forms are not contracted.

The 2nd pers. sing. in the Passive ends in -ris or -re ; amābāris, amābāre ; but in Pres. Indic. the ending in -re is rare.

> *Note.*—An old form in -ier of the Pres. Infin. Passive is sometimes found in poetry: amārier for amāri.
>
> Poets sometimes use old forms in the Future of I- Stems; as audībo, audībor, for audiam, audiar.
>
> The Gerundive sometimes ends in -undus in Consonant and I- Stems.

114

PERIPHRASTIC CONJUGATION.

The Active Future Participle and the Gerundive may be used with all the Tenses of the Verb sum :

amaturus, -a sum,	*I am about to love.*
amaturus, -a es,	*thou art about to love.*
amaturus, -a est,	*he (she) is about to love.*
amaturi, -ae sumus,	*we are about to love.*
etc.	
amandus, -a sum,	*I am meet to be loved.*
etc.	

In the same way the Participle futurus may be used with the tenses of sum : futurus sum, *I am about to be.*

The Active Future Participle with fuisse forms an Imperfect Future Infinitive, which is only used conditionally

115

This verb is formed from two roots, ĕs, *to be*, and fŭ, *to be* or the Perfect and Participial Stems from the root fŭ. In the tense forms

TENSE.	INDICATIVE.
Present.	sum, *I am.* ĕs, *thou art.* est, *he is.* sŭmŭs, *we are.* estĭs, *ye are.* sunt, *they are.*
Future Simple.	ĕro, *I shall be.* erĭs, *thou wilt be.* erĭt, *he will be.* erĭmŭs, *we shall be.* erĭtĭs, *ye will be.* erunt, *they will be.*
Imperfect.	eram, *I was.* erās, *thou wast.* erăt, *he was.* erāmŭs, *we were.* erātĭs, *ye were.* erant, *they were.*
Perfect.	fŭī, *I have been* or *I-was.* fuistī, *thou hast been* or *thou wast.* fŭĭt, *he has been* or *he was.* fŭĭmŭs, *we have been* or *we were.* fuistĭs, *ye have been* or *ye were.* fuērunt, *they have been* or *they were.*
Future Perfect.	fŭĕro, *I shall have been.* fŭĕrĭs, *thou wilt have been.* fŭĕrĭt, *he will have been.* fŭĕrĭmŭs, *we shall have been.* fŭĕrĭtĭs, *ye will have been.* fŭĕrint, *they will have been.*
Pluperfect.	fŭĕram, *I had been.* fŭĕrās, *thou hadst been.* fŭĕrăt, *he had been.* fŭĕrāmŭs, *we had been.* fŭĕrātĭs, *ye had been.* fŭĕrant, *they had been.*

* Before the regular Verbs it is necessary to conjugate the
   as an auxiliary in the conjugation of other Verbs.

(sum, fui, esse, futurus).

become. The Present Stem is formed from the root **ĕs-.**
es- sometimes drops e: sum, sumus; sometimes **s** changes to **r**: ĕram.

CONJUNCTIVE.	IMPERATIVE.
sim sīs sĭt sīmŭs sītĭs sint	ĕs, estō, *be thou.* estō, *let him be.* estĕ, estōtĕ, *be ye.* suntō, *let them be.*
	THE VERB INFINITE. Infinitives. Present } Imperf. } essĕ, *to be.*
essem *or* fŏrem essēs *or* fŏrēs essĕt *or* fŏrĕt essēmŭs essētĭs essent *or* fŏrent	Perfect } Pluperf. } fuissĕ, *to have been.* Future { fŭtūrŭs essĕ } *to be about to be.* { forĕ } Participles. Present (*none*). Future. fŭtūrŭs, *about to be.*
fuĕrim fuĕris fuĕrĭt fuĕrimŭs fuĕritĭs fuĕrint	Gerunds and Supines. (*None.*)
	Note.—There is no present participle of sum. It is only seen in the compounds, ab-sens, prae-sens.
fuissem fuissēs fuissĕt fuissēmŭs fuissētĭs fuissent	Like Sum are conjugated its compounds: absum, *am absent*; adsum, *am present*; dēsum, *am wanting*; insum, *am in* or *among*; intersum, *am among*; obsum, *hinder*; praesum, *am set over*; prōsum, *am of use*; subsum, *am under*; supersum, *survive.* In prōsum the final **d** of the old preposition is kept before **e**: prodes.

irregular Verb of Being, sum, *I am*, esse, *to be*, because it is used

116

TENSE.		INDICATIVE.
Present	ămō, amās, amăt, amāmŭs, amātĭs, amant,	*I love* or *am loving.* *thou lovest* or *art loving.* *he loves* or *is loving.* *we love* or *are loving.* *ye love* or *are loving.* *they love* or *are loving.*
Future Simple.	amābo, amābĭs, amābĭt, amābĭmŭs, amābĭtĭs, amābunt,	*I shall love.* *thou wilt love.* *he will love.* *we shall love.* *ye will love.* *they will love.*
Imperfect.	amābam, amābās, amābăt, amābāmŭs, amābātĭs, amābant,	*I was loving* or *I loved.* *thou wast loving* or *thou lovedst.* *he was loving* or *he loved.* *we were loving* or *we loved.* *ye were loving* or *ye loved.* *they were loving* or *they loved.*
Perfect.	amāvī, amāvistī, amāvĭt, amāvĭmŭs, amāvistĭs, amāvērunt,	*I have loved* or *I loved.* *thou hast loved* or *thou lovedst.* *he has loved* or *he loved.* *we have loved* or *we loved.* *ye have loved* or *ye loved.* *they have loved* or *they loved.*
Future Perfect.	amāvĕrǫ, amāvĕrĭs, amāvĕrĭt, amāvĕrĭmŭs, amāvĕrĭtĭs, amāvĕrint,	*I shall have loved.* *thou wilt have loved.* *he will have loved.* *we shall have loved.* *ye will have loved.* *they will have loved.*
Pluperfect.	amāvĕram, amāvĕrās, amāvĕrăt, amāvĕrāmŭs, amāvĕrātĭs, amāvĕrant,	*I had loved.* *thou hadst loved.* *he had loved.* *we had loved.* *ye had loved.* *they had loved.*

A- Stems.

VOICE.

Conjunctive.	Imperative.
amem amēs amĕt amēmŭs amētĭs ament	amā, amātō, *love thou.* amātō, *let him love.* amātĕ, amātōtĕ, *love ye.* amantō, *let them love.*

The Verb Infinite.

Infinitives.

Present
Imperf. } amārĕ, *to love.*

Perfect
Pluperf. } amāvissĕ, *to have loved.*

Future   amātūrŭs essĕ, *to be about to love.*

amārem amārēs amārĕt amārēmŭs amārētĭs amārent

Gerunds.

Nom. Acc. amandum, *the loving.*

Gen.   amandī, *of loving.*

Dat. Abl. amando, *for* or *by loving.*

amāvĕrim amāvĕrĭs amāvĕrĭt amāvĕrĭmŭs amāvĕrĭtĭs amāvĕrint

Supines.

amātum, *in order to love.*

amātū, *in* or *for loving.*

Participles.

Pres. amans, *loving.*

Fut. amātūrŭs, *about to love.*

amāvissem amāvissēs amāvissĕt amāvissēmŭs amāvissētĭs amāvissent

F

117 SECOND CONJUGATION

ACTIVE

TENSE.	INDICATIVE.	
Present.	mŏneō, monēs, monĕt, monēmŭs, monētĭs, monent,	*I advise* or *am advising.* *thou advisest* or *art advising.* *he advises* or *is advising.* *we advise* or *are advising.* *ye advise* or *are advising.* *they advise* or *are advising,*
Future Simple.	monēbō, monēbĭs, monēbĭt, monēbĭmŭs, monēbĭtĭs, monēbunt,	*I shall advise.* *thou wilt advise.* *he will advise.* *we shall advise.* *ye will advise.* *they will advise.*
Imperfect.	monēbam, monēbās, monēbăt, monēbāmŭs, monēbātĭs, monēbant,	*I was advising* or *I advised.* *thou wast advising* or *thou advisedst.* *he was advising* or *he advised.* *we were advising* or *we advised.* *ye were advising* or *ye advised.* *they were advising* or *they advised.*
Perfect.	monuī, monuistī, monuĭt, monuĭmŭs, monuistĭs, monuērunt,	*I have advised* or *I advised.* *thou hast advised* or *thou advisedst.* *he has advised* or *he advised.* *we have advised* or *we advised.* *ye have advised* or *ye advised.* *they have advised* or *they advised.*
Future Perfect.	monuĕro, monuĕrĭs, monuĕrĭt, monuĕrĭmŭs, monuĕrĭtĭs, monuĕrint,	*I shall have advised.* *thou wilt have advised.* *he will have advised.* *we shall have advised.* *ye will have advised.* *they will have advised.*
Pluperfect.	monuĕram, monuĕrās, monuĕrăt, monuĕrāmŭs, monuĕrātĭs, monuĕrant,	*I had advised.* *thou hadst advised.* *he had advised.* *we had advised.* *ye had advised.* *they had advised.*

E- Stems.

VOICE.

Conjunctive.	Imperative.
moneam moneās moneăt moneāmŭs moneătĭs moneant	monĕ, monētō, *advise thou.* monētō, *let him advise.* monētĕ, monētōtĕ, *advise ye.* monentō, *let them advise.*

The Verb Infinite.

Infinitives.

| monērem
monērēs
monērĕt
monērēmŭs
monērētĭs
monērent | Present }
Imperf. } monērĕ, *to advise.*

Perfect }
Pluperf. } monuissĕ, *to have advised.*

Future monĭtūrŭs essĕ, *to be about to advise.* |

| monuĕrim
monuĕris
monuĕrĭt
monuĕrĭmŭs
monuĕrĭtĭs
monuĕrint | **Gerunds.**

Nom. Acc. monendum, *the advising.*
Gen. monendī, *of advising.*
Dat. Abl. monendō, *for* or *by advising.*

Supines.

monĭtum, *in order to advise.*
monĭtū, *in* or *for advising.* |

| monuissem
monuissēs
monuissĕt
monuissēmŭs
monuissētĭs
monuissent | **Participles.**

Pres. monens, *advising.*
Fut. monĭtūrŭs, *about to advise.* |

118

Tense.		Indicative.
Present.	rĕgō regĭs, regĭt, regĭmŭs, regĭtĭs, regunt,	*I rule* or *am ruling.* *thou rulest* or *art ruling.* *he rules* or *is ruling.* *we rule* or *are ruling.* *ye rule* or *are ruling.* *they rule* or *are ruling.*
Future Simple.	regam, regēs, regĕt, regēmŭs, regētĭs, regent,	*I shall rule.* *thou wilt rule.* *he will rule.* *we shall rule.* *ye will rule.* *they will rule.*
Imperfect.	regēbam, regēbās; regēbăt, regēbāmŭs, regēbātĭs, regēbant,	*I was ruling* or *I ruled.* *thou wast ruling* or *thou ruledst.* *he was ruling* or *he ruled.* *we were ruling* or *we ruled.* *ye were ruling* or *ye ruled.* *they were ruling* or *they ruled.*
Perfect.	rēxī, rexistī, rexĭt, rexĭmŭs, rexistĭs, rexērunt,	*I have ruled* or *I ruled.* *thou hast ruled* or *thou ruledst.* *he has ruled* or *he ruled.* *we have ruled* or *we ruled.* *ye have ruled* or *ye ruled.* *they have ruled* or *they ruled.*
Future Perfect.	rexĕro, rexĕrĭs, rexĕrĭt, rexĕrĭmŭs, rexĕrĭtĭs, rexĕrint,	*I shall have ruled.* *thou wilt have ruled.* *he will have ruled.* *we shall have ruled.* *ye will have ruled.* *they will have ruled.*
Pluperfect.	rexĕram, rexĕrās, rexĕrăt, rexĕrāmŭs, rexĕrātĭs, rexĕrant,	*I had ruled.* *thou hadst ruled.* *he had ruled.* *we had ruled.* *ye had ruled.* *they had ruled.*

Note.—Facio. dīco, dūco, and the compounds of duco, in the 2nd person

CONSONANT STEMS.

VOICE.

CONJUNCTIVE.	IMPERATIVE.
regam regās regăt regāmŭs regātĭs regant	regĕ, regĭtō, *rule thou.* regĭtō, *let him rule.* regĭtĕ, regĭtōtĕ, *rule ye.* reguntō, *let them rule.*

THE VERB INFINITE.

Infinitives.

regĕrem regĕrēs regĕrĕt regĕrēmŭs regĕrētĭs regĕrent	Present Imperf. } regĕrĕ, *to rule.* Perfect Pluperf. } rexissĕ, *to have ruled.*

Future   rectūrŭs essĕ, *to be about to rule.*

Gerunds.

rexĕrim rexĕris rexĕrĭt rexĕrĭmŭs rexĕrĭtĭs rexĕrint	Nom. Acc. regendum, *the ruling.* Gen. regendī, *of ruling.* Dat. Abl. regendō, *for* or *by ruling.*

Supines.

rectum, *in order to rule.*

rectū,   *in* or *for ruling.*

Participles.

rexissem rexissēs rexissĕt rexissēmŭs rexissētĭs rexissent	Present regens, *ruling.* Future rectūrŭs, *about to rule.*

of the Pres. Imperative make făc, or făcĕ, dīc, dūc, &c.

119   Fourth Conjugation

ACTIVE

Tense.		Indicative.
Present.	audĭō,	I hear or am hearing.
	audīs,	thou hearest or art hearing.
	audĭt,	he hears or is hearing.
	audīmŭs,	we hear or are hearing.
	audītĭs,	ye hear or are hearing.
	audĭunt,	they hear or are hearing.
Future Simple.	audĭam,	I shall hear
	audĭēs,	thou wilt hear.
	audĭĕt,	he will hear.
	audĭēmŭs,	we shall hear.
	audĭētĭs,	ye will hear.
	audĭent,	they will hear.
Imperfect.	audĭēbam,	I was hearing or I heard.
	audĭēbās,	thou wast hearing or heardest.
	audĭēbăt,	he was hearing or he heard.
	audĭēbāmŭs,	we were hearing or we heard.
	audĭēbātĭs,	ye were hearing or ye heard.
	audĭēbant,	they were hearing or they heard.
Perfect.	audīvī,	I have heard or I heard.
	audīvistī,	thou hast heard or thou heardest.
	audīvĭt,	he has heard or he heard.
	audīvĭmŭs,	we have heard or we heard.
	audīvistĭs,	ye have heard or ye heard.
	audīvērunt,	they have heard or they heard.
Future Perfect.	audīvĕro,	I shall have heard.
	audīvĕrĭs,	thou wilt have heard.
	audīvĕrĭt,	he will have heard.
	audīvĕrĭmŭs,	we shall have heard.
	audīvĕrĭtĭs,	ye will have heard.
	audīvĕrint,	they will have heard.
Pluperfect.	audīvĕram,	I had heard.
	audīvĕrās,	thou hadst heard.
	audīvĕrăt,	he had heard.
	audīvĕrāmŭs,	we had heard.
	audīvĕrātĭs,	ye had heard.
	audīvĕrant,	they had heard.

I- STEMS.

VOICE.

CONJUNCTIVE.	IMPERATIVE.
audĭam audĭās audĭăt audĭămŭs audĭătĭs audĭant	audī, audītō, *hear thou.* ʼaudītō, *let him hear.* audītĕ, audītōtĕ, *hear ye.* audiuntō, *let them hear.*

THE VERB INFINITE.

Infinitives.

Present
Imperf. } audīre, *to hear.*

audīrem
audīrēs
audīrĕt
audīrēmŭs
audīrētĭs
audīrent

Perfect
Pluperf. } audīvissĕ, *to have heard.*

Future   audītūrŭs essĕ, *to be about to hear.*

Gerunds.

audīvĕrim
audīvĕrĭs
audīvĕrĭt
audīvĕrĭmŭs
audīvĕrĭtĭs
audīvĕrint

Nom. Acc. audiendum, *the hearing.*
Gen.   audiendī,   *of hearing.*
Dat. Abl. audiendō,   *for* or *by hearing.*

Supines.

audītum, *in order to hear.*
audītū,   *in* or *for hearing.*

audīvissem
audīvissēs
audīvissĕt
audīvissēmŭs
audīvissētĭs
audīvissent

Participles.

Present   audiens, *hearing.*
Future   audītūrŭs, *about to hear.*

120

TENSE.	INDICATIVE.	
Present.	ămor, amāris, amātŭr, amāmŭr, amāmĭnī, amantŭr,	*I am* or *I am being loved.* *thou art* or *thou art being loved.* *he is* or *he is being loved.* *we are* or *we are being loved.* *ye are* or *ye are being loved.* *they are* or *they are being loved.*
Future Simple.	amābŏr, amābĕrĭs, amābĭtŭr, amābĭmŭr, amābĭmĭnī, amābuntŭr,	*I shall be loved.* *thou wilt be loved.* *he will be loved.* *we shall be loved.* *ye will be loved.* *they will be loved.*
Imperfect.	amābăr, amābārĭs, amābātŭr, amābāmŭr, amābāmĭnĭ, amābantŭr,	*I was being* or *I was loved.* *thou wast being* or *thou wast loved.* *he was being* or *he was loved.* *we were being* or *we were loved.* *ye were being* or *ye were loved.* *they were being* or *they were loved.*
Perfect.	amātŭs sum, amātŭs ĕs, amātŭs est, amātī sŭmŭs, amātī estĭs, amātī sunt,	*I have been* or *I was loved.* *thou hast been* or *thou wast loved.* *he has been* or *he was loved.* *we have been* or *we were loved.* *ye have been* or *ye were loved.* *they have been* or *they were loved.*
Future Perfect.	amātŭs ĕrō, amātŭs ĕrĭs, amātŭs ĕrĭt, amātī ĕrĭmŭs, amātī ĕrĭtĭs, amātī ĕrunt,	*I shall have been loved.* *thou wilt have been loved.* *he will have been loved.* *we shall have been loved.* *ye will have been loved.* *they will have been loved.*
Pluperfect.	amātŭs ĕram, amātŭs ĕrăs, amātus ĕrăt, amātī ĕrāmŭs, amātī ĕrātĭs, amātī ĕrant,	*I had been loved.* *thou hadst been loved.* *he had been loved.* *we had been loved.* *ye had been loved.* *they had been loved.*

A. STEMS.

VOICE.

CONJUNCTIVE.	IMPERATIVE.
amĕr amērĭs amētŭr amēmŭr amēmĭnī amentŭr	amārĕ, amātŏr, *be thou loved.* amātŏr, *let him be loved.* amāmĭnī, *be ye loved.* amantŏr, *let them be loved.*
amārĕr amārērĭs amārētŭr amārēmŭr amārēmĭnī amārentŭr	
amātŭs sim amātŭs sīs amātŭs sĭt amātī sīmus amātī sītis amātī sint	
amātŭs essem amātŭs essēs amātŭs essĕt amātī essēmŭs amātī essētĭs amātī essent	

THE VERB INFINITE.

Infinitives.

Present Imperf.} amārī, *to be loved.*

Perfect Pluperf.} amātŭs essĕ, *to have been loved.*

Future amātum īrī. (See **387**).

Participle.

Perfect amātŭs, *loved,* or *having been loved.*

Gerundive.

amandŭs, *meet to be loved.*

121   SECOND CONJUGATION

PASSIVE

TENSE.	INDICATIVE.	
Present.	mŏnĕŏr,	*I am* or *I am being advised.*
	monēris,	*thou art* or *thou art being advised.*
	monētŭr,	*he is* or *he is being advised.*
	monēmŭr,	*we are* or *we are being advised.*
	monēmĭnī	*ye are* or *ye are being advised.*
	monentŭr,	*they are* or *they are being advised.*
Future Simple.	monēbŏr,	*I shall be advised.*
	monēbĕris,	*thou wilt be advised.*
	monēbĭtŭr,	*he will be advised.*
	monēbĭmŭr,	*we shall be advised.*
	monēbĭmĭnī,	*ye will be advised.*
	monēbuntŭr,	*they will be advised.*
Imperf.	monēbăr,	*I was being* or *I was advised.*
	monēbăris,	*thou wast being* or *thou wast advised.*
	monēbătŭr,	*he was being* or *he was advised.*
	monēbămŭr,	*we were being* or *we were advised.*
	monēbămĭnī,	*ye were being* or *ye were advised.*
	monēbantŭr,	*they were being* or *they were advised.*
Perfect.	monĭtŭs sum	*I have been* or *I was advised.*
	monĭtŭs ĕs,	*thou hast been* or *thou wast advised.*
	monĭtŭs est,	*he has been* or *he was advised.*
	monĭtī sŭmŭs,	*we have been* or *we were advised.*
	monĭtī estĭs,	*ye have been* or *ye were advised.*
	monĭtī sunt,	*they have been* or *they were advised.*
Future Perfect.	monĭtŭs ĕrō,	*I shall have been advised.*
	monĭtŭs ĕrĭs,	*thou wilt have been advised.*
	monĭtŭs ĕrĭt,	*he will have been advised.*
	monĭtī ĕrĭmŭs,	*we shall have been advised.*
	monĭtī ĕrĭtĭs,	*ye will have been advised.*
	monĭtī ĕrunt,	*they will have been advised.*
Pluperf.	monĭtŭs ĕram,	*I had been advised.*
	monĭtŭs ĕrăs,	*thou hadst been advised.*
	monĭtŭs ĕrăt,	*he had been advised.*
	monĭtī ĕrămus,	*we had been advised.*
	monĭtī ĕrătĭs,	*ye had been advised.*
	monĭtī ĕrant,	*they had been advised.*

E- Stems.

VOICE.

Conjunctive.	Imperative.
monĕăr monĕārĭs monĕātŭr monĕāmŭr monĕāmĭnī monĕantŭr	monērĕ, monētŏr, *be thou advised.* monētŏr, *let him be advised.* monēmĭnī, *be ye advised.* monentŏr, *let them be advised.*
monērĕr monērērĭs monērētŭr monērēmŭr monērēmĭnĭ monērentŭr	**The Verb Infinite.** Infinitives.
monĭtŭs sim monĭtŭs sīs monĭtŭs sĭt monĭtī sīmus monĭtī sītis monĭtī sint	Present ⎫ Imperf. ⎬ monērī, *to be advised.* Perfect ⎫ Pluperf. ⎬ monĭtŭs essĕ, *to have been advised.* Future monĭtum īrī. (See **387.**) Participle. Perfect monĭtŭs, *advised,* or *having been advised.*
monĭtŭs essem monĭtŭs essēs monĭtŭs essĕt monĭtī essēmŭs monĭtī essētĭs monĭtī essent	Gerundive. monendŭs, *meet to be advised.*

122

PASSIVE

Tense.	Indicative.	
Present.	rĕgŏr,	*I am* or *I am being ruled.*
	regĕrĭs,	*thou art* or *thou art being ruled.*
	regĭtŭr,	*he is* or *he is being ruled.*
	regĭmŭr,	*we are* or *we are being ruled.*
	regĭmĭnĭ,	*ye are* or *ye are being ruled.*
	reguntŭr,	*they are* or *they are being ruled.*
Future Simple.	regăr,	*I shall be ruled.*
	regērĭs,	*thou wilt be ruled.*
	regētŭr,	*he will be ruled.*
	regēmŭr,	*we shall be ruled.*
	regēmĭnĭ,	*ye will be ruled.*
	regentŭr,	*they will be ruled.*
Imperfect.	regēbăr,	*I was being* or *I was ruled.*
	regēbărĭs,	*thou wast being* or *thou wast ruled.*
	regēbātŭr,	*he was being* or *he was ruled.*
	regēbāmŭr,	*we were being* or *we were ruled.*
	regēbămĭnĭ,	*ye were being* or *ye were ruled.*
	regēbantŭr,	*they were being* or *they were ruled.*
Perfect.	rectŭs sum,	*I have been* or *I was ruled.*
	rectŭs ĕs,	*thou hast been* or *thou wast ruled.*
	rectŭs est,	*he has been* or *he was ruled.*
	rectī sŭmŭs,	*we have been* or *we were ruled.*
	rectī estĭs,	*ye have been* or *ye were ruled.*
	rectī sunt,	*they have been* or *they were ruled.*
Future Perfect.	rectŭs ĕrō,	*I shall have been ruled.*
	rectŭs ĕrĭs,	*thou wilt have been ruled.*
	rectŭs ĕrĭt,	*he will have been ruled.*
	rectī ĕrĭmŭs,	*we shall have been ruled.*
	rectī erĭtĭs,	*ye will have been ruled.*
	rectī ĕrunt,	*they will have been ruled.*
Pluperfect.	rectŭs ĕram,	*I had been ruled.*
	rectŭs ĕrās,	*thou hadst been ruled.*
	rectŭs ĕrăt,	*he had been ruled.*
	rectī ĕrāmŭs,	*we had been ruled.*
	rectī ĕrātĭs,	*ye had been ruled.*
	rectī ĕrant,	*they had been ruled.*

Consonant Stems

VOICE.

Conjunctive.	Imperative.
regăr regārĭs regătŭr regămŭr regămĭnī regantŭr	regĕrĕ, regĭtŏr, *be thou rule.l.* regĭtŏr, *let him be ruled.* regĭmĭnī, *be ye ruled.* reguntŏr, *let them be ruled.*
regĕrĕr regĕrērĭs regĕrētŭr regĕrēmŭr regĕrēmĭnī regĕrentŭr	
rectŭs sim rectŭs sīs rectŭs.sĭt rectī sīmŭs rectī sītĭs rectī sint	
rectŭs essem rectŭs essēs rectŭs essĕt rectī essēmŭs rectī essētĭs rectī essent	

The Verb Infinite.

Infinitives.

Present }
Imperf. } rĕgī, *to be ruled.*

Perfect }
Pluperf. } rectŭs essĕ, *to have been ruled.*

Future rectum īrī. (See **387**.)

Participle.

Perfect rectŭs, *ruled,* or *having been ruled.*

Gerundive.

rĕgendŭs, *meet to be ruled.*

123

TENSE.	INDICATIVE.	
Present.	audĭŏr,	*I am or I am being heard.*
	audīrĭs,	*thou art or thou art being heard.*
	audītŭr,	*he is or he is being heard.*
	audīmŭr,	*we are or we are being heard.*
	audīmĭnī,	*ye are or ye are being heard.*
	audiuntŭr,	*they are or they are being heard.*
Future Simple.	audĭăr,	*I shall be heard.*
	ăudiērĭs,	*thou wilt be heard.*
	audiētŭr,	*he will be heard.*
	audiēmŭr,	*we shall be heard.*
	audiēmĭnī,	*ye will be heard.*
	audientŭr,	*they will be heard.*
Imperf.	audiēbăr,	*I was being or I was heard.*
	audiēbārĭs,	*thou wast being or thou wast heard.*
	audiēbātŭr,	*he was being or he was heard.*
	audiēbāmŭr,	*we were being or we were heard.*
	audiēbāmĭnī,	*ye were being or ye were heard.*
	audiēbāntŭr,	*they were being or they were heard.*
Perfect.	audītŭs sum,	*I have been or I was heard.*
	audītŭs ĕs,	*thou hast been or thou wast heard.*
	audītŭs est,	*he has been or he was heard.*
	audītī sŭmŭs,	*we have been or we were heard.*
	audītī estĭs,	*ye have been or ye were heard.*
	audītī sunt,	*they have been or they were heard.*
Future Perfect.	audītŭs ĕrō,	*I shall have been heard.*
	audītŭs ĕrĭs,	*thou wilt have been heard.*
	audītŭs ĕrĭt,	*he will have been heard.*
	audītī ĕrĭmŭs,	*we shall have been heard.*
	audītī ĕrĭtĭs,	*ye will have been heard.*
	audītī ĕrunt,	*they will have been heard.*
Pluperf.	audītŭs ĕram,	*I had been heard.*
	audītŭs ĕrās,	*thou hadst been heard.*
	audītŭs ĕrăt,	*he had been heard.*
	audītī ĕrāmŭs,	*we had been heard.*
	audītī ĕrātĭs,	*ye had been heard.*
	audītī ĕrant,	*they had been heard.*

I-Stems.

VOICE.

Conjunctive.	Imperative.
audiär audiārĭs audiätür audiämür audiämĭnĭ audiantür	audirĕ, auditŏr, *be thou heard.* auditŏr, *let him be heard.* audimĭnĭ, *be ye heard.* audiuntŏr, *let them be heard.*
audirĕr audirērĭs audirētür audirēmür audirēmĭnī audirentür	

THE VERB INFINITE.

Infinitives.

audītŭs sim audītŭs sīs audītŭs sĭt audītī sīmŭs audītī sītĭs audītī sint		

Present
Imperf. } audiri, *to be heard.*

Perfect
Pluperf. } auditŭs essĕ, *to have been heard.*

Future auditum iri. (See **387**).

Participle.

Perfect auditŭs, *heard,* or *having been heard.*

Gerundive.

audītŭs essem
audītŭs essēs
audītŭs essĕt
audītī essēmŭs
audītī essētĭs
audītī essent

audiendŭs, *meet to be heard.*

124　　　　　　　　　　Ūtor, ūti, ūsus, *use*.

DEPONENT VERB, HAVING THE FORMS OF THE PASSIVE

TENSE.	INDICATIVE.	
Present.	ūtŏr,	*I use.*
	utĕris,	*thou usest.*
	utĭtŭr,	*he uses.*
	utĭmŭr,	*we use.*
	utĭmĭnī,	*ye use.*
	utuntŭr,	*they use.*
Future Simple.	utăr,	*I shall use.*
	utēris,	*thou wilt use.*
	utētŭr,	*he will use.*
	utēmŭr,	*we shall use.*
	utēmĭnī,	*ye will use.*
	utentŭr,	*they will use.*
Imperfect.	utēbăr,	*I was using* or *I used.*
	utēbārĭs,	*thou wast using* or *thou didst use.*
	utēbātŭr,	*he was using* or *he used.*
	utēbāmŭr,	*we were using* or *we used.*
	utēbāmĭnī,	*ye were using* or *ye used.*
	utēbantŭr,	*they were using* or *they used.*
Perfect.	ūsŭs sum,	*I have used* or *I used.*
	usŭs es,	*thou hast used* or *thou didst use.*
	usŭs est,	*he has used* or *he used.*
	usī sumŭs,	*we have used* or *we used.*
	usī estis,	*ye have used* or *ye used.*
	usī sunt,	*they have used* or *they used.*
Future Perfect.	usŭs ĕrō,	*I shall have used.*
	usŭs ĕrĭs,	*thou wilt have used.*
	usŭs ĕrĭt,	*he will have used.*
	usī ĕrĭmŭs,	*we shall have used.*
	usī ĕrĭtĭs,	*ye will have used.*
	usī ĕrunt,	*they will have used.*
Pluperfect.	usŭs ĕram,	*I had used.*
	usŭs ĕrās,	*thou hadst used.*
	usŭs ĕrăt,	*he had used.*
	usī ĕrāmŭs,	*we had used.*
	usī ĕrātĭs,	*ye had used.*
	usī ĕrant,	*they had used.*

Deponent Verbs have Gerunds, Supines, Present and Future Participles

(THIRD CONJUGATION).

VOICE, WITH THE MEANING OF THE ACTIVE.

CONJUNCTIVE.	IMPERATIVE.
ūtăr utărĭs utātŭr utāmŭr utāmĭnī utantŭr	utĕrĕ, utĭtŏr, *use thou.* utĭtŏr, *let him use.* utĭmĭnī, *use ye.* utuntŏr, *let them use.*

THE VERB INFINITE.

Infinitives.

Present Imperf. } utī, *to use.*

utĕrĕr
utĕrērĭs
utĕrētŭr
utĕrēmŭr
utĕrēmĭnī
utĕrentŭr

Perfect Pluperf. } usŭs esse, *to have used.*

Future   usūrŭs essĕ, *to be about to use.*

Gerunds.

usŭs sim
usŭs sīs
usŭs sĭt
usī sīmŭs
usī sītĭs
usī sint

Nom. Acc. utendum, *using.*
Gen.   utendī, *of using.*
Dat. Abl.   utendō, *for or by using.*

Supines.

usum, *to use.*
usū,   *in or for using.*

Participles.

Present   utens, *using.*
Future   usūrŭs, *about to use.*

usŭs essem
usŭs essēs
usŭs essĕt
usī essēmŭs
usī essētĭs
usī essent

Perfect   usŭs, *having used.*

Gerundive.

utendŭs, *meet to be used.*

Active; their Perfect Participles have the meaning of the Active Voice.

G

125 DEPONENT VERBS of the four Conjugations.

Vēnŏr   vēnātŭs sum   vēnāri, *hunt.*   Utŏr   ūsŭs sum   ūti, *use.*
Vereŏr verĭtŭs sum verērī, *fear.* Partiŏr partītŭs sum partīrī, *divide*

INDICATIVE.

TENSE	1st CONJ.	2nd CONJ.	3rd CONJ.	4th CONJ.
Pres.	vēnor	vereor	ūtor	partior
	venāris (re)	verēris (rĕ)	utĕris (rĕ)	partīris (ire)
Fut. S.	venābor	verēbor	utar	partiar
Imperf.	venābar	verēbar	utēbar	partiēbar
Perf.	venātus sum	verĭtus sum	usus sum	partītus sum
Fu' Perf.	venātus ero	verĭtus ero	usus ero	partītus ero
Pluperf.	venātus eram	verĭtus eram	usus eram	partītus eram

CONJUNCTIVE.

Pres.	vener	verear	utar	partiar
Imperf.	venārer	verērer	utĕrer	partīrer
Perf.	venātus sim	verĭtus sim	usus sim	partītus sim
Pluperf.	venātus essem	verĭtus essem	usus essem	partītus essem

IMPERATIVE.

	venāre	verēre	utĕre	partīre
	venātor	verētor	utĭtor	partītor

THE VERB INFINITE.

Infinitives.

Pres. & Imp.	venāri	verēri	uti	partiri
Perf. & Plup.	venātus esse	verĭtus esse	usus esse	partītus esse
Fut.	venāturus esse	verĭturus esse	usurus esse	partīturus esse

Participles.

Pres.	venans	verens	utens	partiens
Fut.	venāturus	verĭturus	usurus	partīturus
Perf.	venātus	verĭtus	usus	partītus

Gerundive.

	venandus	verendus	utendus	partiendus

Gerunds.

venandum, -i, -o verendum, -i, -o utendum, -i, -o partiendum, -i, -o

Supines.

in -um	venātum	verĭtum	usum	partītum
in -u	venātu	verĭtu	usu	partītu

Note.—Some Deponents have an Active form also: pūnior and pūnio, *punish.*

126 Many Perf. Participles of Deponent Verbs are used passively as well as actively; as confessus from confiteor, *confess*; imitātus from imitor, *imitate*; mĕrĭtus from mĕreor, *deserve*; pollĭcĭtus from pollĭceor, *promise.*

127 Some Verbs have a Perfect of Passive form with a Present of Active form; they are called **Semi-deponents**

audeo, *dare*	ausus sum, *I have dared* or *I dared.*
gaudeo, *rejoice*	gāvīsus sum, *I have rejoiced* or *I rejoiced.*
sŏleo, *am wont*	solĭtus sum, *I have been wont* or *I was wont.*
fīdo, *trust*	fīsus sum, *I have trusted* or *I trusted.*

128 Some Verbs have an Active form with Passive meaning; they are called Quasi-Passive:

exŭlo,	*am banished.*	līceo,	*am put up for sale.*
vāpŭlo,	*am beaten.*	vēnĕo,	*am on sale.*
fīo,	*am made.*		

129 Some Verbs have Perfect Participles with Active meaning, like the Deponent Verbs:

jūro,	*swear.*	jurāvi,	*I swore.*	jurātus,	*having sworn.*
cēno,	*sup.*	cenāvi,	*I supped.*	cenātus,	*having supped.*
prandeo,	*dine.*	prandi,	*I dined.*	pransus,	*having dined.*

130 Inceptive Verbs, with Present Stem in **-sco** (Third Conjugation), express beginning of action, and are derived from Verb-Stems or from Nouns:

pallesco,	*turn pale,*	from palleo.
131 nigresco,	*turn black,*	from niger.

Frequentative Verbs (First Conj.) express repeated or intenser action, and are formed from Supine Stems:

rŏgito, *ask repeatedly* (rogo); canto, *sing with energy* (căno).

132 Desiderative Verbs (Fourth Conj.) express desire of action, and are formed from the Supine Stem:

ēsŭrio, *am hungry* (ĕdō, ēsŭrus).

133 VERBS IN -io (THIRD CONJUGATION).

Forms from Present Stem, cap-i-, *take*.

	ACTIVE VOICE			PASSIVE VOICE	
	INDIC.	CONJUNC.		INDIC.	CONJUNC.
Present	căpio capis capit capĭmus capitis capiunt	capiam capias capiat capiamus capiatis capiant	**Present**	capior capĕris capĭtur capimur capimini capiuntur	capiar capiaris capiatur capiamur capiamini capiantur
Fut. Simple	capiam capies capiet capiēmus capietis capient		**Fut. Simple**	capiar capiĕris capietur capiemur capiemini capientur	
Imperf.	capiebam capiebas capiebat capiebamus capiebatis capiebant	capĕrem caperes caperet caperemus caperetis caperent	**Imperf.**	capiēbar capiebaris capiebatur capiebamur capiebamini capiebantur	capĕrer capereris caperetur caperemur caperemini caperentur

Imper. cape, capite.
    capito, capitōte, capiunto.
			Imper. capĕre, capĭmini.
			    capitor, capiuntor.		

Infin. Pres. căpĕre. Gerund. capiendum. Pres. Partic. capiens.			Infin. Pres. capi. Gerundive capiendus.		

Capio has Perfect cēpi; Supine captum.

The Verbs in -io are :

căpio, cŭpio *and* făcio, fŏdio, fŭgio *and* jăcio, părio, răpio, săpio, quătio, *and their* compounds,	take, desire, make, dig, fly, throw, bring forth, seize, know, shake.
Compounds of spĕcio *and* lăcio {obsolete Verbs,	look at, entice.
Deponent : grădior, pătior, mŏrior, And in some tenses, pŏtior, ŏrior,	step, suffer, die. get possession of, arise.

Note.—Orior is an I-stem, but has some forms like capior : ŏrĕris, orītur, ortus. Potior has potītur or potĭtur, potīmur or potĭmur, potīrer or potĕrer.

134

Irregular Verbs.

Verbs are called irregular :

(1) Because they are formed from more than one root, as **sum**.

(2) Because their tense-forms differ from those of regular verbs.

135   **Possum**, *I can*, **potui, posse.**

The Pres. Indic. possum is compounded of sum, *I am*, and the adjective potis *or* poti, *able.*

	Indic.	Conjunc.		Indic.	Conjunc.
Present	possum pŏtĕs potest possŭmus potestis possunt	possim possis possit possĭmus possitis possint	**Perfect**	potui potuisti potuit potuimus potuistis potuĕrunt	potuerim potueris potuerit potuerimus potueritis potuerint
Fut. Simp.	potero poteris poterit poterĭmus poterĭtis potĕrunt		**Fut. Perf.**	potuero potueris potuerit potuerimus potueritis potuerint	
Imperf.	poteram poteras poterat poteramus poteratis poterant	possem posses posset possemus possetis possent	**Pluperf.**	potueram potueras potuerat potueramus potueratis potuerant	potuissem potuisses potuisset potuissemus potuissetis potuissent

Infinitive Pres. and Imperf. posse (pot-esse), Perf. and Pluperf. potuisse.

Potens is used as an Adjective, *powerful*, *able*, never as a Participle.

136

Fĕro, *bear*, ferre, tŭli, lātum.

	ACTIVE VOICE			PASSIVE VOICE	
	INDIC.	CONJUNC.		INDIC.	CONJUNC.
Present	fĕro fers fert ferĭmus fertis ferunt	feram feras ferat ferāmus ferātis ferant	**Present**	feror ferris fertur ferĭmur ferĭmĭni feruntur	ferar ferāris feratur feramur feramini ferantur
Fut. Simple	feram feres feret ferēmus ferētis ferent		**Fut. Simple**	ferar ferēris feretur feremur feremini ferentur	
Imperf.	ferēbam ferebas ferebat ferebamus ferebatis ferebant	ferrem ferrēs ferret ferrēmus ferrētis ferrent	**Imperf.**	ferēbar ferebāris ferebatur ferebamur ferebamini ferebantur	ferrer ferrēris ferretur ferremur ferremini ferrentur

Imper. fer, ferte.
     ferto, fertote, ferunto.
	Imper. ferre, ferimini.
	     fertor, feruntor.

Infin. Pres. ferre. Gerund. ferend-um, -i, -o. Pres. Partic. ferens.	Infin. Pres. ferri. Gerundive ferendus.

The Perfect-Stem forms are regular :

tul-i   -ero   -eram   -erim   -issem

Also the Supine-Stem forms :

Supines { latum / latu   Participles { latus / laturus   Infin. { tulisse / latus esse / latum iri

latus sum, ero, eram, sim, essem.

137   Eo (for eio), *go*, īre, īvi or ii, ĭtum.

	INDIC.	CONJUNC.	IMPERATIVE
Present	eo īs ĭt imus ītis eunt	eam eas eat eāmus eātis eant	ī, īto. īto. īte, ītōte. eunto.
Fut. Simple	ībo ibis ibit ibimus ibitis ibunt		THE VERB INFINITIVE. Infinitives. Present } īre. Imperf. Perfect } isse, ivisse. Pluperf.
Imperf.	ībam ibas ibat ibamus ibatis ibant	īrem ires iret irēmus iretis irent	Future ĭturus esse. Gerunds. Nom. Acc. eundum. Gen. eundi. Dat. Abl. eundo.
Perf.	ii or īvi iisti, ivisti iit, ivit iimus, ivĭmus iistis, ivistis iērunt, ivērunt	ĭerim ieris ierit ierĭmus ieritis ierint	Supines. ĭtum. ĭtu. Participles. Pres. ĭens (Acc. euntem). Future ĭturus.

138

In the Perfect Tense of **eo** the forms ii, iisti &c. are more usual than īvi &c.; also in the compounds redii, rediisti, redisti.

The Impersonal Passive, ītur, ĭtum est, is often used.

Queo, *can,* **nequeo,** *cannot,* are conjugated like eo in the forms which are found, but many are wanting; they have no Imperative and no Gerunds.

Ambio, *go round, canvass,* is conjugated like audio,

139   **Vŏlo**, *am willing, wish.*

Nōlo, *am unwilling, do not wish.*

Mālo, *prefer, wish rather.*

Nolo is compounded of ne and volo. Malo of magis and volo.

	INDICATIVE			IMPERATIVE
Present	vŏlo	nōlo	mālo	nōlī, nōlīto
	vīs	nonvis	mavis	nolīto
	vult	nonvult	mavult	
	volŭmus	nolŭmus	malŭmus	nolīte
	vultis	nonvultis	mavultis	nolitōte, nolunto
	volunt	nolunt	malunt	Volo and malo have
Fut. Simple	vŏlam	(nōlam)	(mālam)	no Imperative.
	volēs	noles	males	
	volet	nolet	malet	
	volēmus	nolēmus	malēmus	THE VERB INFINITE.
	volētis	nolētis	malētis	Infinitive.
	volent	nolent	malent	
Imperf.	volēbam	nolebam	malebam	Present { velle
	volebas	nolebas	malebas	Imperfect { nolle
	&c.	&c.	&c.	{ malle
	CONJUNCTIVE			
Present	vĕlim	nōlim	mālim	Gerunds.
	velis	nolis	malis	volendum, -i, -o
	velit	nolit	malit	nolendum, -i, -o
	velīmus	nolīmus	malīmus	malendum, -i, -o
	velītis	nolītis	malītis	Supines.
	velint	nolint	malint	None.
Imperf.	vellem	nollem	mallem	Participles.
	velles	nolles	malles	
	vellet	nollet	mallet	Present { vŏlens
	vellemus	nollemus	mallemus	{ nōlens
	velletis	nolletis	malletis	{ —
	vellent	nollent	mallent	

The Pèrfect-Stem forms are regular :

Vŏlŭ-i	-ero	-eram	-erim	-issem	Infin. { vŏluisse
Nōlŭ-i	-ero	-eram	-erim	-issem	{ nōluisse
Mālŭ-i	-ero	-eram	-erim	-issem	{ māluisse

140   Ĕdo, *I eat,* esse (for ĕdere), ēdi, ēsum.

2nd Pers. S. Pres. Act. ēs   for ed-i-s.
3rd   ,,   ,,   ,,   est,   for ed-i-t.
2nd Pers. Pl. ,,   ,,   estis   for ed-i-tis.
Imperf. Conj.   ,,   essem   for ed-e-rem.
Imperat. Pres.   ,,   este   for ed-i-te.
   ,,   Fut.   ,,   esto, estote for edĭto, edĭtote.
Inf. Pres.   .   ,,   esse   for ed-e-re.
3rd Pers. S. Pres. Pass. estur   ed-i-tur.

The other forms of this Verb are regular; except that **edim, edis, edit,** are usually found in the Present Conjunctive.

141   Fīo, *am made, become,* fieri, factus sum.

The Present-Stem tenses of **fio** supply a Passive to the Active verb **facio,** *make.* The Perfect tenses are borrowed from the Perfect Passive of facio formed from the Supine-Stem **facto-.**

	INDIC.	CONJUNC.	IMPERATIVE
Present	fīo fīs fĭt (fimus) (fitis) fiunt	fīam fias fiat fiamus fiatis fiant	fī fite
Fut. Simple	fīam fies fiet fiemus fietis fient		THE VERB INFINITE. Infinitives. Present } Imper. } fĭeri. Perfect } Pluperf. } factus esse.
Imperf.	fīebam fiebas fiebat fiebamus fiebatis fiebant	fĭerem fieres fieret fieremus fieretis fierent	Future factum iri. Participle. Perfect factus. Gerundive. faciendus.
Perf.	factus sum, &c.	factus sim, &c.	

142

DEFECTIVE VERBS.

Defective Verbs are those of which only some forms are used.

Coepi, *begin*   ⎫ have only Perfect-Stem forms; but the
Memĭni, *remember* ⎬ Perfect forms are used with Present
Odi, *hate*   ⎭ meaning.

Indicative.

Perfect.	**coepi,** *I begin.*	**memini,** *I remember.*	**ōdi,** *I hate.*
Fut. Perf.	**coepero,** *I shall begin.*	**meminero,** *I shall remember.*	**odero,** *I shall hate.*
Pluperf.	**coeperam,** *I began.*	**memineram,** *I remembered.*	**oderam,** *I hated.*

Conjunctive.

Perfect.	**coeperim**	**meminerim**	**oderim**
Pluperf.	**coepissem**	**meminissem**	**odissem**
Infin.	**coepisse,** *to begin.*	**meminisse**	**odisse**
Fut. Part.	**coeptūrus,** *about to begin.*	—	**osurus,** *about to hate.*

Coepi has a participle **coeptus.** **Odi** sometimes has **osus sum.**
Memini has Imperative **memento,** Plur. **mementote.**

Nōvi (Perf. of nosco) is used with Present meaning, *I know.*

novero, $\begin{Bmatrix} \text{noveram} \\ \text{noram} \end{Bmatrix}$ noverim $\begin{Bmatrix} \text{novissem} \\ \text{nossem} \end{Bmatrix}$ Infin. $\begin{Bmatrix} \text{novisse} \\ \text{nosse} \end{Bmatrix}$

Aio, *I say* or *affirm.*

Ind. Pres. **aio, ais, ait, — — aiunt.**

Impf. **aiebam, aiebas, aiebat, aiebamus, aiebatis, aiebant.**

Conj. Pres. — — **aiat,** — — **aiant.**

Participle. **aiens.**

Inquam, *I say.*

Ind. Pres. **inquam, inquis, inquit, inquĭmus, inquĭtĭs, inquiunt.**

Impf. — — **inquiebat —** — **inquiebant**

Fut. S. — **inquies, inquiet**

Perf. — **inquisti, inquit**

Imper. **inque —** **inquĭto**

Fari, *to speak.*

Indic. Pres. **faris, fatur.**

„ Fut. **fabor — fabitur.**

Imper. **fare,** *speak thou.*

Participles, Pres. Acc. **fantem.** Perf. **fatus.**

Gerund. **fandi, fando.** Gerundive. **fandus.**

Quaeso, *entreat* (an old form of quaero), has first pers. plur. **quaesŭmus.**

The following Imperatives are found :

apăgĕ, *be gone.*

avē (havē), avēte, *hail.* Infin. avēre, *to have a desire.*

cĕdo, cedĭtĕ (cette), *give.*

salvē, salvēte. Infin. salvēre, *to be well.*

Note.—Age, ăgĭte, *come*; vale, valēte, *farewell*, are used with special meaning; but the verbs ago, *I do*, văleo, *I am well*, are fully conjugated.

143   Impersonal Verbs.

Impersonal Verbs are used only in the forms of the Third Person Singular of each tense, and do not refer to a Subject in the Nominative. They have also Infinitive and Gerund (**288-295**).

The principal are the following: **144**

Present.		Perfect.	Infinitive.
misĕret,	*it moves to pity.*	(miseruit)	(miserēre)
piget,	*it vexes.*	piguit	pigēre
paenĭtet,	*it repents.*	paenituit	paenitēre
pudet,	*it shames.*	puduit	pudēre
taedet,	*it wearies.*	taeduit	taedēre
dĕcet,	*it is becoming.*	decuit	decēre
dēdecet,	*it is unbecoming.*	dedecuit	dedecēre
libet,	*it pleases.*	libuit	libēre
licet,	*it is lawful.*	licuit	licēre
oportet,	*it behoves.*	oportuit	oportēre

145   *Note.* 1.—Decet, dedecet have also 3rd. pers. plur., decent, dedecent.

Note 2.—Active Impersonals have no Passive Voice, but some passive forms are found: misereor, *I pity,* miserētur; miserĭtum est, pigĭtum est, pudĭtum est, pertaesum est. Other forms are occasionally found: paenitendus, pudendus.   **146**

Some Impersonals express change of weather and time:

fulgurat,	*it lightens.*	**tonat,**	*it thunders.*
ningit,	*it snows.*	**lucescit,**	*it dawns.*
pluit,	*it rains.*	**vesperascit,**	*it grows late.*

Of some Verbs which have all the personal forms, the Third Person Singular is used impersonally with special meaning:

accēdit,	*it is added.*	expĕdit,	*it is expedient.*
accĭdit,	*it happens.*	fallit, fugit,	*it escapes one.*
apparet,	*it is evident.*	interest,	*it concerns.*
attinet,	*it belongs.*	juvat,	*it delights.*
constat,	*it is agreed.*	pertinet,	*it pertains.*
contingit,	*it befalls.*	placet,	*it seems good.*
convĕnit,	*it suits.*	rēfert,	*it matters.*
delectat,	*it charms.*	restat,	*it remains.*
ēvĕnit,	*it turns out.*		

Intransitive Verbs are used impersonally in the Passive (**299**).

147 DERIVATION FROM THE THREE TENSE STEMS.

I. From the **Present-Stem**.

Pres. Indic. Act.	ăm(a)-o	mŏnĕ-o	rĕg-o	audĭ-o
„ „ Pass.	-ŏr	ĕ-or	-ŏr	ĭ-ŏr
„ Conj. Act.	-em	ĕ-am	-am	ĭ-am
„ „ Pass.	-ĕr	ĕ-ăr	-ăr	ĭ-ăr
Imperf. Indic. Act.	ā-bam	ē-bam	-ēbam	ĭ-ēbam
„ „ Pass.	ā-băr	ē-băr	-ēbăr	ĭ-ēbar
„ Conj. Act.	ā-rem	ē-rem	-ĕrem	ī-rem
„ „ Pass.	ā-rĕr	ē-rĕr	-ĕrĕr	ī-rĕr
Fut. Indic. Act.	ā-bo	ē-bo	-am	ĭ-am
„ „ Pass.	ā-bŏr	ē-bŏr	-ăr	ĭ-ăr
Imperative Act.	ā	ē	-ĕ	ī
„ Pass.	ā-rĕ	ē-rĕ	-ĕrĕ	ī-rĕ
Infin. Pres. Act.	ā-rĕ	ē-rĕ	-ĕrĕ	ī-rĕ
„ „ Pass.	ā-rī	ē-rī	-ī	ī-rī
Partic. Pres. Act.	a-ns	e-ns	-ens	ĭ-ens
Gerund	a-ndo	e-ndo	-endo	ĭ-endo

II. From the **Perfect-Stem**.

Perfect Indic. Act.	ămāv-ī	monŭ-ī	rex-ī	audīv-ī
„ Conj. „	-ĕrim	-ĕrim	-ĕrim	-ĕrim
Fut. Perf. Indic. Act.	-ĕro	-ĕro	-ĕro	-ĕro
Plup. „ „	-ĕram	-ĕram	-ĕram	-ĕram
„ Conj. „	-issem	-issem	-issem	-issem
Infin. Perf. „	-issĕ	-issĕ	-issĕ	-issĕ

III. From the **Supine-Stem**.

Supine I.	ămāt-um	monĭt-um	rect-um	audīt-um
Infin. Fut. Pass. }	-um īrī	-um īrī	-um īrī	-um īrī
Supine II.	-ū	-ū	-ū	-ū
Partic. Fut. Act. }	-ūrŭs	-ūrŭs	-ūrŭs	-ūrŭs
Partic. Perf. Pass. }	-ŭs	-ŭs	-ŭs	-ŭs
Perf. Indic. Pass. }	-ŭs sum	-ŭs sum	-ŭs sum	-ŭs sum
Perf. Conj. Pass. }	-ŭs sim	-ŭs sim	-ŭs sim	-ŭs sim
Fut. Perf. Pass. }	-ŭs ĕro	-ŭs ĕro	-ŭs ĕro	-ŭs ĕro
Plup. Ind. Pass. }	-ŭs ĕram	-ŭs ĕram	-ŭs ĕram	-ŭs ĕram
Plup. Conj. Pass. }	-ŭs essem	-ŭs essem	-ŭs essem	-ŭs essem
Infin. Pass.	-ŭs essĕ	-ŭs essĕ	-ŭs essĕ	-ŭs essĕ

148 FORMATION OF THE THREE STEMS IN VERBS.

The forms of the Latin Verb vary in many respects from those of the parent and related languages. Both in the Past and in the Future tenses the Latin has developed new endings of its own, so that the original forms are only seen in the Present.

The Verbs in the older language were divided into two principal classes:

I. In which the Personal endings were formed by Pronouns joined immediately to the Root, the tenses being partly formed by changes in the root vowel.

II. In which the Verb-Stem was formed by a so-called Thematic vowel added to the root.

Of the first class there are very few remains in Latin, most of the Verbs which belonged to it having gone over into the second class.

The old ending -m (for -mi) of the First Person Singular is seen in sum, *I am*, and in other tenses, as eram, amem. A few Verbs retain part of their old forms side by side with later forms borrowed from the Thematic Verbs. These are:

Vowel-ending Stems:

eo, *I go*; dō, *I give*; stō, *I stand.*

Consonant-ending Stems:

edo, *I eat*; fero, *I carry*; volo, *I will*; nōlo, *will not*; mālo, *I prefer.*

(For the forms of these Verbs see **115** and **136** to **140**.)

PERSONAL ENDINGS IN UNTHEMATIC AND THEMATIC VERBS.

		ACTIVE VOICE.		PASSIVE VOICE.
		Unthematic.	Thematic.	
Singular 1		-m	-o	-r
2		-s	-s	-ris *or* -re
3		-t	-t (-d)	-tur
Plural 1		-mus (-mos)	-mus (-mos)	-mur
2		-tis	-tis	-mini
3		-nt	-unt (-ont)	-ntur

The -r of the Passive probably comes from an old form of a third Voice, called the Middle Voice, which is not preserved in Latin.

149

Present-Stem Formation.

The Thematic Verbs are divided into six groups according to the formation of their Present Stems.

I. The Present Stem is the same as the Verb-Stem, being formed by the addition of the thematic vowel to the Stem-syllable either with or without lengthening of the Stem-vowel: peto, veho, cēdo, fendo, dīco, fīdo, dūco, claudo, ago, alo, rudo, etc.

Note.—This class had originally two divisions: (*a*) with long root vowel, (*b*) with short root vowel, but in Latin the distinction between them is not clear.

II. Reduplicated Presents. Of this class very few are preserved in Latin: gigno for gi-g(e)no (gĕnus, *race*); si-sto; bi-bo.

III. With suffix -to added to the Stem-syllable: plecto, flecto, necto.

IV. Nasalised Stems:

a) with addition of the suffix -no: cerno, sterno, sperno, temno, and two roots ending in -i: sino, lino. Verbs in -llo, fallo, pello, percello, etc., also belong to this class, -llo standing for older -lno.

(*b*) Verbs in which the n is inserted in the Stem-syllable, as plango (Verb-Stem plag-), jungo, findo, scindo. The n becomes m before Labials, as in rumpo. In some of these Verbs the Nasal goes through all the tenses, as in ungo, unxi, unctum. In others it appears only in the Present Stem, as in frango, frēgi, fractum. A few have the Nasal in the Perfect, but not in the Supine, as pingo, pinxi, pictum.

V. With suffix -sco. This class also has two divisions:

(*a*) With the suffix joined immediately to the root-syllable: nosco, cresco, disco, pasco.

(*b*) Derivative Verbs in -asco, -esco, -isco, derived from other Verbs or from Nouns: congelasco, from gelo; calesco, from caleo; gemisco, from gemo; duresco, from durus, etc.

VI. With suffix -io. The Verbs in -io of the 3rd Conj. (Consonant-Stems) belong to this class. Capio, facio, etc.

It included originally the large number of derivative Verbs with Vowel-Stems, as amo (for ama-io), moneo (for mone-io) **(14)**.

149 PRESENT-STEM FORMATION.

The Thematic Verbs are divided into six groups according to the formation of their Present Stems.

I. The Present Stem is the same as the Verb-Stem, being formed by the addition of the thematic vowel to the Stem-syllable either with or without lengthening of the Stem-vowel: peto, veho, cēdo, fendo, dīco, fīdo, dūco, claudo, ago, alo, rudo, etc.

> *Note.*—This class had originally two divisions: (*a*) with long root vowel, (*b*) with short root vowel, but in Latin the distinction between them is not clear.

II. Reduplicated Presents. Of this class very few are preserved in Latin: gigno for gi-g(e)no (gĕnus, *race*); si-sto; bi-bo.

III. With suffix -to added to the Stem-syllable: plecto, flecto, necto.

IV. Nasalised Stems:

a) with addition of the suffix -no: cerno, sterno, sperno, temno, and two roots ending in -i: sino, lino. Verbs in -llo, fallo, pello, percello, etc., also belong to this class, -llo standing for older -lno.

(*b*) Verbs in which the n is inserted in the Stem-syllable, as plango (Verb-Stem plag-), jungo, findo, scindo. The n becomes m before Labials, as in rumpo. In some of these Verbs the Nasal goes through all the tenses, as in ungo, unxi, unctum. In others it appears only in the Present Stem, as in frango, frēgi, fractum. A few have the Nasal in the Perfect, but not in the Supine, as pingo, pinxi, pictum.

V. With suffix -sco. This class also has two divisions:

(*a*) With the suffix joined immediately to the root-syllable: nosco, cresco, disco, pasco.

(*b*) Derivative Verbs in -asco, -esco, -isco, derived from other Verbs or from Nouns: congelasco, from gelo; calesco, from caleo; gemisco, from gemo; duresco, from durus, etc.

VI. With suffix -io. The Verbs in -io of the 3rd Conj. (Consonant-Stems) belong to this class. Capio, facio, etc.

It included originally the large number of derivative Verbs with Vowel-Stems, as amo (for ama-io), moneo (for mone-io) **(14).**

Weak Formation of the Perfect.

I. The Perfect suffix in -si is joined to the Clipt Stem of many E- and some I- Verbs; also to a large number of Consonant-Stems with which it combines according to the laws of Consonant change. Thus gs, cs, hs, become x, as in rexi, pinxi, duxi, vexi. Also qs in coxi. The guttural drops after l, r in fulsi, mersi, also in vixi from Stem gvigv—(compare Old English cwĭcu, *quick*). In struxi, fluxi, the Perfect preserves the guttural sound which is lost in the Present. Dental sounds are dropped, plausi, flexi; with lengthening of short vowels, as in mīsi. The labial p remains unchanged, as in sculpsi, but b becomes p, scripsĭ, nupsi. After m, p is inserted, in sumpsi, tempsi; s remains, as in gessi, ussi, where in the Present it changes to r. It becomes single after a long vowel or diphthong, as haesi, hausi.

II. The weak Perfect forms in -vi and -ui are peculiar to the Latin language. They were probably formed by analogy from the V- and U- Stems like favi, acui, and extended to a very large number of Verbs. All the A- and I- Stems which keep their character vowel throughout the tenses as amavi, audivi, form their Perfect tense in -vi as well as many Consonant-Stems. The Perfect in -ui is joined to the Clipt E- Stems, as mon-ui, also to a few Clipt Stems in A- and E-, and to a large number of Consonant Verbs. This form had a tendency to spread in later Latin, and many Verbs formed new Perfects in -ui after the classical period.

151　　The Supine Stem.

The Supine or Participial Stem ends in -to. This suffix is joined to the Verb-Stem or to the Clipt Stem, either immediately or by the vowel i. When it is joined immediately to the Vowel-Stem, as in most of the A-, I- and U- Stems, the character vowel is lengthened. When it is joined to a Consonant-Stem, the laws of consonant change again come into force : g before t becomes c; the guttural is dropped after l or r, fultum, tortum; p is inserted between m and t, emptum. In a few Verbs the Stem-vowel is changed, as in lăvo, which has besides lavatum a contracted Supine form lautum, afterwards becoming lōtum: in sătum (from sĕro), cultum (from cŏlo).

The Supine in -sum was formed in Dental Stems by a regular change of medial -dt-, -tt- *to* ss; thus ced-to-, mit-to-, would become cesso-, misso-, and the double s would become single after a long vowel or diphthong (20). From the Dental Stems the Supine in -sum spread to many other Verbs by analogy. It combines with Consonant-Stems according to the same laws of letter change as the Perfect in -si.

H

152 TABLE OF VERB PERFECTS AND SUPINES.

I. A- Stems.

Present	Infin.	Perfect	Supine	
		Usual Form.		
-ō(-a-io)	-ārĕ	-āvi	-ā-tum	
amō	amārĕ	amāvi	amātum	

Exceptions.

		-ŭī	-ĭtum	
crĕpo	-āre	crepui	crepitum	*creak*
cŭbo	-āre	cubui	cubitum	*lie down*
dŏmo	-āre	domui	domitum	*tame*
plīco	-āre	-plicavi / -plicui }	-plicatum / -plicitum }	*fold*
sŏno	-āre	sonui	sonitum	*sound*
tŏno	-āre	tonui	tonitum	*thunder*
vĕto	-āre	vetui / vetavi }	vetitum	*forbid*

		-ŭī	-ātum	
mĭco	-āre	micui / micavi }	-micatum	*glitter*

		-ŭī	-tum	
enĕco	-āre	enecui	enectum	*kill*
frĭco	-āre	fricui	frictum / fricatum }	*rub*
sĕco	-āre	secui	sectum	*cut*

		-ī	-tum	
	(a) Reduplicated		-tum	
dō	-āre	dĕdī	dătum	*give*
stō	-āre	stĕti	stătum	*stand*

	(b) Lengthened Stem		-tum	
jŭvo	-āre	jūv -i	jūtum	*help*
lăvo	-āre	lāv -i	lavātum / lautum / lōtum }	*wash*

Note.--Jŭvo, lăvo have Fut. Part. juvaturus, lavaturus.

For very many Supines no authority exists; but the form is inferred from the Perfect Participle Passive, or from the Future Participle, or the Verbal Substantive.

Forms printed with a hyphen, as -plicavi, -plicatum, are only used in compounds.

153   II. E- Stems.

Present	Infin.	Perfect	Supine	
			Usual Form.	
-ĕō (-e-io)	-ērĕ	-ŭī	-ĭtum	
mŏnĕō	monēre	mŏnŭī	monĭtum	

Exceptions.

		-ŭī	-tum	
arceo	-ēre	arcui		*ward off*
dŏceo	-ēre	docui	doctum	*teach*
ferveo	-ēre	ferbui } fervi		*be hot*
misceo	-ēre	miscui	mistum } mixtum	*mix*
sorbeo	-ēre	sorbui		*swallow*
tĕneo	-ēre	tenui	tentum	*hold*
torreo	-ēre	torrui	tostum	*scorch*
		-ui	-sum	
censeo	-ēre	censui	censum	*deem, vote*
		-vī	-tum	
aboleo	-ēre	abolevi	abolitum	*destroy*
cieo	-ēre	cīvi	cītum	*stir up*
dēleo	-ēre	delevi	deletum	*blot out*
fleo	-ēre	flevi	fletum	*weep*
neo	-ēre	nevi		*spin*
-pleo	-ēre	-plevi	-pletum	*fill*
		-sī	-tum	
augeo	-ēre	auxi	auctum	*increase* (tr.)
conīveo	-ēre	conixi	—	*wink*
frīgeo	-ēre	frixi	—	*freeze*
lūgeo	-ēre	luxi	—	*mourn*
pollūceo	-ēre	—	polluctum	*make a feast*
fulgeo	-ēre	fulsi	—	*shine*
indulgeo	-ēre	indulsi	—	*indulge*
mulgeo	-ēre	mulsi	—	*milk*
torqueo	-ēre	torsi	tortum	*twist*
		-si	-sum	
algeo	-ēre	alsi	—	*be cold*
ardeo	-ēre	arsi	—	*burn* (intr.)
haereo	-ēre	haesi	—	*stick*
jŭbeo	-ēre	jussi	jussum	*command*
lūceo	-ere	luxi	—	*shine*
mǎneo	-ēre	mansi	mansum	*remain*
mulceo	-ēre	mulsi	mulsum	*soothe*
rīdeo	-ēre	risi	risum	*laugh*
suādeo	-ēre	suasi	suasum	*advise*
tergeo	-ēre	tersi	—	*wipe*
turgeo	-ēre	tursi	—	*swell*
urgeo	-ēre	ursi	—	*press*

Note.—Ardeo, haereo have Fut. Part. arsurus, haesurus.

Present	Infin.	Perfect	Supine	
		-i	-tum *or* -sum	

(a) Lengthened Stem   -tum

căveo	-ēre	cāv-i	cautum	*beware*
făveo	-ēre	fāv-i	fautum	*favour*
fŏveo	-ēre	fōv-i	fotum	*cherish*
mŏveo	-ēre	mōv-i	motum	*move* (tr.)
păveo	-ēre	pāv-i	—	*quake*
vŏveo	-ēre	vōv-i	votum	*vow*

(b) Reduplicated   -sum

pendeo	-ēre	pĕpendi	pensum	*hang* (intr.)
mordeo	-ēre	mŏmordi	morsum	*bite*
spondeo	-ēre	spŏpondi	sponsum	*pledge*
tondeo	-ēre	tŏtondi	tonsum	*shear*

(c) Lengthened Stem   -sum

sĕdeo	-ēre	sēdi	sessum	*sit*
vĭdeo	-ēre	vīdi	vīsum	*see*
prandeo	-ēre	prandi	pransum	*lunch, dine*
strīdeo	-ēre	stridi	—	*creak*

154   III. Consonant and U- Stems.

Consonant Stems.

Present	Infin.	Perfect	Supine	
rĕgo	rĕgĕre	rexī	rectum	
		-si	-tum	
cŏquo	-ĕre	coxi	coctum	*cook*
dīco	-ĕre	dixi	dictum	*say*
dīlĭgo	-ĕre	dilexi	dilectum	*love*
dŭco	-ĕre	duxi	ductum	*lead*
afflīgo	-ĕre	-flixi	-flictum	*smite down*
frīgo	-ĕre	frixi	frictum	*roast*
intellĕgo	-ĕre	intellexi	intellectum	*understand*
neglĕgo	-ĕre	neglexi	neglectum	*neglect*
pergo	-ĕre	perrexi	perrectum	*proceed*
sūgo	-ĕre	suxi	suctum	*suck*
surgo	-ĕre	surrexi	surrectum	*arise*
tĕgo	-ĕre	texi	tectum	*cover*
trăho	-ĕre	traxi	tractum	*draw*
vĕho	-ĕre	vexi	vectum	*carry*
vīvo	-ĕre	vixi	victum	*live*
fluo	-ĕre	fluxi	fluctum	*flow*
struo	-ĕre	struxi	structum	*build*

Present	Infin.	Perfect	Supine	
carpo	-ĕre	carpsi	carptum	*pluck*
nūbo	-ĕre	nupsi	nuptum	*marry*
rēpo	-ĕre	repsi	reptum	*creep*
scalpo	-ĕre	scalpsi	scalptum	*scratch*
sculpo	-ĕre	sculpsi	sculptum	*carve*
scrībo	-ĕre	scripsi	scriptum	*write*
gĕro	-ĕre	gessi	gestum	*carry on*
ūro	-ĕre	ussi	ustum	*burn* (tr.)
cōmo	-ĕre	compsi	comptum	*adorn*
dēmo	-ĕre	dempsi	demptum	*take away*
prōmo	-ĕre	prompsi	promptum	*bring out*
sūmo	-ĕre	sumpsi	sumptum	*take*
temno	-ĕre	-tempsi	-temptum	*despise*
ango	-ĕre	—	—	*pain*
clango	-ĕre	—	—	*clash*
cingo	-ĕre	cinxi	cinctum	*surround*
exstinguo	-ĕre	exstinxi	exstinctum	*quench*
fingo	-ĕre	finxi	fictum	*feign*
jungo	-ĕre	junxi	junctum	*join*
pango	-ĕre	panxi / pēgi }	pactum	*fasten*
pingo	-ĕre	pinxi	pictum	*paint*
stringo	-ĕre	strinxi	strictum	*bind*
tingo	-ĕre	tinxi	tinctum	*dye*
unguo (ungo)	-ĕre	unxi	unctum	*anoint*
ninguit (ningit)	-ĕre	ninxit	—	*it snows*
		-sī	**-sum**	
fīgo	-ĕre	fixi	fixum	*fix*
mergo	-ĕre	mersi	mersum	*drown*
spargo	-ĕre	sparsi	sparsum	*sprinkle*
cēdo	-ĕre	cessi	cessum	*yield*
claudo	-ĕre	clausi	clausum	*shut*
divĭdo	-ĕre	divīsi	divīsum	*divide*
laedo	-ĕre	laesi	laesum	*hurt*
lūdo	-ĕre	lusi	lusum	*play*
mitto	-ĕre	mīsi	missum	*send*
plaudo	-ĕre	plausi	plausum	*applaud*
rādo	-ĕre	rasi	rasum	*scrape*
rōdo	-ĕre	rosi	rosum	*gnaw*
trūdo	-ĕre	trusi	trusum	*thrust*
vādo	-ĕre	(in)vasi	(in)vasum	*go (attack)*
prĕmo	-ĕre	pressi	pressum	*press*
flecto	-ĕre	flexi	flexum	*bend*
necto	-ĕre	nexi / nexui }	nexum	*bind*
pecto	-ĕre	pexi	pexum	*comb*
quătio	-ĕre	quassi	quassum	*shake* (tr.)
concŭtio	-ĕre	concussi	concussum	*shake together*

Note.—Nexui, the more usual Perf. of necto, is from an obsolete verb, nexo.

Present	Infin.	Perfect -vī	Supine -tum	
sĕro	-ĕre	sēvī	sătum	sow
cerno	-ĕre	crēvī	crētum	sift, discern
sperno	-ĕre	sprēvi	sprētum	despise
sterno	-ĕre	strāvi	strātum	strew
lĭno	-ĕre	lēvi livi }	lĭtum	smear
sĭno	-ĕre	sīvi	sĭtum	allow
cognosco	-ĕre	cognōvi	cognĭtum	know
cresco	-ĕre	crēvi	crētum	grow
nosco	-ĕre	nōvi	nōtum	know
pasco	-ĕre	pāvi	pastum	feed (tr.)
abolesco	-ĕre	abolēvi		decay
adolesco	-ĕre	adolēvi		grow up
obsolesco	-ĕre	obsolēvi	—	grow out of use
quiesco	-ĕre	quiēvi	quietum	rest
suesco	-ĕre	suēvi	suētum	grow accustomed

Note.—Adolesco has adjective adultus.

		-īvī	-ītum	
arcesso	-ĕre	arcessīvi	arcessitum	send for
incesso	-ĕre	incessīvi	—	attack
lăcesso	-ĕre	lacessīvi	lacessitum	provoke
căpesso	-ĕre	capessīvi	capessitum	take in hand
cŭpio	-ĕre	cupīvi	cupitum	desire
săpio	-ĕre	sapīvi		be wise
quaero	-ĕre	quaesīvi	quaesitum	seek
tĕro	-ĕre	trīvi	tritum	rub

		-ŭī	-tum	
ălo	-ĕre	alui	altum	nourish
cŏlo	-ĕre	colui	cultum	till, worship
consŭlo	-ĕre	consului	consultum	consult
occŭlo	-ĕre	occului	occultum	hide
pinso	-ĕre	pinsui pinsi }	pistum	beat, pound
sĕro	-ĕre	serui	sertum	join
texo	-ĕre	texui	textum	weave
răpio	-ĕre	rapui	raptum	seize

		-ŭī	-ĭtum	
frĕmo	-ĕre	fremui	fremitum	bellow
gĕmo	-ĕre	gemui	gemitum	groan
mŏlo	-ĕre	molui	molitum	grind
strĕpo	-ĕre	strepui	strepitum	roar
trĕmo	-ĕre	tremui		tremble
vŏmo	-ĕre	vomui	vomitum	vomit
gigno	-ĕre	genui	genitum	produce
pōno	-ĕre	posui	positum	place
compesco	-ĕre	compescui		restrain

		-ŭī	-sum	
mĕto	-ĕre	messui	messum	reap
excello	-ĕre	excellui		excel

Present	Infin.	Perfect	Supine	
		-ī	-tum	

(a) Reduplicated -tum

căno	-ĕre	cĕcĭni	cantum	*sing*
pungo	-ĕre	pŭpŭgi	punctum	*prick*
tango	-ĕre	tĕtĭgi	tactum	*touch*
tendo	-ĕre	tĕtendi	tentum (tensum)	*stretch*
disco	-ĕre	dĭdĭci	—	*learn*
posco	-ĕre	pŏposci	—	*demand*
părio	-ĕre	pĕpĕri	partum	*bring forth*
			-sum	
cădo	-ĕre	cĕcĭdi	cāsum	*fall*
caedo	-ĕre	cĕcīdi	caesum	*beat, kill*
curro	-ĕre	cucurri	cursum	*run*
fallo	-ĕre	fĕfelli	falsum	*deceive*
parco	-ĕre	pĕperci	parsum	*spare*
pello	-ĕre	pĕpŭli	pulsum	*drive*
pendo	-ĕre	pĕpendi	pensum	*hang*
tundo	-ĕre	tŭtŭdi	tūsum tunsum }	*bruise*

Compounds of dō

abdo	-ĕre	abdĭdi	abdĭtum	*hide*
addo	-ĕre	addidi	additum	*add*
condo	-ĕre	condidi	conditum	*found, hide*
crēdo	-ĕre	crēdidi	crēditum	*believe*
dēdo	-ĕre	dēdidi	dēditum	*give up*
ēdo	-ĕre	ēdidi	ēditum	*give forth*
perdo	-ĕre	perdidi	perditum	*lose*
prōdo	-ĕre	prōdidi	prōditum	*betray*
reddo	-ĕre	reddidi	redditum	*restore*
subdo	-ĕre	subdidi	subditum	*substitute*
trādo	-ĕre	trādidi	trāditum	*deliver*
vendo	-ĕre	vendidi	venditum	*sell*

Note.—Pereo, *perish*, veneo, *go for sale*, are used as Passives of perdo and vendo.

Reduplicated from stō

sisto	-ĕre	-stĭti	-stātum	*make to stand*

(b) Lengthened Stem, -tum

ĕmo	-ĕre	ēmi	emptum	*buy*
lĕgo	-ĕre	lēgi	lectum	*choose,* **read**
rumpo	-ĕre	rūpi	ruptum	*break*
vinco	-ĕre	vīci	victum	*conquer*
linquo	-ĕre	-līqui	-lictum	*leave*
căpio	-ĕre	cēpi	captum	*take*
fŭgio	-ĕre	fūgi	fugitum	*fly*
ăgo	-ĕre	ēgi	actum	*do*
frango	-ĕre	frēgi	fractum	*break* (tr.)
făcio	-ĕre	fēci	factum	*make*
jăcio	-ĕre	jēci	jactum	*throw*

Present	Infin.	Perfect	Supine	
		Lengthened Stem -ī -sum		
fundo	-ĕre	fūdi	fusum	*pour*
retundo	-ĕre	rettŭdi	retusum	*beat back*
fŏdio	-ĕre	fōdi	fossum	*dig*
ĕdo	-ĕre	ēdi	esum	*eat*
		-ī -tum, -sum		
bĭbo	-ĕre	bĭbi	bibitum	*drink*
īco	-ĕre	īci	ictum	*strike*
cūdo	-ĕre	cudi	cusum	*stamp*
sīdo	-ĕre	sīdi	—	*settle*
viso	-ĕre	vīsi	visum	*visit*
psallo	-ĕre	psalli	—	*play on strings*
verro	-ĕre	verri	versum	*sweep*
verto	-ĕre	verti	versum	*turn* (tr.)
cendo	-ĕre	-cendi	-censum	*kindle*
fendo	-ĕre	-fendi	-fensum	*strike*
findo	-ĕre	fīdi	fissum	*cleave*
mando	-ĕre	mandi	mansum	*chew*
pando	-ĕre	pandi	pansum } passum }	*open, spread*
prĕhendo	-ĕre	prehendi	prehensum	*grasp*
scando	-ĕre	scandi	scansum	*climb*
scindo	-ĕre	scĭdi	scissum	*tear*
percello	-ĕre	percŭli	perculsum	*thrill*
vello	-ĕre	velli (vulsi)	vulsum	*rend*
		U- Stems. -ī -tum		
acŭo	-ĕre	acŭi	acūtum	*sharpen*
arguo	-ĕre	argui	argutum	*prove*
congruo	-ĕre	congrui	—	*come together*
exuo	-ĕre	exui	exutum	*put off*
induo	-ĕre	indui	indutum	*put on*
imbuo	-ĕre	imbui	imbutum	*tinge*
luo	-ĕre	lui	-lutum	*wash, atone*
mĕtuo	-ĕre	metui	—	*fear*
mĭnuo	-ĕre	minui	minutum	*lessen*
adnuo	-ĕre	adnui	—	*nod*
pluo	-ĕre	plui pluvi	—	*rain*
ruo	-ĕre	rui	rŭtum } ruitum }	*rush, fall*
spuo	-ĕre	spui	sputum	*spit*
statuo	-ĕre	statui	statutum	*set up*
sternuo	-ĕre	sternui	—	*sneeze*
suo	-ĕre	sui	sutum	*sew*
tribuo	-ĕre	tribui	tributum	*assign, render*
solvo	-ĕre	solvi	solutum	*loosen, pay*
volvo	-ĕre	volvi	volutum	*roll* (tr.)

155   IV. I- Stems.

Present	Infin.	Perfect	Supine	
		Usual Form.		
-ĭō (-i-io)	-īre	-īvī	-ītum	
audio	audīre	audīvi	audītum	

Exceptions.

		-īvi	-tum	
sĕpĕlio	-īre	sepelivi	sepultum	*bury*
		-vi	-tum	
scio	-īre	scivi	scitum	*know*
		-ui	-tum	
sălio	-īre	salui	—	*dance*
apĕrio	-īre	aperui	apertum	*open*
opĕrio	-īre	operui	opertum	*cover*
		-si	-tum	
amĭcio	-īre	amixi ⎫ amicui ⎭	amictum	*clothe*
fulcio	-īre	fulsi	fultum	*prop*
haurio	-īre	hausi	haustum	*drain*
saepio	-īre	saepsi	saeptum	*hedge in*
sarcio	-īre	sarsi	sartum	*patch*
sancio	-īre	sanxi	sanctum	*hallow*
vincio	-īre	vinxi	vinctum	*bind*
		-si	-sum	
sentio	-īre	sensi	sensum	*feel*
		-i	-tum	
vĕnio	-īre	vēni	ventum	*come*
compĕrio	-īre	comperi	compertum	*find*
repĕrio	-īre	repperi	repertum	*discover*

156   DEPONENT VERBS.

A- Stems (Perfect -ātus sum).
About 160, all regular.

157   E- Stems (Perfect -ĭtus sum).

Present	Infin.	Perfect	
făteor	-ērī	fassus sum	*confess*
lĭceor	-ērī	licitus sum	*bid in auction*
mĕdeor	-ērī	—	*heal*
mĕreor	-ērī	meritus sum	*deserve*
mĭsĕreor	-ērī	miseritus ⎫ misertus ⎭ sum	*have pity on*
tueor	-ērī	tuitus sum	*protect*
vĕreor	-ērī	veritus sum	*fear*
reor	-ērī	rătus sum	*think*

158   Semi-deponent Verbs.

Present	*Infin.*	*Perfect*		
audeo	-ēre	ausus sum	—	*dare*
gaudeo	-ēre	gāvīsus sum	—	*rejoice*
sŏleo	-ēre	sŏlitus sum	—	*be wont*

159   Consonant and U- Stems (Perfect -tŭs *or* -sŭs sum).

amplector	-ī	amplexus sum	*embrace*
ăpiscor	-ī	aptus sum	*acquire*
expergiscor	-ī	experrectus sum	*waken*
fătiscor	-ī	fessus sum	*grow weary*
fruor	-ī	fruitus sum	*enjoy*
fungor		functus sum	*perform*
grădior	-ī	gressus sum	*step*
īrascor	-ī	iratus sum	*be angry*
lābor	-ī	lapsus sum	*glide*
-miniscor	-ī	-mentus sum	*have in mind*
morior	-ī	mortuus sum	*die*
nanciscor	-ī	nactus nanctus } sum	*obtain*
nascor	-ī	natus sum	*be born*
nītor	-ī	nisus (nixus) sum	*strive*
păciscor	-ī	pactus sum	*bargain*
pătior	-ī	passus sum	*suffer*
profīciscor	-ī	profectus sum	*set out*
quĕror	-ī	questus sum	*complain*
ulciscor	-ī	ultus sum	*avenge*
ūtor	-ī	usus sum	*use*
vescor	-ī	—	*feed on*
līquor	-ī	—	*melt*
lŏquor	-ī	locutus sum	*speak*
sĕquor	-ī	secutus sum	*follow*

Note.—The form gressus is very rarely found except in Compounds
Morior has Future Participle morīturus.

160   Semi-deponent.

fīdo	-ī	fīsus sum	*trust*

161   I- Stems (Perfect -ītus, -tus, *or* -sus sum).

blandior	-īrī	blandītus sum	*flatter*
expĕrior	-īrī	expertus sum	*try*
largior	-īrī	largitus sum	*bestow*
mōlior	-īrī	molitus sum	*contrive*
oppĕrior	-īrī	oppertus sum	*wait for*
ŏrior	-īrī	ortus sum	*arise*
partior	-īrī	partitus sum	*distribute*
pŏtior	-īrī	potitus sum	*acquire*
pūnior	-īrī	punitus sum	*punish*
sortior	-īrī	sortitus sum	*take by lot*
assentior	-īrī	assensus sum	*agree*
mētior	-īrī	mensus sum	*measure*
ordior	-īrī	orsus sum	*begin*

162 PARTICLES.

The Particles are for the most part old cases of Substantives or Adjectives, which have become limited to special uses as Adverbs, Prepositions or Conjunctions.

The oldest of these is the adverbial use, which was originally to limit or qualify the action expressed by the Verb, but was afterwards extended to qualify Adjectives, and sometimes other Adverbs.

Prepositions are Adverbs which have acquired the special use of standing before Nouns to express relations of place and time.

Many Conjunctions are also Adverbs which have come to be used merely as links between words or sentences.

163 ADVERBS.

Adverbs are formed either from cases of Substantives, Adjectives or Participles, or from Pronoun roots. Those which are formed from Adjectives or Participles generally have comparison (85). Those which are derived from Pronoun roots have no comparison.

In regard to meaning, they are divided chiefly into Adverbs of (1) Manner; (2) Degree; (3) Cause; (4) Place; (5) Time; (6) Order.

The following are a few of each class :

164
Adverbs of Manner:

lentē, *slowly.*
facilĕ, *easily.*
falso, *falsely.*
ultro, *spontaneously.*

aequē, perindĕ, proindĕ, } *in like manner.*
similiter, ĭtĭdem, } *in the same manner.*
quam, *how ?*

celeriter, *quickly.*
sapienter, *wisely.*
vementer, *strongly.*

aliter, secus, } *otherwise. differently.*
ita, sic, tam, } *so.*
adeo, *so far.*
ut, *as, how.*

165
Adverbs of Degree:

multum, *much.*
quantum, *how much.*
satis, *enough.*
nimis, nimium, } *too much.*
valde, *very.*
ferme, fere, } *almost.*

paullum, *little.*
tantum, *so much.*
magis, *more.*
potius, *rather.*
potissimum, *by preference.*
parum, *too little.*
magnopere, *greatly.*
vix, aegre, } *scarcely.*

166
Adverbs of Cause:

ideo, idcirco, propterea, *on that account.*

Adverbs of Place:

167

Where: ubi, *where?*   hic, *here.*
      ibi, } *there.*   ibidem, *in the same place.*
      illic, }   alibi, *elsewhere.*
      usquam, *anywhere.*   nusquam, *nowhere.*

Whither: quo, *whither?*   huc, *hither.*
      eo, } *thither.*   eodem, *to the same place.*
      illuc, }   usque, *so far.*

Whence: unde, *whence?*   hinc, *hence.*
      inde, } *thence.*   indidem, *from the same place.*
      illinc, }   hac, *by this way.*
      quā, *by what way?*   eā, illac, *by that way.*

Adverbs of Time:

168

When: quando, ubi, *when?*   tum, tunc, *then.*
      nunc, modo, *now.*   jam, *now, already.*
      simul, *at the same time.*   alias, *at another time.*
      umquam, *ever.*   numquam, *never.*
      semper, *always.*   interdum, *now and then.*
      olim, } *at some time.*   mox, *by and bye.*
      quondam, }   nuper, *lately.*
      ante, *before.*   post, *after.*
      demum, *at length.*   nondum, *not yet.*

How long: quam diu, *how long?*   tamdiu, *so long.*
      diu, *long.*   usque, *continuously.*
      jamdiu, *long since.*

How often: quotiens, *how often?*   totiens, *so often.*
      semel, *once.*   iterum, *a second time.*
      saepe, *often.*   raro, *seldom.*

169   crebro, *frequently.*   identidem, *repeatedly.*

Adverbs of Order:

primum, *first.*   primo, *in the beginning.*
deinde, *in the next place.*   praeterea, } *moreover.*
deinceps, *afterwards.*   insuper, }

170   tertio, *thirdly.*   denique, } *lastly.*
          postremo, }

Sometimes an Adverb qualifies a sentence or phrase, rather than any particular word.

Adverbs of

Affirmation: etiam, *also*; quidem, equidem, *indeed*; vero, *but*; plane, *quite*; sane, *certainly*; profecto, omnino, certe, *surely, by all means.*

Limitation: pariter, *alike*; simul, *together*; plerumque, *usually*; solum, tantum, modo, *only.*

Negation: non, haud, *not*; haudquaquam, neutiquam, *by no means.*

Doubt: fortasse, forsan, forsitan, *perhaps*; forte, *by chance.*

Question: cur, quare, quamobrem? *why?* quomodo, quemadmodum, quam, ut? *how?*

171 PREPOSITIONS.

Prepositions are placed before Nouns to show their relation to other words in the sentence. They are also compounded with Verbs to modify their meaning.

172 The following Prepositions are used with the Accusative:

ăd	to, at	juxtā	next to, beside
adversŭs	{ towards, against	ŏb	over against, on account of
adversum }	{ opposite to	pĕnĕs	in the power of
antĕ	before	pĕr	through
ăpŭd	at, near, among	pōnĕ	behind
circum	around	post	after, behind
circā, circĭtĕr	about	praetĕr	beside, past
cĭs, cītrā	on this side of	prŏpĕ	near
contrā	against	proptĕr	near, on account of
ergā	towards	sĕcundum	next, along, according to
extrā	outside of, without	suprā	above
infrā	below	trans	across
intĕr	between, amidst	ultrā	beyond
intrā	within	versŭs, versum	towards

173 The following are used with the Ablative:

ā, ăb, abs	by, from	ex, ē	out of, from
absquĕ	without	palam	in sight of
clam	unknown to	prae	before, in front of
cōram	in the presence of	prō	before, for
cum	with	sĭnĕ	without
dē	from, concerning	tĕnŭs	as far as, reaching to

Note.—Clam is also used with the accusative, but more rarely; tĕnŭs is placed after the Noun; it is sometimes used with the Genitive.

174 The following take the Accusative when they denote motion towards, and the Ablative when they denote rest:

in	into, against, in, on	sŭper	over, upon
sŭb	up to, under	subtĕr	under

175 Prepositions used only in Verb compounds are:

ambi, amb-, am-, an-	around	ambio,	go around
dis-	apart	dissolvo,	separate; **dirigo,** direct
rĕd-, rĕ-	back, again	red-eo,	go back; **refero,** bring back
sĕd-, sē-	apart	secedo,	step apart

176   CONJUNCTIONS.

Conjunctions are: I. Co-ordinative (**400**); II. Subordinative (**421–429**).

177   I. Co-ordinative Conjunctions are:

Connective: et, -que, atque (adque), ac, } *and.*
         neque, nec, } *nor.*
         etiam, quoque, item, } *also.*

Separative: aut, vel, -ve, } *or, either.*
         sive, seu, } *whether, or.*

Adversative: sed, at (ast), } *but.*
     atqui, *but yet.*
     at enim, *but it will be said.*
     tamen, { *yet, however, nevertheless.*
         autem, *but, now, however.*
         ceterum, verum, vero, } *but, moreover.*
         attamen, verumtamen, } *but nevertheless.*

Causal: nam, namque, enim, etenim, } *for.*
         enimvero, *for indeed.*

Conclusive: ergo, itaque, igitur, } *therefore.*
         quare, quamobrem, quapropter, quocirca, } *wherefore.*

Comparative: ut, uti, velut, veluti, sicut, sicuti, ceu, } *as*
     utpote, *as being.*
         quomodo, quemadmodum, } *as, how.*
         quam, *than, as.*
         quasi, tamquam, } *as it were.*

Interrogative: num, -ne, nonne, }
         utrum—an? *whether—or.*
         necne, *or not?*

178   II. Subordinative Conjunctions are:

Consecutive: ut, *so that.*
     ut non, *so that not.*
         quin, { *that not. but that.*

Final: ut, *in order that.*
     neve, neu, { *and that not. and lest.*
     quo, { *whereby. in order that.*
         ne, *lest.*
         ut ne, *that not, lest.*
         quominus, { *whereby not. in order that not.*

Causal: quod, *because.* quia, *because.*

cum, *since.* quoniam, quandoquidem, } *since.*

quippe, { *for as much as.* *seeing that.* siquidem, *inasmuch as.*

Temporal: cum (quum), *when.* quando, *when.*
ut, *when.* ubi, *when.*
dum, doneo, quoad, } *while.* *so long as.* dum, donec, quoad, } *until.*
  quatenus, *how long.*

antequam, priusquam, } *before that.* postquam, *after that.*
simul ac, *as soon as.* quotiens, *as often as.*

Conditional: si, *if.* sin (si ne), *but if.*
sive, seu, } *whether.* *or if.* nisi, ni, *unless.*
  si non, *if not.*
si modo, *if only.* modo, tantum, } *only.*
modo, dummodo, *provided that.*

Concessive: etsi, etiamsi, } *even if, although.* tametsi, *although.*
quamquam, utut, } *however,* *although.* quamvis, } *although.* *however much.*
cum, *whereas, although.*
ut, licet, *granting that, although.*

Comparative: quasi (quam si), ut si, velut si, } *as if.* ceu, tamquam, } *as though.*

179 The following pairs are often used as Correlatives:

et . . . . et que . . . que que . . . et } *both . . . and*   sive . . . sive seu . . . seu } *whether . . . or*

aut . . . aut vel . . . vel } *either . . . or*   sic . . . ut,   *so . . . as*
  ut . . . ita,   *as . . . so*

neque . neque nec . . . . . nec neve . . . neve } *neither . . . nor*   ita . . . ut,   *so . . . that*
  adeo . . . ut, *so far . . . that*

180   INTERJECTIONS.

An Interjection is an exclamatory word, used either to draw attention or to express feeling. The most usual are:

O, *O! oh!*   prō *or* prōh, *forbid it!*
A *or* āh, *alas!*   vae, *woe!*
ēheu, heu, ei, *alas!*   ēn, eccĕ, *lo! behold!*

SYNTAX.

THE SIMPLE SENTENCE.

181 ### Introductory Outline.

SYNTAX teaches how **Sentences** are made.

182 Sentences are **Simple** or **Compound**.

A Simple Sentence has two parts:

1. The **Subject**: the person or thing spoken about;

2. The **Predicate**: that which is said about the

183 Subject.

1. The **Subject** must be a **Substantive**, or some word or words taking the place of a Substantive:

A **Substantive**: lex, *the law*;

A **Substantive Pronoun**: ego, *I*;

An **Adjective, Participle, or Adjectival Pronoun**: Romanus, *a Roman*; iratus, *an angry man*; ille, *that* (*man*);

A **Verb Noun Infinitive**: navigare, *to sail*, or *sailing*;

A **Phrase**: satis temporis, *enough time*.

184

2. The **Predicate** must either be a **Verb** or contain a Verb, because it makes a statement or assertion about the Subject; and it is usually a Verb Finite, which alone has the power of making direct statements.

I

185

Subject.	Predicate.	Subject.	Predicate.
Lex	jubet.	Navigare	delectat.
Law	*commands.*	*Sailing*	*delights.*
Nos	paremus.	Satis temporis	datur.
We	*obey.*	*Enough time*	*is given.*

Note.—A single Verb may be a sentence. Veni, vidi, vici, *I came, I saw, I conquered*, comprises three sentences.

186 Some Verbs cannot by themselves form complete Predicates. The Verb sum is a complete Predicate only when it implies mere existence :

Seges	est	ubi	Troja	fuit. Ov.
Corn	*is*	*where*	*Troy*	*was.*

It more often links the Subject with the **Complement**, which completes what is said about it.

187 Verbs which link a Subject and Complement are called **Copulative Verbs.**

Others besides sum are :—

appareo, *appear* ;   audio, *am called* ; maneo, *remain* ;
evado, existo, *turn out* ;   videor, *seem.*

The Passives of Verbs of *making, saying, thinking* (**Factitive Verbs***) are also used as Copulative Verbs (**206**) :

fio (facio), *become* or *am made* ;   feror, *am reported* ;
appellor, *am called* ;   legor, *am chosen* ;
creor, *am created* ;   putor, *am thought* ;
declaror, *am declared* ;   vocor, *am called.*

188 Copulative Verbs have the same Case after them as before them.

* These Verbs are called Factitive from facere, *to make*, because they contain the idea of making.

189   The Complement may be—

1. An **Adjective** or **Adjectival Word**.
2. A **Substantive**.

Subject.	Predicate.	
	Copulative Verb	Complement.
1. Leo	est	validus.
The lion	*is*	*strong.*
2. Illi	appellantur	philosophi.
They	*are called*	*philosophers.*

190   Many Verbs usually require another Verb in the Infinitive to carry on their construction; such are: soleo, *am wont*; possum, *am able*; queo, *can*; debeo, *ought*; volo, *wish*; conor, *endeavour.*

Solet legere.   Possum ire.
He is wont to read.   *I am able to go.*

These Verbs are called **Indeterminate**, and the Infinitive following them is called **Prolative**, because it carries on (profert) their construction.

191   A Simple Sentence may be enlarged in many ways.

The **Subject** may be qualified by Adjectives or Pronouns in Agreement, or may have words in Apposition added to it.

The **Verb** may be qualified by Adverbs or Adverbial phrases; it may have a Preposition with a Case, or some part of the Verb Infinite depending on it; if Transitive, it has a Nearer Object and may have also a Remoter Object; if Intransitive, it may have a Remoter Object in the Dative.

The **Complement** may again be qualified by an Adjective or an Adverb, or by a Case of a Noun, or a Preposition with a Case.

AGREEMENT.

RULES OF THE FOUR CONCORDS.

192   I. A Verb agrees with its Subject in Number and Person :

Tempus fugit.   Libri leguntur.
Time flies.   *Books are read.*

193   II. An Adjective or Participle agrees in Gender, Number, and Case with the Substantive it qualifies :

Vir bonus bonam uxorem habet.
The good man has a good wife.

Verae amicitiae sempiternae sunt.   Cic.
True friendships are everlasting.

194   III. When a Substantive or Pronoun is followed by another Substantive, so that the second explains or describes the first, and has the same relation to the rest of the sentence, the second Noun agrees in Case with the first, and is said to be in Apposition :

Nos liberi patrem Lollium imitabimur.
We children will imitate our father Lollius.

Procas, rex Albanorum, duos filios, Numitorem et
   Amulium, habuit.   Liv.
Procas, king of the Albans, had two sons, Numitor and Amulius.

195   IV. The Relative qui, quae, quod, agrees with its Antecedent in Gender, Number and Person; in Case it takes its construction from its own clause (**330**) :

Amo te, mater, quae me amas.
I love you, mother, who love me.

Quis hic est homo quem ante aedes video ?   Plaut.
Who is this man whom I see before the house?

Arbores multas serit agricola, quarum fructus non adspiciet.   Cic.
The farmer plants many trees, of which he will not see the fruit.

196   Notes on the Concords.

I. 1.—The Verb est, sunt, is often understood, not expressed :

Nihil bonum nisi quod honestum. Cic.
Nothing is good except what is virtuous.

2. A Copulative Verb occasionally agrees with the Complement rather than with the Subject :

Amantium irae amoris integratio est. Ter.
The quarrels of lovers are the renewal of love.

197   III. 1. A Substantive often agrees in Number and Gender with the Noun to which it is in apposition :

Stilus, optimus et praestantissimus dicendi magister. Cic.
The pen, best and chief teacher of oratory.

Philosophia, vitae magistra. Cic.
Philosophy, the mistress of life.

2. A Noun may be in apposition to a Personal Pronoun understood :

Hannibal peto pacem. Liv.
I Hannibal sue for peace.

Composite Subject.

198   1. When two or more Nouns are united as the Subject, the Verb and Adjectives are usually in the Plural :

Veneno absumpti sunt Hannibal et Philopoemen. Liv.
Hannibal and Philopoemen were cut off by poison.

Aetas, metus, magister eum cohibebant. Ter.
Age, fear, and a tutor were restraining him.

2. If the Persons of a Composite Subject are different, the Verb agrees with the first person rather than the second ; with the second rather than the third :

Si tu et Tullia valetis, ego et Cicero valemus. Cic.
If you and Tullia are well, I and Cicero are well.

3. When the Genders are different, Adjectives agree with the Masculine rather than with the Feminine :

> Rex regiaque classis una profecti. Liv.
> *The king and the royal fleet set out together.*

4. If the things expressed are without life, the Adjectives are generally Neuter :

> Regna, honores, divitiae, caduca et incerta sunt. Cic.
> *Kingdoms, honours, riches, are frail and fickle things.*

199   Notes on the Composite Subject.

1. When several Subjects of the third person are united, the Verb is sometimes found in the Singular, agreeing with one only :

> Nunc mihi nihil libri, nihil litterae, nihil doctrina prodest. Cic.
> *Now neither do books avail me, nor letters, nor* does *learning.*

2. If the union of two Subjects forms a single notion, the Verb may be Singular :

> Senatus populusque Romanus intellegit. Cic.
> *The Roman senate and people understand.*

3. But sometimes when a Collective Noun is the Subject, although it is Singular in form, the Verb and Adjectives are Plural :

> Pars militum capti, pars occisi sunt. Liv.
> *Part of the soldiers were taken captive, part were slain.*

Observe that the Adjectives agree in Gender with the individuals of which the Collective Noun is made up.

THE CASES.

200 ### THE NOMINATIVE AND VOCATIVE CASES.

The Subject of a Finite Verb is in the Nominative Case:

Anni fugiunt.   Labitur aetas. Ov.
Years flee.   *Time glides away.*

Note.—When an Infinitive, called Historic, is used for the Imperfect of a Finite Verb, the Nominative remains as the Subject (**372**):

Tum pius Aeneas umeris abscindere vestem. VERG.
Then the pious Aeneas began to tear his vest from his shoulders.

201

·A Substantive joined to the Subject by a Copulative Verb is in the Nominative Case:

Cicero declaratus est consul. CIC.
Cicero was declared consul.

202

The Vocative stands apart from the construction of the sentence, with or without an Interjection (**404**):

O sol pulcher, o laudande! HOR.
O beauteous sun, worthy of praise!

Pompei, meorum prime sodalium! HOR.
O Pompeius, earliest of my comrades

Note.—The Nominative sometimes takes the place of the Vocative:

Audi, tu, populus Albanus. LIV.
Hear, thou people of Alba.

203 ### THE ACCUSATIVE CASE.

The Accusative Case is used to express:

A. The Nearer Object of the Verb.
B. Place to which there is motion.
C. The idea contained in the Verb (Cognate Accusative).
D. Adverbial Relations.

A. Accusative of Nearer Object.

204   The nearer Object of a Transitive Verb is in the Accusative Case :

> Agricola colit agros; uxor domum tuetur.
> *The farmer tills the fields ; his wife takes care of the house.*
>
> Haec studia adulescentiam alunt, senectutem oblectant.
> *These studies nurture youth, and delight old age.*   [Cic.

205   *Note* 1.—Intransitive Verbs when compounded with Prepositions are often transitive :

> Antonius oppugnat Brutum, Mutinam circumsedet.   Cic.
> *Antonius is making war on Brutus, and besieging Mutina.*

Note 2.—Some Compounds take two Accusatives :

> Caesar equites flumen transjecit.   Caes.
> *Caesar threw his cavalry across the river.*

206   Factitive Verbs (verbs of *making, saying, thinking*) have a second Accusative in agreement with the Object :

> Ciceronem consulem populus declaravit.   Sall.
> *The people declared Cicero consul.*
>
> Socrates totius se mundi civem arbitrabatur.   Cic.
> *Socrates considered himself a citizen of the whole world.*

207   *Note.*—The Accusative is used as the Subject of the Infinitive to form a Clause which may be the Object of Verbs of *saying, thinking,* and *perceiving,* or the Subject of Impersonal Verbs **(414).**

> Solem fulgere videmus.
> *We see that the sun shines.*

208   Some Verbs of *teaching, asking, concealing* (doceo, *teach,* flagito, *demand,* rogo, *ask,* oro, *pray,* celo, *conceal*), take two Accusatives, one of the Person, the other of the Thing :

> Racilius primum me sententiam rogavit.   Cic.
> *Racilius asked me first my opinion.*

Quid nunc te litteras doceam ? Cic.
Why should I now teach you letters ?

Antigonus iter omnes celat. Nep.
Antigonus conceals from all his line of march.

In the Passive they keep the Accusative of the Thing:

Primus a Racilio sententiam rogatus sum.
I was asked my opinion first by Racilius.

Note.—Quaero, peto, take Ablative of the Person with a or ab : hoc a te peto, *this I ask of you.*

209 *Note.*—Intransitive Verbs which express feeling sometimes take an Accusative of the Object which excites the feeling :

Non omnia quae dolemus queri possumus. Cic.
We cannot complain of all things which we grieve for.

Virgas ac secures dictatoris horrent et tremunt. Liv.
They shudder and tremble at the rods and axes of the dictator.

Note.—An Accusative is used in exclamations, with or without an Interjection : Me miserum, *O wretched me !* O fragilem fortunam ! *O fickle fortune !*

210 *Note.*—Some Passive Verbs in poetry take an Accusative, when used reflexively. Such verbs are induor, *dress oneself*, exuor, *undress oneself*, cingor, *gird oneself :*

Inutile ferrum cingitur. Verg.   Exuitur cornua. Ov.
He girds on the useless steel.   *She puts off her horns.*

A similar construction is frequently used with Passive Participles :

Virgines longam indutae vestem canentes ibant. Liv.
Virgins marched singing, arrayed in long robes.

Nascuntur flores inscripti nomina regum. Verg.
Flowers spring up inscribed with names of kings.

This construction is analogous to that of the Greek Middle Voice.

211 **B. Place to which Motion is directed is in the Accusative :** eo Romam, *I go to Rome* (**269, 273**).

Note.—Similar are the phrases: pessum ire, *to go to the bad* ; inftias ire, *to deny* ; suppetias ire, *to march in aid* ; venum ire, *to be sold.*

C. Cognate Accusative.

212   Many Intransitive Verbs take an Accusative containing the same idea as the Verb, and often from the same stem :

> Fortuna ludum insolentem ludit. Hor.
> *Fortune plays an insolent game.*

> Modice et modeste melius est vitam vivere. Plaut.
> *It is best to live one's life temperately and modestly.*

> Itque reditque viam totiens. Verg.
> *He goes and returns the same way as often.*

Note.—The Cognate Accusative must have some more limited meaning than that which is contained in the Verb, either expressed by an Adjective or implied in the Noun itself : ludum insolentem ludere, *to play an insolent game* ; dicta dicere, *to say witty sayings.*

D. Adverbial Accusative.

213   The Accusative of Respect is joined to Verbs and Adjectives, especially in poetry :

> Tremit artus. Verg.   Nūdae lacertos. Tac.
> *He trembles in his limbs.*   *Bare as to the arms.*

> Omnia Mercurio similis vocemque coloremque. Verg.
> *In all points like Mercury, both in voice and complexion.*

Note 1.—Adverbial Accusatives with Verbs and Nouns are very numerous : multum, *much* ; aliquid, *in some degree* ; cetera, *in other respects* ; id genus, *of that kind* ; id temporis, *at that time* : multum amare, *to love much* ; quid refert ? *what does it matter ?*

Note 2.—Neuter Adjectives and Pronouns are used in the Accusative by poets like Adverbs :

> Dulce ridere.   Lucidum fulgere. Hor.
> *To smile sweetly.*   *To shine brightly.*

> Dulce ridentem Lalagen amabo, dulce loquentem. Hor.
> *I will love the sweetly smiling, sweetly speaking Lalage.*

(For the Accusative of Extent see Time, **278**, and Space, **281-3**.)

214 THE DATIVE CASE.

The Dative is the Case of the Person or Thing for whose interest anything exists or is done. It expresses :

A. The person or thing *to* whom or which something is done : Dative of the Remoter Object.

B. The person or thing *for* whom or which something is done : Dative of Advantage.

Special uses are : (*a*) Dative of Agent, (*b*) Ethic Dative, (*c*) Dative of Possessor, (*d*) Dative of Result, (*e*) Dative of Purpose.

A. Dative of the Remoter Object.

215 **The Dative of the Remoter Object** is used :

1. With Transitive Verbs of *giving, telling, showing, promising,* which take also an Accusative of the Nearer Object :

Tibi librum sollicito damus aut fesso. HOR.
We give you a book when you are anxious or weary.

Saepe tibi meum somnium narravi. CIC.
I have often told you my dream.

Nobis spondet fortuna salutem. VERG.
216 *Fortune guarantees safety to us.*

2. With Intransitive Verbs of *pleasing, helping, sparing, pardoning, appearing, speaking, believing, obeying,* and their opposites. These Verbs have the Dative as their only Object :

Victrix causa deis placuit sed victa Catoni. LUCAN.
The conquering cause pleased the gods, but the conquered pleased Cato.

Imperio parent. CAES. Parce pio generi. VERG.
They obey the command. *Spare a pious race.*

Imperat aut servit collecta pecunia cuique. HOR.
Money amassed rules or serves every man.

Non possum dolori tanto resistere. CIC.
I cannot withstand so great a sorrow.

Note.—These Verbs contain the ideas of *being pleasing to, helpful to, obedient to,* &c.

Note.—Delecto, juvo, *delight*, laedo, *hurt*, guberno, *govern*, rego, *rule*, jubeo, *command*, take an Accusative :

217

Multos castra juvant. Hor.   Animum rege. Hor.
The camp delights many.   *Rule the temper.*

Tempero, moderor, *govern*, *restrain*, take sometimes the Accusative, sometimes the Dative :

218

Hic moderatur equos qui non moderabitur irae. Hor.
This man controls horses who will not restrain his anger.

3. With Adjectives implying *nearness, fitness, likeness, nelp, kindness, trust, obedience,* or any opposite idea :

Hortus ubi et tecto vicinus jugis aquae fons. Hor.
Where is a garden, and near to the house a fount of flowing water.

Quis amicior quam frater fratri? Sall.
Who [is] more friendly than a brother to a brother ?

Homini fidelissimi sunt equus et canis. Plin.
The horse and the dog are most faithful to man.

Turba gravis paci, placidaeque inimica quieti. Lucan.
The crowd hostile to peace, unfriendly to tranquil rest.

Note.—The following take Genitive or Dative : communis, *common*, proprius, *proper*. Affinis, *akin*, alienus, *foreign*, par, *equal*, sacer, *sacred*, superstes, *surviving*, take usually Dative, sometimes Genitive. Similis, *like*, takes usually Genitive, sometimes Dative. Adjectives of fitness as aptus, sometimes take Accusative with ad.

4. More rarely with Substantives or Adverbs :

219

Nulla fides regni sociis. Lucan.
No reliance is to be placed on partners in government.

Justitia est obtemperatio legibus. Cic.
Justice is obedience to laws.

Congruenter naturae vivendum est. Cic.
We must live agreeably to nature.

Note 1.—Some Verbs, as credo, *believe*, *entrust*, fido, *trust*, suadeo, *persuade,* minor, *threaten*, gratulor, *congratulate*, are used both transitively and intransitively :

Perfidis se credidit hostibus. Hor.
He trusted himself to treacherous enemies.

Non est, crede mihi, sapientis dicere : Vivam. Mart.
It is not, believe me, the part of a wise man to say, ‘ I will live.’

Note 2.—Nubo, *marry* (lit. *take the veil for*), and vaco, *have leisure for,* take the Dative :

His duobus fratribus duae Tulliae nupserant. LIV.
The two Tullias had married these two brothers.

220 Philosophiae semper vaco. CIC.
I have always leisure for philosophy.

Note 3.—The Verbs irascor, *feel angry,* pugno, *fight,* certo, *strive,* some-
tives take a Dative : sibi irascitur, *he is angry with himself.*

The Dative of the Remoter Object is used with Compound Verbs, Transitive and Intransitive, formed with the
following Prepositions (including compounds of esse) :

ad, ante, ab, sub, super, ob,
in, inter, de, con, post, and prae.

Also with the compounds of bene, male, satis.

(*a*) Transitive :

Gigantes bellum dis intulerunt. CIC.
The giants waged war against the gods.

Praesentia confer praeteritis. LUCR.
Compare present things with past.

(*b*) Intransitive :

His negotiis non interfuit solum sed praefuit. CIC.
He not only took part in these affairs, but directed them.

Nullus in orbe sinus Baiis praelucet amoenis. HOR.
No bay in the world outshines the pleasant Baiae.

Ceteris satisfacio semper, mihi numquam. CIC.
I always satisfy others, myself never.

221 B. **Dative of Advantage.**

The person or thing for whose advantage or disad-
vantage something is done is in the Dative Case :

Tibi aras, tibi seris, tibi eidem metis. PLAUT.
*For yourself you plough, for yourself you sow, for the same self
you reap.*

Non solum nobis divites esse volumus. CIC.
We do not wish to be rich for ourselves alone.

Sic vos non vobis mellificatis, apes! VERG.
Thus ye make honey not for yourselves, O bees!

Special Uses of the Dative.

222 (*a*) A Dative, commonly called the **Dative of the Agent**, is often used with the Gerundive, and occasionally with Passive Participles and with Adjectives in -bilis (**381**) :

> Ut tibi ambulandum, sic mihi dormiendum
> *As you have to walk, I have to sleep.*

> Magnus civis obit et formidatus Othoni. Juv.
> *A great citizen and one dreaded by Otho has died.*

> Multis ille bonis flebilis occidit. Hor.
> *He died a cause of weeping to many good men.*

Note.—Rarely, in poetry, a Personal Passive takes a Dative :

> Non intellegor ulli. Ov.
> *I am intelligible to none.*

223 (*b*) A Dative, called the **Ethic Dative**, is used, in familiar talk or writing, to express interest or call special attention :

> Quid mihi Celsus agit ? Hor.
> *Tell me what is Celsus about ?*

> Haec vobis per biduum eorum militia fuit. Liv.
> *This, mind you, was their style of fighting for two days.*

224 (*c*) The **Dative of the Possessor**, with esse, is used when emphasis is laid on the thing possessed, not on the possessor :

> Est mihi plenus Albani cadus. Hor.
> *I have a cask full of Alban wine.*

> Fons cui nomen Arethusa fuit. Cic.
> *A fountain of which the name was Arethusa.*

Note.—With such phrases as 'cui nomen est' a second Dative is sometimes joined by attraction: Volitans cui nomen asilo Romanum est (Verg.), *an insect of which the Roman name is 'asilus.* A like attraction occurs with other factitive and copulative verbs': Huic ego diei nomen Trinummo faciam (Plaut.), *I will give to this day the name Trinummus.* Analogous to these are the attractions: Hoc mihi volenti est, non invito, *this is with my good will, not against it.* Mihi non licet esse neglegenti (Cic.), *I must not be negligent.*

225' (*d*) The Dative is used to express the Result of action :

> Nimia fiducia calamitati solet esse. Nep.
> *Too great confidence is wont to become a calamity.*

> Exemplo est magni formica laboris. Hor.
> *The ant affords an example of great labour.*

Note.—It is often found in connexion with the Dative of the Person interested :

> Exitio est avidum mare nautis. Hor.
> *The greedy sea is a destruction to sailors.*

> L. Cassius quaerere solebat, 'cui bono fuisset.' Cic.
> *Lucius Cassius used to ask who had been the gainer* (lit. '*to whom had it been for a good*').

226 (*e*) The Dative may express the Purpose of action :

> Equitatum auxilio Caesari miserunt. Caes.
> *They sent the cavalry as a help to Caesar.*

Note.—Observe the phrases, receptui canere, *to give the signal for retreat*; alimento serere, *to sow for food*; laudi vertere alicui, *to turn to the praise of someone*; vitio vertere alicui, *to impute as a fault to someone.*

227 Sometimes the Dative is used in poetry for the place towards which there is motion :

> It clamor caelo, Verg., *a shout ascends towards heaven.*

THE ABLATIVE CASE.

228 The Ablative is the Case which defines circumstances; it is rendered by many Prepositions, *from, with, by, in.* Its uses may be divided into :

> A. Ablative of Separation (*from, of*).
> B. Ablative of Association (*with*).
> C. Instrumental Ablative (*by, with*).
> D. Ablative of 'Place where' (Locative, *in, at*).

A. Pure Ablative.

229   1. The **Ablative of Separation** is used with Verbs meaning *to remove, release, deprive*; with Adjectives such as liber, *free*, solutus, *released*, and also the Adverb procul, *far from*:

> Cedes coemptis saltibus et domo. Hor.
> *You will depart from purchased glades and house.*

> Populus Atheniensis Phocionem patriā pepulit. Nep.
> *The Athenian people drove Phocion from his country.*

> Vacare culpā maximum est solacium. Cic.
> *To be free from blame is a very great comfort.*

> Procul negotiis, solutus omni fenore. Hor.
> *Far from business, freed from all usury.*

230   2. The **Ablative of Origin** is used with Verbs, chiefly Participles, implying descent or origin :

> Atreus, Tantalo prognatus, Pelope natus. Cic.
> *Atreus, descended from Tantalus, and son of Pelops.*

231   3. The **Ablative of Comparison** (expressing Difference) is used with Comparative Adjectives and Adverbs:

> Nihil est amabilius virtute. Cic.
> *Nothing is more amiable than virtue.*

> Neminem Lycurgo utiliorem Sparta genuit. Val. Max.
> *Sparta produced no man more serviceable than Lycurgus.*

Note.—This construction is equivalent to quam, *than*, with the Nominative or Accusative. 'Virtute' equals 'quam virtus;' 'Lycurgo,' 'quam Lycurgum.' With other cases than Nom. or Accus. quam must be used for comparison :

> Nihilo amicior est Phaedriae quam Antiphoni. Ter.
> *He is in no degree more friendly to Phaedria than to Antipho.*

(For '**Place whence**' see 270, 274.)

B. Ablative of Association.

232 *Note.*—This includes the uses of an old case called the Sociative Case, expressing the circumstances associated with the Subject or the action of the Sentence.

233 1. The **Ablative of Association** is used with Verbs and Adjectives denoting *plenty*, *fulness*, *possession* : abundo, *abound*, dono, *present*, praeditus, *endowed with* (253) :

Villa abundat gallinā, lacte, caseo, melle. Cic.
The farm abounds in poultry, milk, cheese, honey.

Juvenem praestanti munere donat. Verg.
He presents the youth with a noble gift.

Legiones pulchris armis praeditae. Plaut.
Legions furnished with splendid armour.

Note.—Dono also takes the Accusative of the thing with Dative of the Person: Caesar praedam militibus donat, *Caesar gives the booty to the soldiers.*

234 2. The **Ablative of Quality** is used with an Adjective in agreement (255) :

Senex promissā barbā, horrenti capillo. Plin. Min.
An old man with long beard and rough hair.

Habuit fratrem Dumnorigem summā audaciā. Caes.
He had a brother Dumnorix of supreme audacity.

235 3. **Ablative of Respect:**

Pauci numero.　　　　　Natione Medus.
Few in number.　　　　*By birth a Mede.*

Et corde et genibus tremit. Hor.
It trembles both in heart and knees.

Ennius, ingenio maximus, arte rudis. Ov.
Ennius, mighty in genius, in art (is) rude.

Note.—In the phrases natu major, *older*, natu minor, *younger*, natu is an Ablative of Respect.

236 4. The **Ablative of the Manner** in which something happens or is done has an Adjective in agreement with it ; or it follows the Preposition **cum**, *with* :

Jam veniet tacito curva senecta pede. Ov.
Presently bent old age will come with silent foot.

Athenienses summā vi proelium commiserunt. Nep.
The Athenians began the battle with the greatest vigour.

Magnā cum curā atque diligentiā scripsit. CIC.
He wrote with great care and attention.

Note.—More majorūm, *in the fashion of our ancestors*, pace tuā, *with your leave*, jure, *by right*, injuriā, *wrongfully*, ratione, *on principle*, are Ablatives of Manner.

237 5. The **Ablative Absolute** is a phrase, consisting of a Noun in the Ablative Case and a Participle, or another Noun, in agreement with it :

Regibus exactis consules creati sunt. LIV.
Kings having been abolished, consuls were elected.

Pereunte obsequio imperium intercidit. TAC.
Obedience failing, government falls to pieces.

Caesare venturo, Phosphore, redde diem. MART.
Caesar being on his way, star of morn, restore the day.

Nil desperandum Teucro duce et auspice Teucro. HOR.
There must be no despair, Teucer being leader and Teucer omen-giver.

Natus est Augustus consulibus Cicerone et Antonio.
SUETON.
Augustus was born when Cicero and Antonius were consuls.

Quid dicam hac juventute? CIC.
What can I say when our young men are of this stamp?

Note.—The Ablative Absolute is equivalent to a shortened Adverbial Clause within the Sentence, serving to explain some circumstance which indirectly affects the action of the Sentence. It is called Absolute because it is independent in construction of the rest of the Sentence. A dependent clause joined to the Sentence by a Conjunction may be used instead of the Ablative Absolute. In the above example 'Regibus exactis' could be replaced by 'Cum reges exacti essent,' *when kings had been driven out.*

C. Instrumental Ablative.

238 *Note.*—This Ablative includes the uses of the old Instrumental Case.

239 The **Agent** by whom something is done is in the Ablative Case, with the Preposition a, ab, after a Passive or Quasi passive Verb (**296, 300, 303**).

240　1. The **Instrument** by means of which something is done is in the Ablative Case without a Preposition:

> Hi jaculis, illi certant defendere saxis. VERG.
> *These strive to defend with javelins, those with stones.*
>
> Dente lupus, cornu taurus petit. HOR.
> *The wolf attacks with his teeth, the bull with his horns.*
>
> Opportuna loca armatis hominibus obsidet. SALL.
> *He occupies convenient posts with armed men.*

241　2. The **Ablative of the Cause** is used with Adjectives, Passive Participles, and Verbs:

> Coeptis immanibus effera Dido. VERG.
> *Dido driven wild by her horrible designs.*
>
> Oderunt peccare mali formidine poenae. HOR.
> *The bad hate to sin through fear of punishment.*

242　3. The Deponent Verbs fungor, *perform*, fruor, *enjoy*, vescor, *feed on*, utor, *use*, potior, *possess oneself of* (**253**), take an Ablative:

> Hannibal cum victoriā posset uti frui maluit. LIV.
> *Hannibal, when he could use his victory, preferred to enjoy it.*
>
> Numidae ferinā carne vescebantur. SALL.
> *The Numidians used to feed on the flesh of wild animals.*

243　4. The Adjectives dignus, *worthy*, indignus, *unworthy*, and the Transitive Verb dignor, *deem worthy*, also contentus, *contented*, and fretus, *relying on*, take an Ablative:

> Dignum laude virum Musa vetat mori. HOR.
> *A man worthy of praise the Muse forbids to die.*
>
> Haud equidem tali me dignor honore. VERG.
> *I do not indeed deem myself worthy of such honour.*

Note.—Opus est, usus est, *there is need of*, take the Ablative.

> Ubi res adsunt, quid opus est verbis? SALL.
> *When things are present, what is the need of words?*

244　5. An **Ablative of the Measure** of difference is joined as an Adverb with Comparatives and Superlatives and, rarely, with Verbs:

> Sol multis partibus major est quam luna. CIC.
> *The sun is many degrees larger than the moon.*

Especially the Ablatives :

| altero, hoc, eo, quo, | dimidio, duplo, quanto, tanto, |
| nihilo and nimio, | paullo, multo, aliquanto. |

Quo plus habent, eo plus cupiunt.
The more they have, the more they desire.

Hibernia dimidio minor est quam Britannia. CAES.
Ireland is smaller by half than Britain.

245 6. The **Ablative of Price** is used with Verbs and Adjectives of *buying* and *selling* :

Vendidit hic auro patriam. VERG.
This man sold his country for gold.

Multorum sanguine victoria stetit. LIV.
The victory cost (literally *stood at*) *the blood of many.*

Note.—Ablatives of price are magno, *at a high price*; parvo, minime, vili, *at a low price* (257) :

Parvo fames constat, magno fastidium. SEN.
Hunger costs little, daintiness much.

D. The Locative Ablative.

246 The Locative is the Case of the Place at which something is or happens. Its distinct forms remain in the Singular in names of towns and small islands: Romae, *at Rome*; Corcyrae, *at Corcyra*; and in a few other words, as domi, *at home.* For the most part its uses have passed to the Ablative, and it is often difficult to distinguish between the two Cases, especially in the Plural, where their forms are identical. The Locative is sometimes used for a point of time : die septimi, *on the seventh day*; Kalendis, *on the Kalends*; Idibus, *on the Ides.*

Note.—The word animi in such phrases as anxius animi, *anxious;* pendēre animi, *to waver in mind*, is probably Locative.

(For ' Place where,' see 268, 272[a].)

THE GENITIVE CASE.

247   The Genitive is used to define or complete the meaning of another Noun on which it depends. It also follows certain Verbs.

The uses of the Genitive may be divided into:

A. Genitive of Definition.   D. Partitive Genitive.
B. Possessive Genitive.   E. Objective Genitive.
C. Genitive of Quality.

A. Genitive of Definition.

248   1. The Genitive of Definition follows the Noun on which it depends:

Vox voluptatis.   Nomen regis.
The word pleasure.   *The name of king.*

Note.—But the name of a city is always placed in Apposition: urbs Roma, *the city of Rome.*

249   2. The **Attributive Genitive** defines the Noun on which it depends like an Adjective:

Lux solis.   Anni labor.
The light of the sun.   *A year's toil.*

250   3. The **Genitive of the Author**:

Ea statua dicebatur esse Myronis. CIC.
That statue was said to be Myro's.

Legendi sunt vobis Platonis libri. CIC.
You should read the works of Plato.

251   4. The Genitive is often used in Impersonal construction with a Copulative Verb, followed by an Infinitive, where in English a word such as nature, part, characteristic, or mark, must be supplied to complete the meaning:

Cujusvis hominis est errare. CIC.
It is (the nature) of any man to err.

Est adulescentis majores natu vereri. Cic.
It is a young man's (part) to reverence his elders.

Tempori cedere habetur sapientis. Cic.
To yield to occasion is held (the mark) of a wise man.

Note.—The word proprium is often used:

Sapientis est proprium nihil quod paenitere possit facere. Cic.
It is the characteristic of a wise man to do nothing which he may repent of.

252 5. Verbs and Adjectives of *accusing, condemning, convicting,* or *acquitting* take a Genitive of the fault or crime:

Alter latrocinii reus, alter caedis convictus est. Cic.
The one was accused of robbery, the other was convicted of murder.

Miltiades capitis absolutus pecunia multatus est. Nep.
Miltiades, acquitted of capital crime, was fined.

Note.—Sometimes the Ablatives nomine, *on the ground of*, crimine, *on the charge of*, are used:

Themistocles crimine proditionis absens damnatus est. Nep.
Themistocles was convicted while absent on the charge of treason.

253 6. Verbs and Adjectives implying *want* and *fulness*, especially ægeo, indigeo, *want*, impleo, *fill*, potior, *get possession of* (242), plenus, *full*, often take a Genitive (233):

Virtus plurimae exercitationis indiget. Cic.
Virtue needs very much practice.

Hanc juventutem spei animorumque implevere. Liv.
They filled these youths with hope and spirit.

Romani signorum et armorum potiti sunt. Sall.
The Romans got possession of standards and arms.

Acerra turis plena. Hor.
A pan full of incense.

254

B. Possessive Genitive.

Regis copiae. Cic. , Contempsi Catilinae gladios. Cic.
The king's forces.   *I have braved the swords of Catiline.*

Singulorum opes divitiae sunt civitatis. Cic.
The means of individuals are the state's riches.

Sometimes the Genitive depends on a Noun understood :

Hectoris Andromache. Verg.
Hector's (wife) Andromache.

Ventum erat ad Vestae. Hor.
We had come to Vesta's (temple).

C. Genitive of Quality.

255   1. The **Genitive of Quality** has an Adjective in agreement :

Ingenui vultus puer ingenuique pudoris. Juv.
A boy of noble countenance and noble modesty.

Memoriae felicioris est nomen Appii. Liv.
The name of Appius is of happier memory.

256   2. Number and age are expressed by the Genitive :

Classis septuaginta navium.   Puer annorum novem.
A fleet of seventy ships.   *A boy of nine years.*

257   3. **Genitives of Value**, magni, parvi, plurimi, minimi, nihili, are used with Verbs of *valuing*; the Genitives tanti, quanti, pluris, minoris, are also used with Verbs of *buying* and *selling*, but not to express definite price.

Voluptatem virtus minimi facit.
Virtue accounts pleasure of very little value.

Emit hortos tanti, quanti Pythius voluit. Cic.
He bought the gardens for as much as Pythius wished.

Quanti id emit? Vili. Plaut.
For how much did he buy it ? For a low price.

Note.—The Genitives flocci, nauci were used in the popular speech to express worthlessness, answering to the English expressions, *not worth a straw, a nut,* &c.

Judices rempublicam flocci non faciunt. Cic.
The judges make the republic of no account.

D. Partitive Genitive.

258 The Genitive of a Noun which is distributed into parts is called a Partitive Genitive.

259 1. Any word denoting a definite part, whether Substantive, Adjective or Pronoun, is used with the Genitive of the whole of which it denotes a part.

(*a*) Substantives :

> Sic partem majorem copiarum Antonius amisit. CIC.
> *Thus Antony lost the greater part of his forces.*

> Nemo mortalium omnibus horis sapit. PLIN.
> *No one of mortals is wise at all times.*

(*b*) Pronouns or Pronominal Adjectives :

> Incertum est quam longa nostrum cujusque vita futura sit.
> *It is uncertain how long the life of each one of us will be.*

> Elephanto beluarum nulla est prudentior. CIC.
> *Of animals none is more sagacious than the elephant.*

(*c*) Numerals and Adjectives of number :

> Sulla centum viginti suorum amisit. EUTR.
> *Sulla lost a hundred and twenty of his men.*

> Multae harum arborum mea manu sunt satae. CIC.
> *Many of these trees were planted by my hand.*

(*d*) Comparatives and Superlatives :

> Major Neronum. HOR.
> *The elder of the Neros.*

> Hoc ad te minime omnium pertinet. CIC.
> *This belongs to you least of all men.*

> Totius Graeciae Plato doctissimus erat. CIC.
> *Plato was the most learned man of all Greece.*

Note 1.—The Genitives gentium, *of nations*, terrarum, *of countries*, depend on Adverbs of Place : ubi, *where*, eo, *thither*, quo, *whither*, longe, *far :*

> Ubinam gentium sumus ? Cic.
> *Where in the world are we ?*

> Migrandum aliquo terrarum arbitror. Cic.
> *I think we must migrate to some part of the world.*

Note. 2.—A Partitive Genitive is found in poetry with Verbs :

> Scribe tui gregis hunc. Hor.
> *Enlist this man in your train.*

> Fies nobilium tu quoque fontium. Hor.
> *Thou too shalt become one of famous fountains.*

260 2. Any word denoting quantity may be used with the Genitive of the whole in which such quantity is contained.

> Aliquid pristini roboris conservat. Cic.
> *He keeps somewhat of his old strength.*

> Dimidium facti qui coepit habet. Hor.
> *He has half done the work who has begun it.*

> Catilinae erat satis eloquentiae, sapientiae parum. Sall.
> *Catiline had plenty of eloquence, of wisdom too little.*

E. The Objective Genitive.

261 *Note.*—The terms Subjective and Objective Genitive are used to express different relations of the Genitive to the Noun on which it depends. Thus amor patris, *the love of a father*, may mean either ' the love felt by a father ' (where patris is a Subjective Genitive), or ' the love felt for a father ' (where patris is an Objective Genitive).

262 An Objective Genitive is used with Verbal Substantives and Adjectives, especially Adjectives in -ax, and Participles which have the meaning of *love, desire, hope, fear, care, knowledge, ignorance, skill, power.*

(*a*) With Substantives :

> Erat insitus menti cognitionis amor. Cic.
> *Love of knowledge had been implanted in the mind.*

Difficilis est cura rerum alienarum. CIC.
The care of other people's affairs is difficult.

(b) With Adjectives:

Avida est periculi virtus. SEN.
Valour is greedy of danger.

Conscia mens recti famae mendacia risit. Ov.
The mind conscious of right smiled at the lies of rumour.

Homo multarum rerum peritus. CIC.
A man skilled in many things.

Vir propositi tenax. HOR.
A man holding to his purpose.

(c) With Participles:

Quis famulus amantior domini quam canis? COL.
What servant is fonder of his master than the dog is?

263   *Note.*—The Genitive of the Gerund is an Objective Genitive : ars scribendi, *the art of writing.* An Objective Genitive also follows the Ablatives causā, gratiā, *by reason of, by favour of, for the sake of*; honoris causā, *on the ground of honour* ; exempli gratiā, *for an example.*

264   Mei, *of me,* tui, *of thee,* sui, *of him, her, them,* nostri, *of us,* vestri, *of you,* are Objective Genitives :

Nicias tuā sui memoriā delectatur. CIC.
Nicias is delighted by your recollection of him.

Si tibi cura mei, sit tibi cura tui. Ov.
If you care for me, take care of yourself.

The Possessive Pronouns, meus, tuus, suus, noster, vester, are used as Adjectives : meus liber, my book.

Note.—A Genitive understood in a Possessive Pronoun often has a Genitive agreeing with it :

Respublica meā unius operā salva erat. CIC.
The state was saved by my own unaided effort.

265 Most Verbs of *remembering, forgetting, reminding*, memini, reminiscor, obliviscor, usually take the Genitive, sometimes the Accusative. Recordor almost always takes the Accusative, rarely the Genitive.

Animus meminit praeteritorum. Cic.
The mind remembers past things.

Res adversae admonent religionum. Cic.
Adversity reminds of religious duties.

Nam modo vos animo dulces reminiscor, amici. Ov.
For now I remember you, O friends, dear to my soul.

The Adjectives corresponding to these Verbs, memor, immemor, always take a Genitive.

Omnes immemorem beneficii oderunt. Cic.
All hate one who is forgetful of a kindness.

266 Verbs of *pitying*, misereor, miseresco, take a Genitive:

Nil nostri miserere. Verg.
You pity me not at all.

Arcadii, quaeso, miserescite regis. Verg.
Take pity, I entreat, on the Arcadian king.

Note 1.—Miseror, commiseror take an Accusative.

267 *Note 2.*—Verbs of *refraining* and *ceasing* and some Adjectives are used by poets with a Genitive in imitation of the Greek use; especially by Horace:

Abstineto irarum. Hor. Fessi rerum. Verg
Refrain from angry words. *Weary of toil.*

Integer vitae, scelerisque purus. Hor.
Virtuous in life and pure from wrong.

Place, Time, and Space.

Place.

268 Place **where** anything is or happens is generally in the Ablative case with a Preposition; sometimes without a Preposition (especially in poetry), an Adjective of place being attached to the Substantive:

> Castra sunt in Italia contra rempublicam collocata. Cic.
> *A camp has been set up in Italy against the republic.*

> Celsa sedet Aeolus arce. Verg.
> *Aeolus is seated on his high citadel.*

> Medio sedet insula ponto. Ov.
> *The island lies in mid ocean.*

269 Place **whither** is in the Accusative with a Preposition; but in poetry the Preposition is sometimes omitted:

> Caesar in Italiam magnis itineribus contendit. Caes.
> *Caesar hastened with long marches into Italy.*

> Italiam fato profugus Lavinaque venit litora. Verg.
> *Driven by fate he came to Italy and the Lavinian shores.*

270 Place **whence** is in the Ablative with **ab, ex,** or **de**:

> Ex Asia transis in Europam. Curt.
> *Out of Asia you cross into Europe.*

271 In names of **towns** and **small islands,** also in **domus** and **rus,** Place **where, whither,** or **whence** is expressed by the Case without a Preposition.

272 (*a*) **Place where,** by the Locative:

> Quid Romae faciam? Juv. | Is habitat Mileti. Ter.
> *What am I to do at Rome?* | *He lives at Miletus.*

> Philippus Neapoli est, Lentulus Puteolis. Cic.
> *Philip is at Naples, Lentulus at Puteoli.*

> Si domi sum, foris est animus; sin foris sum, animus est domi. Plaut.
> *If I am at home, my mind is abroad: if I am abroad, my mind is at home.*

273 (*b*) **Place whither,** by the Accusative :

> Regulus Carthaginem rediit. Cic.
> *Regulus returned to Carthage.*
>
> Vos ite domum; ego rus ibo.
> *Go ye home; I will go into the country.*

274 (*c*) **Place whence,** by the Ablative :

> Video rure redeuntem senem. Ter.
> *I see the old man returning from the country.*
>
> Demaratus fugit Tarquinios Corintho. Cic.
> *Demaratus fled from Corinth to Tarquinii.*

Note.—The Locative domi is used with a Genitive of the Possessor : domi Caesaris, *at the house of Caesar ;* or with the Possessive : domi meae, *at my house.*

275 The road by which one goes is in the Ablative :

> Ibam forte Via Sacra. Hor.
> *I was going by chance along the Sacred Way.*

Time.

276 **Time at which,** in answer to the question When ? is expressed by the Ablative : hieme, *in winter*; solis occasu, *at sunset* :

> Ego Capuam veni eo ipso die. Cic.
> *I came to Capua on that very day.*

277 **Time within which,** generally by the Ablative :

> Quicquid est biduo sciemus. Cic.
> *Whatever it is, we shall know in two days.*

278 **Time during which,** generally by the Accusative :

> Pericles quadraginta annos praefuit Athenis. Cic.
> *Pericles was leader of Athens forty years.*

Note 1.—Often by per with the Accusative : per triduum, *for three days.*

Note 2.—Age is expressed by the participle natus, *born,* used with the Accusative, sometimes with the Ablative :

> Cato quinque et octoginta annos natus excessit e vita. Cic.
> *Cato died aged eighty-five years.*

79 **How long ago**, is in the Accusative or Ablative with **abhinc** :

> Hoc factum est ferme abhinc biennium. PLAUT.
> *This was done about two years ago.*

> Comitia jam abhinc triginta diebus habita. CIC.
> *The assembly was held thirty days ago.*

280 To express **How long before**, **How long after**, the words **ante**, *before*, **post**, *after*, are used either with the Ablative as Adverbs, or with the Accusative as Prepositions, followed by **quam** :

> Numa annis permultis ante fuit quam Pythagoras. CIC.
> *Numa lived very many years before Pythagoras.*
> (*or*, Numa ante permultos annos fuit quam.)

> Post diem tertium gesta res est quam Clodius dixerat. CIC.
> *The affair took place three days after Clodius had spoken.*
> (*or*, Die tertio post gesta res est quam.)

Space.

281 **Space over which** motion takes place, is in the Accusative :

> Milia tum pransi tria repimus. HOR.
> *Then having had luncheon we crawl three miles.*

282 **Space which lies between**, is in the Accusative or in the Ablative :

> Marathon abest ab Athenis circiter milia passuum decem. NEP.
> *Marathon is distant from Athens about ten miles.*

> Aesculapii templum quinque milibus passuum ab Epidauro distat. LIV.
> *The temple of Aesculapius is five miles distant from Epidaurus.*

283 **Space of measurement**, answering the questions how high? how deep? how broad? how long? is generally in the Accusative :

> Erant muri Babylonis ducenos pedes alti. PLIN.
> *The walls of Babylon were two hundred feet high.*

PREPOSITIONS.

284 Prepositions, like the case-endings, shew the relations of Nouns to other words, and they are used where these relations cannot be clearly expressed by the case-endings alone. Almost all Prepositions take the Accusative or the Ablative case; they are usually placed before the Noun.

285 ### Prepositions with Accusative.

Ad, *to, towards,* with Accusative of Motion to; *at*: ad urbem ire, *to go to the city*; ad summam senectutem, *to extreme old age*; ad octingentos caesi, *there were slain to the number of* 800; pugna ad Alliam, *the battle at the Allia*; ad primam lucem, *at daybreak*; ad hoc, *moreover*; ad tempus, *for a time*; ad verbum, *word for word*; nihil ad Atticum, *nothing to (in comparison with) Atticus*; nihil ad rem, *nothing to the purpose.*

Adversus, Adversum, *towards, against, opposite to*: adversum Antipolim, *opposite to Antipolis*; reverentia adversus senes, *respect towards the aged.*

Apud, *at, near* (used chiefly with persons, rarely with places): apud me, *at my house*; apud veteres, *among the ancients*; apud Homerum, *in Homer's works*; but in Iliade Homeri, *in Homer's Iliad.*

Ante, *before*:   **Post,** *behind, after*: ante oculos, *before one's eyes*; ante meridiem, *before noon*; ante aliquem esse, *to surpass someone*; post terga, *behind the back*; post mortem, *after death.*

Pone, *behind*: pone nos, *behind us.*

Circum, Circa, *around, about* (in Place).

Circa, Circiter, *about* (in Time, Number).

Circum caput, *round the head*; circa forum, *around the forum.*

Circa primam lucem, *about daybreak*; circa, circiter triginta, *about thirty.*

Cis, Citra, *on this side of*: cis Alpes, *on this side of the Alps.*

Trans, *across*: trans Rhenum ducere, *to lead across the Rhine*; trans Alpes, *on the further side of the Alps.*

Ultra, *beyond*: ultra Euphratem, *beyond the Euphrates*; ultra vires, *beyond their powers.*

Contra, *against, opposite to*: contra hostem, *against the enemy*; contra arcem, *opposite to the citadel.*

Erga, *towards* (not used of Place): erga aliquem benevolus, *feeling kindly towards someone.*

Extra, *outside of, without*: extra muros, *outside the walls*; extra culpam, *free from blame.*

Intra, *within*: intra muros, *within the walls*; intra viginti dies, *within twenty days.*

Inter, *between* (in Place): *during* (in Time), *among*; inter urbem et Tiberim, *between the city and the Tiber*; inter silvas, *among the woods*; inter cenandum, *during dinner*; constat inter omnes, *all are agreed*; inter nos, *between ourselves*; inter se amant, *they love each other.*

Infra, *under, beneath* : infra caelum, *under the sky* ; infra dignitatem, *beneath one's dignity.*

Supra, *over, above* : supra terram, *above the ground* ; supra milia viginti, *more than twenty thousand.*

Juxta, *adjoining to, beside* : juxta viam, *adjoining the road* ; juxta deos, *next to the gods.*

Ob, *over against, on account of* : mihi ob oculos, *before my eyes* ; quam ob rem, *wherefore.*

Penes, *in the power of* : penes me, *in my power* ; penes te es? *are you in your senses?*

Per, *through (by)* : per vias, *through the streets* ; per vim, *by force* ; per me licet, *I give leave* ; per te deos oro, *I pray you by the gods* ; per exploratores certior fio, *I ascertain through scouts.*

Praeter, *beside, past, along* : praeter ripam, *along the bank* ; praeter omnes, *beyond all others* ; praeter me, *except me* ; praeter opinionem, *contrary to expectation.*

Prope, *near* : prope amnem, *near the river* ; prope lucem, *towards day-break.*

Propter, *on account of,* (rarely of Place) *near, close to* : propter aquam, *close to the water's edge* ; propter hoc, *on that account.*

Secundum, *next, along, according to (following)* : secundum vos, *next to (behind) you* ; secundum litus, *along the shore* ; secundum legem, *in accordance with the law* ; secundum nos, *in our favour.*

Versus, *towards* (following the Noun) : Italiam versus, *towards Italy.*

286   **Prepositions with Ablative.**

A, ab, *from, by* : ab eo loco, *from that place* ; ab ortu ad occasum, *from East to West* ; procul a patria, *far from one's country* ; prope abesse ab, *to be near* ; a tergo, *in the rear* ; a senatu stetit, *he took the side of the senate* ; hoc a me est, *this is in my favour* ; ab urbe condita, *from the foundation of Rome* ; servus ab epistulis, *secretary* ; non ab re fuerit, *it will not be irrelevant* ; ab ira facere, *to do in anger.*

Absque, *without* (rare) : absque vobis esset, *if it were not for you.*

Clam, *unknown to* : clam vobis, *unknown to you.*

Palam, *in sight of* : palam omnibus, *in sight of all.*

Coram, *in the presence of* : coram populo, *in the presence of the people.*

Cum, *with* : cum aliquo congruere, certare, *to agree, strive with someone* ; magno cum periculo, *with great danger* ; with me, te, nobis, vobis, often with quo, quibus, cum follows the Pronoun ; mecum, *with me.*

Sine, *without* : sine regibus, *without kings* ; sine dubio, *without doubt.*

De, *from (down from), concerning* : de monte, *down from the mountain* ; de die, *in the daytime* ; de die in diem, *from day to day* ; unus de multis, *one out of many* ; de marmore signum, *a marble bust* ; de pace, *concerning peace* ; quid de nobis fiet, *what will become of us?* de industria, *on purpose* ; de more, *according to custom* ; de integro, *anew.*

Ex, E, *out of, from*: ex urbe, *out of the city*: e longinquo, *from far*; ex equis pugnant, *they fight on horseback*; diem ex die, *from day to day*; ex eo audivi, *I heard it from him*; unus ex illis, *one of those*; ex quo, *from the time when*; e republica, *for the good of the State*; ex sententia, *satisfactorily*; ex parte, *in part*; ex occulto, *secretly.*

Prae, *before, in front of* (*for*) (Place rarely, chiefly used in idioms): prae se fert speciem viri boni, *he wears the semblance of a good man*; prae nobis beatus es, *you are happy compared with us*; prae gaudio ubi sim nescio, *I do not know where I am for joy.*

Pro, *before, for*: pro foribus, *before the door*; pro patria mori, *to die for one's country* (in defence of); mihi pro parente fuit, *he was in the place of a parent to me*; pro certo hoc habui, *I held this for certain*; pro rata parte, *in proportion*; pro re, *according to circumstances.*

    Note.—**Prae** means *in advance of;* **pro**, *standing for, defending.*

Tenus, *as far as* (always following the Noun): verbo tenus, *so far as the word goes* Sometimes with Genitive: Corcyrae tenus, *as far as Corcyra*; especially with a plural Noun: crurum tenus, *as far as the legs.*

287   Prepositions with Accusative or Ablative.

In, *into, to, towards, against*; with Accusative: ibo in Piraeum, *I will go into the Piraeus*; in orbem ire, *to go round*; liberalis in milites, *liberal towards the troops*; Cicero in Verrem dixit, *Cicero spoke against Verres*; in aeternum, *for ever*; in vicem, *in turn*; in poenam dare, *to deliver to punishment*; venire in conspectum, *to come into sight.*

In, *in, among, on*; with Ablative: in urbe Roma, *in the city of Rome*; in oculis esse, *to be before one's eyes*; in tempore, *at the right time*; in dicendo, *while speaking*; in bonis habere, *to count among blessings*; in Ganymede, *in the case of Ganymede*; in eo reprehendere quod, *to blame on the score that.*

Sub, *up to*; with Accusative: sub montem venire, *to come close to the foot of the mountain*; sub lucem, *towards daybreak*; sub haec dicta, *just after these things were said.*

Sub, *under*; with Ablative: sub terra, *underground*; sub monte esse, *to be beneath the mountain*; sub poena, *under penalty of.*

Subter, *underneath*: with Acc., subter murum venire, *to come close to the wall.* Abl., subter litore esse, *to be close to the shore.*

Super, *over*; with Accusative: super terram, *over the ground*; super omnia, *above all.*

Super, *upon*; with Ablative: super foco, *on the hearth*; super Hectore, *about Hector.*

IMPERSONAL VERBS.

Case Construction.

288 - The following verbs of *feeling* take an Accusative of the person with a Genitive of the cause: **miseret, piget, paenitet, pudet, taedet :**

> Miseret te aliorum, tui te nec miseret nec pudet. Plaut.
> *You pity others, for yourself you have neither pity nor shame.*
>
> Me civitatis morum piget taedetque. Sall.
> *I am sick and weary of the morals of the state.*

289 **Decet, dedecet** take an Accusative of the person with an Infinitive :

> Oratorem irasci minime decet, simulare non dedecet. Cic.
> *It by no means becomes an orator to feel anger, it is not unbecoming to feign it.*
>
> Si me gemmantia dextrā sceptra tenere decet. Ov.
> *If it befits me to hold in my right hand the jewelled sceptre.*

290 **Libet, licet, liquet, contingit, convenit, evenit, expedit,** take a Dative :

> Ne libeat tibi quod non licet. Cic.
> *Let not that please you which is not lawful.*
>
> Licet nemini contra patriam ducere exercitum. Cic.
> *It is not lawful for anyone to lead an army against his country.*

291 **Interest,** *it is of importance, it concerns,* is used with the Genitive of the person or thing concerned, but with the feminine Ablatives **meā, tuā, suā, nostrā, vestrā** of the Possessive Pronouns :

> Interest omnium recte facere. Cic.
> *It is for the good of all to do right.*
>
> Et tuā et meā interest te valere. Cic.
> *It is of importance to you and to me that you should be well.*

292 **Rēfert,** *it concerns, it matters,* is also used with the feminine Ablatives of the Possessive Pronouns :

> Quid me ā rēfert cui serviam? PHAED.
> *What does it matter to me whom I serve?*

Note 1.—Rarely with a Genitive: quorum nihil rēfert, QUINT., *whom it does not at all concern.*

Note 2.—The Genitives of Value, magni, parvi, tanti, quanti, pluris, are often joined with interest and rēfert :

> Illud meā magni interest te ut videam. CIC.
> *It is of great importance to me that I should see you.*
>
> Hoc non pluris rēfert quam si imbrem in cribrum geras. PLAUT.
> *This avails no more than if you pour rain-water into a sieve.*

293 **Pertinet, attinet** take an Accusative with ad :

> Nihil ad me attinet. TER.
> *It does not concern me at all.*

294 **Oportet** is used with the Accusative and Infinitive clause, or with the Conjunctive alone; rarely with the Prolative Infinitive (**369**) :

> Legem brevem esse oportet. CIC.
> *It behoves that a law be brief.*
>
> Me ipsum ames oportet, non mea. CIC.
> *You ought to love me, not my possessions.*
>
> Vivere naturae si convenienter oportet. HOR.
> *If it behoves to live agreeably to nature.*

295 *Note.*—Coepit, debet, desinit, potest, solet are used impersonally with an Impersonal Infinitive :

> Pigere eum facti coepit. JUST.
> *It began to repent him of his deed.*
>
> Pervenīri ad summa sine industria non potest. QUINT.
> *One cannot reach the highest without industry.*

296 PASSIVE CONSTRUCTION.

When a sentence is changed from the Active to the Passive form :

(a) The Object of a Transitive Verb becomes the Subject; the Subject becomes the Agent in the Ablative with the Preposition a or ab :

> { Numa leges dedit. CIC.   *Numa gave laws.*
> { A Numā leges datae sunt.   *Laws were given by Numa.*

297   (*b*) Factitive Verbs and Verbs of saying and thinking become Copulative :

Clodium plebs tribunum creavit. — *The plebs elected Clodius tribune.*

Clodius a plebe creatus est tribunus. — *Clodius was elected tribune by the plebs.*

298   (*c*) Transitive Verbs which have two Objects in the Accusative, the Person and the Thing, keep the Accusative of the Thing in the Passive form :

Rogas me sententiam. — *You ask me my opinion.*
Rogor a te sententiam. — *I am asked by you my opinion.*

299 Intransitive Verbs are used impersonally in the Passive.

300   (*a*) The Subject of an Intransitive Verb in Passive construction becomes the Agent in the Ablative :

Nos currimus.
A nobis curritur. } *We run.*

301   or the Agent may be omitted :

Sic imus ad astra.
Sic itur ad astra. Verg. } *Thus we go to the stars.*

Acriter utrimque usque ad vesperum pugnatum est. Caes.
There was fierce fighting on both sides until the evening.

302   (*b*) Intransitive Verbs which take the Dative keep it in the Passive :

Mihi isti nocere non possunt.
Mihi ab istis noceri non potest. Cic. } *They cannot hurt me.*

Nihil facile persuadetur invitis. Quint.
The unwilling are not easily persuaded of anything.

203   *Note.*—The Ablative of the Agent is used with Quasi-Passive Verbs :

Malo a cive spoliari quam ab hoste venire. Quint.
I would rather be despoiled by a citizen than be sold by a foe.

ADJECTIVES.

304 Some Adjectives are used as Substantives to express persons or things: sapiens, *a wise man*; boni, *the good*; Romani, *the Romans*; omnia, *all things*; multa, *many things*; bona, *goods.*

> Bonos boni diligunt. Cic.
> *The good love the good.*

> Aiunt multum legendum esse, non multa. Cic.
> *They say that much should be read, not many things.*

305 Neuter Adjectives are used for Abstract Substantives: verum or vera, *the truth.*

> Omne tulit punctum qui miscuit utile dulci. Hor.
> *He who has combined the useful with the pleasing has won every vote.*

306 Some Adjectives, when used as Substantives, can be qualified by other Adjectives: amicus, *friend*; vicinus, *neighbour*; dextra, *right hand*; majores, *ancestors.*

> Vetus vicinus ac necessarius. Cic.
> *An old neighbour and intimate acquaintance.*

307 Medius, *middle*, and superlatives of position in place and time, as summus, imus, primus, ultimus, are used with a partitive force: medio ponto, *in mid ocean*; ad imam quercum, *at the foot of the oak*:

> Prima luce summus mons a Labieno tenebatur. Caes.
> *At dawn of day the mountain top was held by Labienus.*

Note.—The singular forms of ceteri, *the rest* (of which the masc. nom. sing. is wanting), are similarly used with collective nouns: cetera turba, *the rest of the crowd*; a cetero exercitu, *by the rest of the army.*

308 Adjectives are used adverbially when they qualify the Verb rather than the Substantive:

> Socrates laetus venenum hausit. Sen.
> *Socrates drank the poison cheerfully.*

> Matutinus ara. Verg. | Vespertinus pete tectum. Hor.
> *Plough at morn.* | *At eventide go home.*

Hannibal primus in proelium ibat, ultimus excedebat. Liv.
Hannibal was the first to go into battle, the last to withdraw.

Comparative and Superlative Adjectives.

309 **Superlatives** often express a very high degree, and not the
highest :

Ego sum miserior quam tu, quae es miserrima. Cic.
I am more wretched than you, who are very wretched.

310 **Comparatives** may also express a certain degree, without
special comparison : longior, *rather long* ; senior, *elderly.*
After a Comparative with quam, a second Comparative
is often used :

Aemilii contio fuit verior quam gratior populo. Liv.
The harangue of Aemilius was more truthful than popular.

Note.—Comparatives and Superlatives are often strengthened by adverbs
and adverbial phrases : multo carior, *much dearer* ; longe carissimus,
far dearest ; vel minimus, *the very least* ; quam maximus, *the greatest
possible.*

Numeral Adjectives.

311 **Cardinals** : Unus, apart from other Numerals, is used only
to give emphasis ; it often means *the one of all others* :

Demosthenes unus eminet inter omnes oratores. Cic.
Demosthenes is pre-eminent among all orators.

Mille is used as an indeclinable Adjective ; sometimes
as a Substantive taking the Genitive after it ; milia is
always used as a Substantive, followed by a Genitive :

Mille greges illi. Ov.   Mille annorum. Plaut.
He had a thousand flocks.   *A thousand years.*
Quattuor milia hominum Capitolium occupavere. Liv.
Four thousand men seized the Capitol.

If a smaller number is added to milia, the compound
number becomes adjectival : tria milia et sexcenti
homines, *three thousand six hundred men.*

312 **Ordinals** are used in expressing time : but in compound
numbers unus is used for primus : uno et octogesimo
anno, *in the eighty-first year* :

Octavus annus est ex quo Britanniam vicistis. Tac.
It is the eighth year since you conquered Britain.

Note.—Unus, alter, tertius, &c., are used for *a first, a second, a third,* where the order is of no importance, as distinguished from the regular ordinals, primus, secundus, tertius, which can only mean *the first, the second,* &c.

313·Distributives express *how many each* or *at a time* :

> Militibus quini et viceni denarii dati sunt. Liv.
> *Twenty-five denarii were given to each soldier.*

Note 1.—With a Substantive of plural form Distributives are used, but the plural of unus is used instead of singuli :

> Una castra jam facta ex binis videbantur. Caes.
> *One camp now seemed to have been formed from two.*

Note 2.—Bini is used for a pair :

> Pamphilus binos habebat scyphos sigillatos. Cic.
> *Pamphilus had in use a pair of embossed cups.*

314 After plus, amplius, minus, quam is often left out before Numerals :

> Romani paulo plus sexcenti ceciderunt. Liv.
> *Rather more than six hundred Romans fell.*

PRONOUNS.

315 The Personal Pronoun is usually expressed only by the Verb ending, but is sometimes added for emphasis :

> Ego reges ejeci, vos tyrannos introducitis. Cic.
> *I expelled kings, ye are bringing in tyrants.*

Note.—Nos is often used for ego, and noster for meus, but vos is not used for tu, nor vester for tuus.

316 The Reflexive Pronoun **se, sese, sui, sibi,** refers to the Subject in a Simple Sentence (464) :

> Fur telo se defendit. Cic.
> *The thief defends himself with a weapon.*
>
> Ira sui impotens est. Sen.
> *Anger is not master of itself.*

Iratus cum ad se rediit, sibi tum irascitur. PUBL. SYR.
When an angry man has come to himself he is angry with himself.

Deforme est de se ipso praedicare. CIC.
It is bad taste to boast of oneself.

Note 1.—There is no Reciprocal Pronoun in Latin; se with **inter** is used reciprocally: inter se amant, *they love each other.*

Note 2.—In the First and Second Persons, me, te, are used reflexively with ipse; me ipse consolor, *I console myself.*

317 The Possessive **suus**, formed from the Reflexive, is used to express *his own, their own,* when emphasis is required and usually refers to the Subject of the Verb:

Nemo rem suam emit.
No one buys what is his own.

sometimes to other cases if the context shows that it cannot be referred to the Subject:

Suis flammis deléte Fidenas. LIV.
With its own flames destroy Fidenae.

Suus is especially used in combination with **quisque**:

Suus cuique erat locus attributus. CAES.
To each man his own place had been assigned.

318 **Ejus** is the Possessive used of the Third Person where no emphasis is required, and does not refer to the Subject.

Chilius te rogat, et ego ejus rogatu. CIC..
Chilius asks you, and I at his request.

Note.—The Possessive Pronouns are often omitted when the meaning is clear without them: fratrem amat, *he loves his brother.*

319 **Hic, ille** are often used in contrast: **hic** usually meaning *the latter,* **ille** *the former*:

Quocumque adspicio, nihil est nisi pontus et aer,
    nubibus hic tumidus, fluctibus ille minax. OV.
*Whithersoever I look, there is nought but sea and sky,
    the latter heaped with clouds, the former threatening with billows.*

Note.—**Iste** is sometimes contemptuous: quid sibi isti miseri volunt? *What do those wretched ones want?* **Ille** may imply respect: philosophus ille, *that famous philosopher.* **Is** often is he antecedent to qui: is cujus, *he whose;* eum cui, *him to whom.*

320   Ipse, *self*, is of all the three Persons, with or without a Personal Pronoun: ipse ibo, *I will go myself.*

> *Note.*—**Ipse** sometimes means *of one's own accord*: ipsi veniunt, *they come of their own accord.* **Ipse, ipsa**, also stand for the chief person (master, mistress): the scholars of Pythagoras used to say 'Ipse dixit,' *The master himself said it.* Sometimes a superlative is formed: ipsissima verba, *the very exact words.*

321   Idem, *the same*, is of all the three Persons; with qui it expresses *the same . . . . as.* It may often be translated *at the same time; also*:

> Ego vir fortis, idemque philosophus. Cic.
> *I a brave man, and also a philosopher.*

322   Of the Indefinite Pronouns Quis, siquis, numquis, quispiam, aliquis, quidam, the most definite is quidam, the least so quis.

Quis, qui, *any,* cannot begin a sentence; they often follow si, num, ne.

> Si mala condiderit in quem quis carmina jus est. Hor.
> *If anyone has composed malicious verses on another, there is a remedy at law.*
>
> Si quid te volam, ubi eris? Plaut.
> *If I want anything of you, where will you be?*

Aliquis means *some one*: dicat aliquis, *suppose some one to say*; si vis esse aliquis, *if you wish to be somebody.*

Quidam means *a certain person* (known but not named):

> Accurrit quidam, notus mihi nomine tantum. Hor.
> *A certain man runs up, known to me only by name.*

Nescio quis, *some one or other* (*I know not who*), used as if one word, forms an Indefinite Pronoun:

> Nescio quid mihi animus praesagit mali. Ter.
> *My mind forebodes I know not what evil.*

823 Quisquam (Substantive),   } *any at all,*
      Ullus (Adjective) :   }

> are often used after a negative word, or a question expecting a negative answer :

> Nec amet quemquam nec ametur ab ullo. Juv.
> *Let him not love anyone nor be loved by any.*
>
> Non ullus aratro dignus honos. Verg.
> *Not any due honour (is given) to the plough.*

Note.—Quisquam and ullus are used after si when negation is implied, or with comparatives :

> Aut nemo aut, si quisquam, Cato sapiens fuit. Cic.
> *Either no man was wise, or, if any, Cato was.*

824 Quivis, quilibet, *any you like* :

> Quivis homo potest quemvis de quolibet rumorem proferre. Cic.
> *Any man can put forth any report of anybody.*
>
> Non cuivis homini contingit adire Corinthum. Hor.
> *It does not happen to every man to go to Corinth.*

325 Quisque, *each* (severally), is often used with se, suus :

> Sibi quisque habeant quod suum est. Plaut.
> *Let them have each for himself what is his own.*

With Superlatives it expresses *every* :

> Epicureos doctissimus quisque contemnit. Cic.
> *All the most learned men despise the Epicureans.*

It also distributes Ordinal numbers :

> Quinto quoque anno Sicilia tota censetur. Cic.
> *A census of all Sicily is taken every fifth year.*

326 Uterque, *each* (of two), *both,* can be used with the Genitive of Pronouns ; but with Substantives it agrees in case :

Uterque parens. Ov.	Utroque vestrum delector. Cic.
Both father and mother.	*I am delighted with both of you.*

327 Uter, *which* (of two), is Interrogative : uter melior ? *which is the better ?*

> Uter utri insidias fecit ? Cic.
> *Which of the two laid an ambush for which ?*

Note.—Utri, plural, is used for *which of two parties,* utrique for *both parties.* So alteri ... alteri, *one party, the other party.*

328 Alter, *the one, the other* (of two), *the second,* is the Demonstrative of uter : a l t e r ego, *a second self.*

> Quicquid negat alter, et a l t e r ; affirmant pariter. Hor.
> *Whatever the one denies, so does the other ; they affirm alike.*

329 Alius, *another* (of any number), *different* :

> Fortuna nunc mihi, nunc a l i i benigna. Hor.
> *Fortune, kind now to me, now to another.*

Alius, alius, repeated in two clauses, mean *one . . . another*; **alii, alii** (plural), *some . . . others* :

> Aliud est maledicere, aliud accusare. Cic.
> *It is one thing to speak evil, another to accuse.*

> Alii Demosthenem laudant, alii Ciceronem.
> *Some praise Demosthenes, others Cicero.*

Note 1.—Alius repeated in different cases in the same sentence, or with one of its derived adverbs, has an idiomatic use :

> Alii alia sentiunt.
> *Some think one thing, some another.*

> Illi alias aliud isdem de rebus judicant. Cic.
> *They judge differently, at different times, about the same things.*

Note 2.—A l i u s expresses comparison and difference : nil a l i u d quam-*nothing else than ;* a l i u s Lysippo, Hor., *other than Lysippus.*

330 The Relative **qui, quae, quod,** is of all three Persons, and when the Antecedent is a Noun either expressed or understood, it may be regarded as standing between two Cases of the same Noun, and agreeing with the second Case.

(*a*) Sometimes both Cases are expressed :

> Erant itinera duo, quibus itineribus exire possent. Caes.
> *There were two roads by which they might go forth.*

(*b*) usually the second is omitted :

> Animum rege qui, nisi paret, imperat. Hor.
> *Rule the temper, which, unless it obeys, commands.*

(*c*) sometimes the first, in poetry :

> Sic tibi dent nymphae quae levet unda sitim. Ov.
> *So may the nymphs give thee water to assuage thirst.*

(d) sometimes both are omitted :

> Sunt quibus in satira videor nimis acer. Hor.
> *There are some to whom I seem too keen in satire.*

331 The following scheme shows this principle fully :

(1) vir quem virum vides rex est (both Cases expressed).
(2) vir quem ...:... vides rex est (second Case omitted) (usual form).
(3) ...quem virum vides rex est (first Case omitted).
(4) ...quem ...... vides rex est (both Cases omitted).

332 *Note 1.*—If the Relative is the Subject of a Copulative Verb, it often agrees in Gender and Number with the Complement :

> Thebae, quod Boeotiae caput est. Liv.
> *Thebes, which is the capital of Boeotia.*

Note 2.—When an Adjective qualifying the Antecedent is emphatic, as unus, solus, or is a Superlative, it is often attracted to the Clause of the Relative, agreeing with it in Case :

> Si veniat Caesar cum copiis quas habet firmissimas. Cic.
> *Should Caesar come with the very strong forces that he has.*

Note 3.—If the Antecedent consists of two or more Nouns, or is a Collective Noun, the rules for the Agreement of the Relative are the same as for the Agreement of Adjectives with the Composite Subject (see **198, 199**).

Note 4.—If the Relative refers to a Sentence or Clause it is Neuter; sometimes id quod is used, id being in apposition to the Clause :

> Diem consumi volebat, id quod est factum. Cic.
> *He wished the day to be wasted, which came to pass.*

Note 5.—The Relative clause sometimes comes first :

> Quam quisque norit artem, in hac se exerceat. Cic.
> *Let everyone practise the art which he knows.*

(For other uses of the Relative see **403, 450, 451**.)

CORRELATION.

333 Pronouns and Pronominal Adverbs are said to be Correlatives when they correspond to one another as Antecedent and Relative **(102)**.

334 The Pronoun Antecedent to qui is usually the Demonstrative is; sometimes hic, ille, idem :

> Is minimo eget qui minimum cupit. Pub. Syr.
> *He wants for least who desires least.*

335 **Talis ... qualis**, means *of such a kind ... as* ; **tantus ... quantus,** *as much* or *as great ... as* : **tot ... quot,** *as many ... as :*

> Talis est qualem tu eum esse scripsisti. Cic.
> *He is such as you wrote word that he was.*

> Tanto brevius omne, quanto felicius tempus. Plin.
> *The happier a time is, so much the shorter is it.*

> Quot homines, tot sententiae. Ter.
> *So many men, so many minds.*

Tam ... quam, means *so ... as* or *as ... as* ; **ut ... ita,** means *as ... so :*

> Tam ego ante fui liber quam gnatus tuus. Plaut.
> *I was formerly as free as your son.*

> Ut optasti, ita est. Cic.
> *As you wished, so it is.*

TENSES.

336 The **Present** expresses :

> (1) What happens at the present moment : jacio, *I throw.*
>
> (2) What is going on at the present time : scribo, *I am writing.*
>
> (3) What is habitually or always : quod semper movetur aeternum est, *that which is always in motion is eternal.*

337 The Historic Present is used for a Past by orators, historians, and poets, to give variety, or call up a vivid picture :

> Dimisso senatu decemviri prodeunt in contionem abdicantque se magistratu. Liv.
> *When the senate was dismissed the decemvirs go forth to the assembled people and resign office.*

338 *Note.*—Dum, *while*, is used with the Historic Present in speaking of Past Time : Dum Romani consultant, Saguntum oppugnabatur, Liv., *While the Romans were consulting, Saguntum was being besieged* (see **430**). With jam, jamdiu (dudum, pridem) the Present expresses what has long been and still continues : Jamdudum video, Hor., *I have seen it this long time.*

339 The **Perfect** expresses :

As Primary, from the point of the present moment what has just been done : scripsi, *I have written.*

As Historic, simply a past action, which happened at some indefinite time : scripsi, *I wrote.*

Note.—The Perfect is used in poetry to express past existence which has ceased : Fuimus Troes ; fuit Ilium, VERG., *We Trojans were* (i.e. are no longer) ; *Troy was* (exists no longer).

340 The **Imperfect** expresses what was continued or repeated in past time, as opposed to the completed or momentary past :

Aequi se in oppida receperunt murisque se tenebant. LIV.
The Aequi retreated into their towns and remained within their walls.

Carthagine quotannis bini reges creabantur. NEP.
At Carthage two rulers were elected annually.

341 The **Future Simple** is used in Latin where in English the Present is used with Future meaning :

Ut voles me esse, ita ero. PLAUT.
As you wish me to be, so I shall be.

342 The **Future Perfect** expresses action to be completed in the future ; if two actions are spoken of, one of which will take place before the other, the prior one is in the Future Perfect :

Ut sementem feceris, ita metes. CIC.
As you shall have sown, so will you reap.

343 *Note.*—The Romans, in writing letters, often speak of the time of writing in a Past Tense, because it would be past when a letter would be received.

Res, cum haec scribebam, erat in extremum adducta discrimen. CIC.
At the time I write, the affair has been brought to a crisis.

MOODS.

344 The **Indicative** is the Mood which makes a statement with regard to a fact, or to something which is dealt with by the speaker as a fact.

345 *Note.*—Verbs expressing *duty, fitness, possibility,* as possum, debeo, decet, licet, oportet, are often used in the Indicative tenses of past time, to express that it was proper or possible at that time to do something which in fact was not done. Phrases such as necesse est, fuit; aequum, longum, melius, satius est, fuit, are similarly used in the Indicative (**440** *c*) :

> Hic tamen hanc mecum poteras requiescere noctem. VERG.
> *Yet you might have rested here with me this night.*
> Et vellem et fuerat melius. VERG.
> *I should have wished, and it would have been better.*
> Longum est ea dicere: sed hoc breve dicam. CIC.
> *It would be tedious to speak of those things, but this little I will say.*

Compare with these :

> Non Asiae nomen obiciendum Murenae fuit. CIC.
> *Murena should not have been reproached with the mention of Asia.*

346 The **Imperative** is the Mood of positive command or direct request :

> I, sequere Italiam. VERG.   Pergite, adulescentes. CIC.
> *Go, seek Italy.*   *Proceed, O youths.*

347 Prohibitions in the second person are expressed by **ne** with the Perfect Conjunctive, or by **noli** with the Infinitive :

> Ne feceris quod dubitas. PLIN.
> *Never do anything about which you are doubtful.*
> Nolite id velle quod fieri non potest. CIC.
> *Do not wish what cannot be.*

348 but in poetry **ne** is often used with the Imperative :

> Equo ne credite, Teucri. VERG.
> *Do not trust the horse, O Trojans.*

349   The forms in **-to**, **-tote** are specially used in laws; but they are also often used for emphasis.

> Regio imperio duo sunto, iique consules appellantor. Cic.
> *Let there be two with royal power, and let them be called consuls.*

350   *Note 1.*—The following Imperatives are joined with the Infinitive or Conjunctive of other Verbs to form Imperatives; fac, fac ut, cura ut, with the Conjunctive; memento with Infinitive or Conjunctive. In prohibitions fac ne, cave, take the Conjunctive; and in poetry fuge, mitte, parce, take the Infinitive:

> Magnum fac animum habeas. Cic.
> *Mind you have a lofty spirit.*

Note 2.—For a courteous Imperative the Future Indicative is often used: · facies ut sciam, Cic., *you will please let me know.*

351 The **Conjunctive Mood** makes a statement or asks a question, not so much with regard to a fact as with regard to something thought of or imagined by the speaker, often with some condition expressed or implied.   It expresses a modified or conditional command or desire.

Note.—The Conjunctive is so called because it joins with the other moods and adds to their power of expression.

The Conjunctive has two general uses :

352   Pure or Independent : velim, *I could wish*; vellem, *I could have wished.*

353   Subjunctive or Dependent on another Verb : cura ut facias, *take care that you do it.*

354   The Pure Conjunctive must generally be rendered in English with auxiliaries, *may, might, could, would, should.*

Note.—The Conjunctive makes a Statement :

355   (*a*) With a condition expressed or implied (Conditional use) :
> Ita amicos pares. Cic.
> *Thus you may get friends.*
> Crederes victos. Liv.
> *You would have supposed them conquered (from their appearance).*

356   (*b*) Or in a modified tone, to avoid positiveness (Potential use) :
> Dubitem haud equidem. Verg.
> *For my part I should not hesitate.*

The Perfect Conjunctive is especially so used:

Forsitan quispiam dixerit. Cic.
Perhaps someone may say.

357 (c) Conveying an admission or supposition (Concessive use):

Haec sint falsa sane. Cic. Fuerit malus civis. Cic.
Granting this to be quite   Suppose he was a bad citizen,
untrue.

358 It asks a Question (Deliberative use):

Faveas tu hosti? Cic. Quid facerem? Verg.
Would you befriend an   What was I to do?
enemy?

It expresses a Desire or Command:

359 (a) A Wish or Prayer (Optative use): often with utinam, *Oh that!*

Sis felix. Hor. Utinam potuissem.
May you be happy.   Oh that I had been able.

Doceas iter et sacra ostia pandas. Verg.
Pray shew me the road and open the sacred doors.

360 (b) An Exhortation (Hortative use) chiefly in the 1st Person Plural

Amemus patriam, pareamus senatui. Cic.
Let us love our country, let us obey the senate.

361 (c) A modified Command (Jussive use) in the 3rd Person:

Sit sermo lenis. Cic.
Let speech be calm.

Vilicus ne sit ambulator. Cato.
Let not a steward be a loiterer.

362 From the Jussive use comes a further use of the Conjunctive, by which the expression of a wish is conveyed into past time. This use is chiefly in the 2nd Person, but extends also to the others:

Rem tuam curares. Ter.
You should have been minding your own business.

Restitisses, repugnasses, mortem oppetisses. Cic.
You should have resisted, fought against it, braved death.

363 The use of the 2nd Person in the Pres. Conj. is often indefinite, not addressed to anyone in particular, but expressing a general maxim:

Agere decet quod agas considerate. Cic.
Whatever you do, it is proper to do it with consideration.

M

THE VERB INFINITE.

364   The parts of the Verb Infinite have some of the uses of
Verbs, some of the uses of Nouns.

THE INFINITIVE.

365   The **Infinitive** as a Verb has Tenses, Present, Past, or
Future, it governs cases and is qualified by Adverbs; as a
Noun it is neuter, indeclinable, used only as Nominative or
Accusative.

366   The **Infinitive** in the Nominative may be the Subject of
Impersonal Verbs, or of verbs used impersonally:

> Juvat ire et Dorica castra visere. VERG.
> *It is pleasant to go and view the Doric camp.*
>
> Ipsum philosophari nunc displicet. CIC.
> *The very study of philosophy now displeases.*
>
> Dulce et decorum est pro patria mori. HOR.
> *To die for one's country is sweet and seemly.*
>
> Non vivere bonum est sed bene vivere. SEN.
> *It is not living which is a good, but living well.*

> *Note.*—Occasionally the Infinitive is the Complement:

> Homo cui vivere est cogitare. CIC.
> *Man to whom to live is to think.*

367   The **Infinitive** is often one of the two Accusatives
depending on an Active Verb of *saying* or *thinking*:

> Errare, nescire, decipi et malum et turpe ducimus. CIC.
> *To err, to be ignorant, to be deceived, we deem both unfortunate and
> disgraceful.*

368   *Note.*—Sometimes, though rarely, it is a simple Object:

> Hoc ridere meum nulla tibi vendo Iliade. PERS.
> *This laughter of mine I won't sell you for an Iliad.*

The **Prolative Infinitive** is used to carry on the construction of Indeterminate and some other Verbs (190) :

369

Verbs of *possibility, duty, habit* : possum, queo, nequeo, debeo, soleo ;

" of *wishing, purposing* : volo, nolo, malo, cupio, opto, statuo ;

" of *beginning, ceasing, endeavouring, continuing, hastening* ; coepi, *begin* ; desino, *cease*; conor, *try* ; pergo, *proceed* ;

" of *knowing, teaching, learning* : scio, disco, doceo.

Ego plus quam feci f a c e r e non p o s s u m. Cic.
I cannot do more than I have done.

Solent diu cogitare qui magna v o l u n t gerere. Cic.
They are wont to reflect long who wish to do great things.

Praecedere coepit. Hor.	Sapere aude. Hor.
He begins to walk on.	*Dare to be wise.*

Note.—The **Infinitive** of a Copulative Verb used Prolatively is followed by a Complement in the Nominative :

Socrates p a r e n s philosophiae jure d i c i potest. Cic.
Socrates may rightly be called the parent of philosophy.

370 Vis f o r m o s a v i d e r i. Hor.
You wish to seem beautiful.

The **Prolative Infinitive** is also used with the Passives of Verbs of saying and thinking :

Barbara n a r r a t u r venisse venefica tecum. Ov.
A barbarian sorceress is said to have come with thee.

Aristides unus omnium justissimus f u i s s e traditur. Cic.
Aristides is recorded to have been the one man of all most just.

Note.—This construction is called the Nominative with Infinitive, and is used with most Passive Verbs of saying and thinking. A few, however, narror, nuntior, trador, are used Impersonally—always in the Perfect, and often in the Present and Imperfect :

Galbam et Africanum doctos fuisse t r a d i t u m est. Cic.
It has been handed down that Galba and Africanus were learned.

371 With an Infinitive Perfect Passive *esse* is often omitted :

Pons in Ibero prope effectus nuntiabatur. Caes.
The bridge over the Ebro was announced to be nearly finished.

Titus Manlius ita locutus fertur. Liv.
Titus Manlius is reported to have thus spoken.

372 The Historic Infinitive is the Present Infinitive used by historians in vivid description for the Imperfect Indicative :

Multi sequi, fugere, occidi, capi. Sall.
Many were following, flying, being slain, being captured.

373 An Infinitive often follows an Adjective Prolatively, chiefly in poetry :

Audax omnia perpeti. Hor.   Insuetus vinci. Liv.
Bold to endure all things.   *Unused to be conquered.*

Figere doctus erat sed tendere doctior arcūs. Ov.
He was skilled in piercing (with a dart), but more skilled in bending the bow.

Gerund and Gerundive.

374 The Genitive, Dative, and Ablative of the Gerund, and the Accusative with a Preposition, are used as Cases of the Infinitive.

375 The **Accusative** of the Gerund follows some Prepositions, especially ad, ob, inter :

Ad bene vivendum breve tempus satis est longum. Cic.
For living well a short time is long enough.

Mores puerorum se inter ludendum detegunt. Quint.
The characters of boys show themselves in their play.

376 The **Genitive** of the Gerund depends on some Abstract Substantives, and Adjectives which take a Genitive :

Ars scribendi discitur.   Cupidus te audiendi sum. Cic.
The art of writing is learnt.   *I am desirous of hearing you.*

The **Dative** of the Gerund follows a few Verbs, Adjectives, and Substantives implying *help, use, fitness* :

Par est disserendo. Cic.	Dat operam legendo.
He is equal to arguing.	*He gives attention to reading.*

Note.—Observe the phrase: solvendo non est, *he is insolvent.*

The **Ablative** of the Gerund is of Cause or Manner, or it follows one of the Prepositions ab, de, ex, in, cum :

Fugiendo vincimus.	De pugnando deliberant.
We conquer by flying.	*They deliberate about fighting.*

If the Verb is Transitive, the **Gerundive** is more often used than the Gerund, agreeing with the Object as an Adjective. It takes the Gender and Number of the Object, but the Object is drawn into the Case of the Gerundive.

The following examples show how the Gerundive takes the place of the Gerund.

Gerund	*Gerundive*	
Ad petendum pacem	ad petendam pacem	*in order to seek peace.*
Petendi pacem	petendae pacis	*of seeking peace.*
Petendo pacem	petendae paci	*for seeking peace.*
Petendo pacem	petendā pace	*by seeking peace.*
Ad mutandum leges	ad mutandas leges	*in order to change laws*
Mutandi leges	mutandarum legum	*of changing laws.*
Mutando leges	mutandis legibus	*for or by changing laws.*

(becomes)

Note 1.—*In order to seek peace* may also be rendered by the Genitive of the Gerund or Gerundive with causā or gratiā : pacem petendi causā or petendae pacis causā. (See **423**, note 3.)

Note 2.—The Dative of the Gerundive is used with names of office to show the purpose of the office :

Comitia regi creando. Liv.
An assembly for electing a king.

Tres viri agris dividendis. Florus.
Three commissioners for dividing lands.

381 The Gerund and Gerundive are often used to express that something ought or is to be done, the Dative of the Agent being expressed or understood (**222**).

382 If the Verb is **Intransitive** the Gerund is used impersonally :

Eundum est.	Mihi eundum est.
One must go.	*I must go.*

Suo cuique judicio est utendum. Cic.
Each must use his own judgment.

383 If the Verb is **Transitive** the Gerundive is used in agreement :

Caesari omnia uno tempore erant agenda. Caes.
All things had to be done by Caesar at one time.
Principio sedes apibus statioque petenda. Verg.
First of all a site and station must be sought for the bees.

Note 1.—If an Intransitive Verb has an Object in the Dative, the Agent is in the Ablative with the preposition a or ab: patriae est a te consulendum, *you must consult for your country.*

384 *Note 2.*—After some Verbs, as do, trado, curo, the Gerundive is used in the Accusative to express that something is caused to be done :

Caesar pontem faciendum curat. Caes.
Caesar causes a bridge to be made.

SUPINES.

385 The Supines are also used as Cases of the Infinitive :

386 The **Supine in -um** is an Accusative after Verbs of motion, expressing the purpose :

Lusum it Maecenas, dormitum ego. Hor.
Maecenas goes to play, I to sleep.
Athenienses miserunt Delphos consultum. Nep.
The Athenians sent to Delphi to consult.

387 with the Infinitive **iri**, used impersonally, it forms a Future Passive Infinitive :

Aiunt urbem captum iri.
They say that the city will be taken.

Note.—Literally, *they say there is a going to take the city.*

388 The Supine in -u (Dative and Ablative) is used with some Adjectives, such as facilis, dulcis, turpis, and the Substantives fas, nefas : turpe factu, *disgraceful to do.*

| Hoc fas est dictu. | Libertas, dulce auditu nomen. LIV. |
| *It is lawful to say this.* | *Freedom, a name sweet to hear.* |

Nec visu facilis, nec dictu affabilis ulli. VERG.
One not easy for any to gaze on, or to address.

PARTICIPLES.

389 The Present and Perfect Participles of some Verbs are used as Adjectives :

| Homo frugi ac diligens. CIC. | Odorata cedrus. VERG. |
| *A thrifty and industrious man.* | *The fragrant cedar.* |

390 Most Participles which can be used as Adjectives have Comparison : pietate praestantior, *more excellent in piety ;* nocentissima victoria, *a very hurtful victory.*

391 A Participle, agreeing with a Noun in any Case, often expresses within one sentence what might be expressed by a dependent or a co-ordinate clause :

Saepe sequens agnam lupus est a voce retentus. Ov.
Often, when following a lamb, the wolf has been held back by his voice.

Elephantes, amnem transituri, minimos praemittunt. PLIN.
Elephants, intending to cross a river, send forward the smallest ones.

Timotheus a patre acceptam gloriam multis auxit virtutibus. NEP.
Timotheus increased by many virtues the glory which he had received from his father.

Sacras jaculatus arces terruit urbem. HOR.
He has smitten the sacred towers and terrified the city.

Caesar milites hortatus castra movit. CAES.
Caesar addressed the soldiers, and moved his camp.

392 *Note* 1.—Only Deponent Verbs have an Active Perfect Participle; in other Verbs its place is supplied either by a Finite Verb Active with the Relative or a Particle, or by the Ablative Absolute Passive:

The enemy, having thrown away their arms, fled,

can be expressed in Latin by

$$\text{Hostes} \begin{cases} \text{qui arma abjecerant} \\ \text{cum arma abjecissent} \\ \text{armis abjectis} \end{cases} \text{terga verterunt.}$$

393 *Note* 2.—Sometimes when a Substantive has a Perfect Participle in agreement, the Substantive must be rendered in English by a Genitive, the Participle by a Substantive: ademptus Hector, *the removal of Hector*; ante urbem conditam, *before the foundation of the city.*

Terra mutata non mutat mores. Liv.
Change of country does not change character.

Note on the Verb Infinite.

394 The Infinitive, the Gerund, the Supine in -um and the Participles govern the same Cases as the Finite Verbs to which they belong.

Ingenuas didicisse fideliter artes emollit mores. Ov.
To have truly learned the liberal arts refines the character.

Cupio satisfacere reipublicae. Cic.
I desire to do my duty to the republic.

Romae privatis jus non erat vocandi senatum. Liv.
At Rome private persons had not the right of summoning the senate.

Ast ego non Graiis servitum matribus ibo. Verg.
But I will not go to be a slave to Greek matrons.

Ausi omnes immane nefas, ausoque potiti. Verg.
All having dared monstrous impiety and having accomplished what they dared.

ADVERBS.

395 Adverbs show how, when, and where the action of the Verb takes place; they also qualify Adjectives or other Adverbs: recte facere, *to do rightly*; huc nunc venire, *to come hither now*; facile primus, *easily first*; valde celeriter, *very swiftly.*

Many words are both Adverbs and Prepositions, as ante, *before*, post, *after*:

Adverbs: multo ante, *long before*; paullo post, *shortly after.*

Prepositions : ante oculos, *before one's eyes*; post tergum, *behind one's back.*

Joined with quam they form Conjunctions : antequam, *before that* . . . postquam, *after that.* . . . (see **428, 431**).

396 **Negative Adverbs** are non, haud, ne.

Non, *not,* is simply negative :

> Nives in alto mari n o n cadunt. PLIN.
> *No snow falls on the high seas.*

Haud, *not,* is used with Adjectives, with other Adverbs, and a few Verbs of knowing and thinking: haud aliter, haud secus, *not otherwise*; res haud dubia, *no doubtful matter*; haud scio an verum sit, *I am inclined to think it is true.*

Ne is used with the second person of the Perfect Conjunctive for prohibitions (**347**) : ne transieris Hiberum (LIV.), *do not cross the Ebro.* With the second person of the Present Conjunctive **ne** often means *lest*: ne forte credas (HOR.), *lest by chance you believe,* or *that you may not by chance believe.*

397 Two Negatives make an Affirmative, as in English : non sum nescius, *I am not unaware,* that is *I am aware.* Non nemo means, *somebody*; nemo non, *everybody*; non-nihil, *something*; nihil non, *everything.*

> In ipsa curia n o n n e m o hostis est. CIC.
> *In the very senate-house there is some enemy.*
>
> N e m o Arpinas n o n Plancio studuit. CIC.
> *Every citizen of Arpinum was zealous for Plancius.*

Note 1.—**Neque, nec,** *nor* (Conjunction) is used for *and not*;

> Rapimur in errorem, neque vera cernimus. CIC.
> *We are hurried into error, and do not perceive truth.*

So also are generally rendered :

and no one,	nec quisquam, nec ullus ;
and nothing,	nec quidquam ;
and never, nowhere,	nec umquam, nec usquam.

398　　*Note 2.*—**Ne** is used with **quidem** to express *not even*, and the word or words on which emphasis is laid comes between them:

> Ne ad Catonem quidem provocabo. Cic.
> *Not to Cato even will I appeal.*

'*Not only not . . ., but not even*' is non modo non . . . sed ne . . . quidem (or ne . . . quidem, non modo non).

> Non modo tibi non irascor, sed ne reprehendo quidem factum tuum. Cic.
> *I am not only not angry with you, but do not even blame your act.*

If the predicate of both clauses is the same, it is often expressed only in the second clause with ne . . . quidem, and also the negative is omitted in the first clause—*i.e.* non modo is used rather than non modo non.

> Assentatio non modo amico, sed ne libero quidem digna est. Cic.
> *Flattering is unworthy, not only of a friend, but even of a free man.*

CONJUNCTIONS.

399　　Conjunctions connect words, sentences, and clauses.

400　　(1) **Co-ordinative** Conjunctions connect two or more Nouns in the same case:

> Miratur portas strepitumque et strata viarum. Verg.
> *He marvels at the gates and the noise and the pavements.*

> Et nostra respublica et omnia regna. Cic.
> *Both our own republic and all kingdoms.*

> Sine imperio nec domus ulla nec civitas stare potest. Cic.
> *Without government neither any house nor any State can be stable.*

Or they join two or more Simple Sentences (**402**):

Note 1.—**Aut . . . aut** are used to mark an emphatic distinction; **vel . . . vel** where the distinction is of little importance:

Aut Caesar aut nullus.	Vel paci decorum vel bello.
Either Caesar or nobody.	*Suitable either for peace or war.*

Note 2.—**Sed** distinguishes with more or less opposition, or passes to a fresh point; while **autem** corrects slightly or continues:

> Non scholae sed vitae discimus. Sen.
> *We learn not for the school but for life.*

Note 3.—**Autem, enim, quidem, vero,** never begin a sentence :

Neque e n i m tu is es qui quid sis nescias. Cɪᴄ.
For you are not the man to be ignorant of your own nature.

401   (2) **Subordinative** Conjunctions join Dependent Clauses to the Principal Sentence.   (See Compound Sentence.)

Co-ordination.

402   When two or more Sentences are joined together by Co-ordinative Conjunctions, so as to form part of one Sentence, they are said to be **Co-ordinate Sentences,** and each is independent in its construction.

E t mihi sunt vires et mea tela nocent. Ov.
I too am not powerless, and my weapons hurt.

Gyges a nullo videbatur, ipse a u t e m omnia videbat. Cɪᴄ.
Gyges was seen by no one, but he himself saw all things.

403   The Relative Pronoun with a Verb in the Indicative often forms a Co-ordinate Sentence :

Res loquitur ipsa, q u a e semper valet plurimum. Cɪᴄ.
The fact itself speaks, and this always avails most.

Constantes amici sunt eligendi, c u j u s generis magna est penuria. Cɪᴄ.
Firm friends are to be chosen, but of such there is great scarcity.

INTERJECTIONS.

404   Interjections are apart from the construction of the sentence. O, ah, eheu, heu, pro, are used with the Vocative, Nominative, or Accusative ; en, ecce, with the Nominative or Accusative ; ei, vae, with the Dative only :

O f o r m o s e p u e r, nimium ne crede colori. Vᴇʀɢ.
O beautiful boy, trust not too much to complexion.

O f o r t u n a t a m Romam ! Cɪᴄ.
O fortunate Rome !

E n e g o vester Ascanius ! Vᴇʀɢ.
Lo here am I your Ascanius !

Ei misero mihi!	Vae victis! Liv.
Alas! wretched me.	*Woe to the vanquished!*

QUESTION AND ANSWER.

405 (*a*) **Single Questions** are asked by:

nonně, expecting the answer *yes.*

nụm,   ,,   ,,   ,,   *no.*

-ně, expecting either answer.

an, expressing surprise and expecting answer *no.*

Canis n o n n e similis lupo est? Cic.
Is not a dog like a wolf?

N u m negare audes? Cic.	Potes n e dicere? Cic.
Do you venture to deny?	*Can you say?*

An tu me tristem esse putas? Plaut.
Do you think I am sad?

Note.—Questions are also asked by Interrogative Pronouns (95, 100, 102, 327) and Adverbs (167, 168).

406 (*b*) **Alternative Questions** are asked by:

utrum   .   .   .   . an (*or*).

num .   .   .   .   . an (*or*).

-ně   .   .   .   .   . an (*or*).

    .   .   .   .   . an, anně (*or*).

Haec u t r u m abundantis an egentis signa sunt? Cic.
Are these the tokens of one who abounds or lacks?

N u m duas habetis patrias a n est illa patria communis? Cic.
Have you two countries, or is that your common country?

Roma m n e venio, a n hic maneo, an Arpinum fugio? Cic.
Do I come to Rome, or stay here, or flee to Arpinum?

Note.—A single question is sometimes asked without any particle:

Infelix est Fabricius quod rus suum fodit? Sen.
Is Fabricius unhappy because he digs his land?

For **Deliberative Questions** the Present or Imperfect Conjunctive is used :

407

Quid faciam? roger anne rogem? Ov.
What shall I do ? Shall I be asked or ask ?

Tibi ego irascerer, mi frater? tibi ego possem irasci? Cic.
Should I be angry with you, my brother ? Could I be angry with you ?

408 Answer Affirmative is expressed :

(a) By repeating the emphatic word of the question, sometimes with vero, sane, inquam.

Estne? . . . est. Liv.	Dasne? . . . Do sane. Cic.
Is it ? . . . . it is.	*Do you grant ? . I grant indeed.*

(b) By ita, ita est, etiam, sane, sane quidem . . .

Visne potiora tantum interrogem ? . . . Sane. Cic.
Would you have me ask only the principal matters ? . . . Certainly.

409 Answer Negative is expressed :

(a) By repeating the emphatic Verb with non.

Estne frater intus ? . . Non est. Ter.
Is my brother within ? . . No.

(b) By non, non ita, minime, minime vero :

Venitne? . . . . . Non. Plaut.
Did he come ? . . . No.

Non pudet vanitatis?   Minime.
Are you not ashamed of your folly ?   *Not at all.*

Note.—**Immo,** *nay rather, yes even,* is used in answers to correct or modify, either by contradicting, or by strengthening :

Ubi fuit Sulla, num Romae ? . . . Immo longe afuit. Cic.
Where was Sulla ? at Rome ? . . . Nay, he was far away from it.

Tenaxne est ? . . . . . . Immo pertinax. Plaut.
Is he tenacious ? . . . . Yes even pertinacious.

410   THE COMPOUND SENTENCE.

A **Compound Sentence** consists of a Principal Sentence with one or more Subordinate Clauses.

Subordinate Clauses depend in their construction on the Principal Sentence. They are divided into:

I. Substantival.   **II. Adverbial.**   **III. Adjectival.**

I. A Substantival Clause stands, like a Substantive, as Subject or Object of a Verb, or in Apposition.

II. An Adverbial Clause qualifies the Principal Sentence like an Adverb, answering the questions *how? why? when?* Adverbial Clauses are introduced by Subordinative Conjunctions, and are (1) Consecutive (*so that*); (2) Final (*in order that*); (8) Causal (*because, since*); (4) Temporal (*when, while, until*); (5) Conditional (*if, unless*); (6) Concessive (*although, even if*); (7) Comparative (*as if, as though*).

III. An Adjectival Clause qualifies the Principal Sentence like an Adjective. It is introduced by the Relative qui or by a Relative Particle, as ubi (*where*), unde (*whence*), quo (*whither*).

411   Sequence of Tenses.

The general rule for the Sequence of Tenses is that a Primary Tense in the Principal Sentence is followed by a Primary Tense in the Clause, a Historic Tense by a Historic Tense.

PRIMARY.

Simple Pres.	rogo	*I ask*	*Act.*	quid agas	*what you are*
Pres. Perf.	rogavi	*I have*	*Pass.*	quid a te agatur	*doing.*
		asked	*Act.*	quid egeris	*what you have*
Simple Fut.	rogabo		*Pass.*	quid a te actum sit	*done.*
Fut. Perf.	rogavero		*Act.*	quid acturus sis	*what you are going to do.*

HISTORIC.

Imperf.	rogabam		*Act.*	quid ageres	*what you were*
Perf.	rogavi	*I*	*Pass.*	quid a te ageretur	*doing.*
		asked	*Act.*	quid egisses	*what you had*
Pluperf.	rogaveram		*Pass.*	quid a te actum esset	*done.*
			Act.	quid acturus esses	*what you were going to do.*

Note.—The Historic Present and Historic Infinitive are generally used with Historic Sequence. The Primary Perfect Indicative has Primary Sequence in most writers, but Cicero often gives it Historic Sequence. The Perfect Conjunctive in its Pure use is always Primary; in its Dependent use, it is generally Primary, sometimes Historic.

412   Tenses of the Infinitive in Oratio Obliqua.

If the time of the Clause is the same as that of the Principal Verb, the Present Infinitive is used.

If the time is before that of the Principal Verb, the Perfect Infinitive.

If the time follows that of the Principal Verb, the Future Infinitive.

Scio	eum amare	amavisse	amaturum esse
	that he is loving	*has loved*	*will love*
I know	copias mitti	missas esse	missum iri
	that forces are being sent	*have been sent*	*will be sent*
Sciebam	eum amare	amavisse	amaturum esse
	that he was loving	*had loved*	*would love*
I knew	copias mitti	missas esse	missum iri
	that forces were being sent	*had been sent*	*would be sent*

Note.—For the Supine in -**um** with iri, may be substituted **fore** or **futurum ut** with the Conjunctive: fore (futurum esse), ut copiae mittantur, ut copiae mitterentur.

413   I. Substantival Clauses.

Substantival Clauses are Indirect Speech (**Oratio Obliqua**). Their forms correspond to the three direct forms of the Simple Sentence.

1. Direct Statement.	**1. Indirect Statement** (Enuntiatio Obliqua).
Valeo. *I am well.*	Scis me valere. *You know that I am well.*
Calet ignis. *Fire is hot.*	Sentimus calere ignem. *We feel that fire is hot.*
2. Direct Positive Command or Request.	**2. Indirect Command or Request** (Petitio Obliqua).
Vale. *Farewell.*	Cura ut valeas. *Take care that you keep well.*
Mane in sententia. *Keep firm in your opinion.*	Oro maneas in sententia. *I beg that you keep firm in your opinion.*
3. Direct Question.	**3. Indirect Question** (Interrogatio Obliqua).
Valesne ? *Are you well?*	Quaero an valeas. *I ask whether you are well.*
Quis est ? *Who is he?*	Incertum est quis sit. *It is doubtful who he is.*

414

1. Indirect Statement.

The **Accusative with Infinitive** is the most usual form of Indirect Statement. It may stand :

    (*a*) As the **Subject** of an Impersonal Verb, or of est with an Abstract Substantive or Neuter Adjective :

Constat leges ad salutem civium inventas esse. Cic.
It is agreed that laws were devised for the safety of citizens.

Nuntiatum est Scipionem adesse. Caes.
It was announced that Scipio was at hand.

Rem te valde bene gessisse rumor erat. Cic.
There was a report that you had conducted the affair very well.

Verum est amicitiam nisi inter bonos esse non posse. Cic.
It is true that friendship cannot exist except between the good.

(*b*) As **Object,** after Verbs of *saying, thinking, feeling, perceiving, knowing, believing, denying* :

Democritus dicit innumerabiles esse mundos. CIC.
Democritus says that there are countless worlds.

Pompeios desedisse terra motu audivimus. SEN.
We have heard that Pompeii has perished in an earthquake.

(*c*) In **Apposition :**

Illud temere dictum, sapientes omnes esse bonos. CIC.
It was rashly said that all wise men are good.

Note.—Verbs of *hoping, promising, swearing, threatening* generally take the Accusative with Future Infinitive :

Sperabam id me assecuturum. CIC.
I hoped to attain this.

415   Pollicebatur pecuniam se esse redditurum. CIC.
He promised that he would return the money.

A **Clause formed by Ut with the Conjunctive** is used as Subject with Impersonal Verbs or phrases which express fact or occurrence ; it is also used in Apposition, but it seldom stands as Object :

Expedit ut civitates sua jura habeant. LIV.
That states should have their own laws is expedient.

Mos erat ut in pace Jani templum clauderetur. LIV.
It was the custom that in time of peace the temple of Janus was shut.

Extremum illud est ut te obsecrem. CIC.
The last thing is for me to beseech you.

Note.—The Accusative with Infinitive, or the Ut Clause, used Inter-rogatively, sometimes expresses indignation :

Mene incepto desistere victam? VERG.
What ! I to be vanquished and abandon my design !

416   Te ut ulla res frangat? CIC.
Can anything break your pride ?

A Clause formed by **Quod with the Indicative** is used as Subject, or in Apposition, where a fact is to be dwelt on :

Accedit huc quod postridie ille venit. CIC.
Add to this that he came the next day.

Hoc praestamus maxime feris, quod loquimur. CIC.
We excel beasts most in this respect, that we speak.

N

Rarely as Object, after Verbs such as addo, mitto, omitto, praetereo :

Adde quod idem non horam tecum esse potes. Hor.
Add moreover that you cannot keep your own company for an hour.

It is also used with Verbs of *rejoicing* and *grieving* :

Dolet mihi quod tu stomacharis. Cic.
It grieves me that you are angry.

Gaude, quod spectant oculi te mille loquentem. Hor.
Rejoice, that a thousand eyes behold you speaking.

Note.—With Verbs of *rejoicing* and *grieving*, the Accusative with Infinitive or the Quod Clause may be used : Salvum te advenire gaudeo (Plaut.), *I rejoice that you arrive in health ;* might be, ' Gaudeo quod salvus advenis.'

2. Indirect Command, Request or Prohibition.

417 A Clause depending on a Verb of *commanding, wishing, exhorting, entreating,* is in the Conjunctive : if positive, with **ut ;** if negative, with **ne.** The Clause may stand

(*a*) as Subject ; (*b*) as Object ; (*c*) in Apposition :

(*a*) Postulatur ab amico ut sit sincerus. Cic.
It is required of a friend that he be sincere.
Nuntiatum est Antonio ne Brutum obsideret. Cic.
An order was sent to Antony that he should not besiege Brutus.

(*b*) Etiam atque etiam te rogo atque oro ut eum juves. Cic.
I urgently beg and pray you to help him.
Mihi ne abscedam imperat. Ter.
He commands me not to go away.

(*c*) Hoc te rogo, ne dimittas animum. Cic.
This I beg you, not to lose heart.

Note 1.—With oro, rogo, moneo, suadeo, sino, impero, curo, volo, nolo, malo, and some other verbs, ut is often omitted. With licet oportet it is not used. Idque sinas oro ; *and I pray that you grant that.*

Haec omnia praetermittas licet. Cic.
It is allowable to omit all these things.

Note 2.—Verbs of *willing* and *desiring,* volo, nolo, cupio, also jubeo and many others, frequently take the Accusative with Infinitive :

Eas res jactari nolebat. Caes.
He was unwilling to have those things discussed.
Eos suum adventum exspectare jussit. Caes.
He desired them to await his arrival.

Note 3.—Verbs of *taking care, effecting*, *causing*, are used with ut; verbs of *guarding against*, with ne:

> Cura et provide ut nequid ei desit. Cic.
> *Take care and provide that nothing be wanting to him.*
>
> Sol efficit ut omnia floreant. Cic.
> *The sun causes all things to bloom.*

Cave, *beware lest*, with ne or without a Conjunction; cave, *take care that*, is used with ut:

> Cave ne portus occupet alter. Hob.
> *Beware lest another forestall you in occupying the harbour.*

Note 4.—Verbs of *fearing* take the Conjunctive: with ne to express fear that something *will* happen; with ut or ne non to express fear that something *will not* happen:

Metuo ne faciat.	Metuo ut faciat (*or* ne non faciat).
I fear he may do it.	*I fear he may not do it.*

418   **Quominus,** *that not* (literally *by which the less*), with the Conjunctive, forms a Clause depending on a Verb or phrase which expresses *hindrance* or *prevention*:

> Senectus non impedit quominus litterarum studia teneamus. Cic.
> *Age does not prevent our continuing literary pursuits.*
>
> Neque repugnabo quominus omnia legant. Cic.
> *Nor will I oppose their reading all things.*
>
> Per Afranium stetit quominus proelio dimicaretur. Caes.
> *It was owing to Afranius that no battle was fought.*

419   **Quin,** *that not*, with the Conjunctive, follows many of the same Verbs, and phrases of similar meaning:

> Nihil abest quin sim miserrimus. Cic.
> *Nothing is wanting to my being most miserable.*
>
> Aegre sunt retenti quin oppidum irrumperent. Caes.
> *They were hardly withheld from bursting into the city.*

Note 1.—The sentence on which **quominus** depends is generally negative or interrogative, but it may be positive; the sentence on which **quin** depends is always negative, or virtually negative.

Note 2.—Many of these Verbs take ne:

> Atticus, ne qua sibi statua poneretur, restitit. Nep.
> *Atticus opposed having any statue raised to him.*

Prohibeo takes quominus or ne, veto more often ne, and both take Accusative with Infinitive.

420   3. Indirect Question.

Indirect Question is formed by a dependent Interrogative Pronoun or Particle with a Verb in the Conjunctive.

The Clause of the Indirect Question may be (*a*) Subject or (*b*) Object or (*c*) in Apposition, and the Question may be single or alternative :

(*a*) Videndum est, quando, et cui, et quemadmodum, et quare demus. Cic.
  Care must be taken, when, to whom, how, and why we give.
  Demus, necne demus, in nostra potestate est. Cic.
  Whether we give or do not give is in our own power.

(*b*) Fac me certiorem quando adfuturus sis. Cic.
  Let me know when you will be here.

  Haud scio an quae dixit sint vera omnia. Ter.
  I am inclined to think that all he has said is the truth.

(*c*) Ipse quis sit, utrum sit, an non sit, id quoque nescit. Catull.
  He knows not even this, who he himself is, whether he is or is not.

421   II. Adverbial Clauses.

1. Consecutive Clauses.

Consecutive Clauses define the consequence of what is stated in the Principal Sentence. They are introduced by **ut**, with a Verb in the Conjunctive; if negative, by **ut non, ut nihil, ut nullus**, &c.

Ut, in Consecutive Clauses, usually follows a Demonstrative, **adeo, eo, huc, ita, tam, sic, tantus, tot**:

  Non sum ita hebes ut istud dicam. Cic.
  I am not so stupid as to say that.

  Quis tam demens est ut sua voluntate maereat? Cic.
  Who is so mad as to mourn of his own free will?

  Nemo adeo ferus est ut non mitescere possit. Hor.
  No one is so savage that he cannot soften.

Note.—Sometimes the Demonstrative is omitted:

Arboribus consita Italia est, u t tota pomarium v i d e a t u r.   VARRO,
Italy is planted with trees, so as to seem one orchard.

Clare, et ut a u d i a t hospes.   PERS.
Aloud, and so that a bystander may hear.

Ut is used in a restrictive sense after ita :

Litterarum i t a studiosus erat u t poetas omnino neglegeret.   CIC.
*He was fond of literature, with the reservation that he cared
nothing for poetry.*

Ut Consecutive sometimes follows quam with a Comparative:

422   Isocrates m a j o r e ingenio est quam ut cum Lysia compare-
tur.   CIC.
Isocrates is of too great genius to be compared with Lysias.

Quin, *but that,* with the Conjunctive, follows phrases and
questions such as non, or haud dubium est; quis dubitat?

Non dubium erat q u i n totius Galliae plurimum Helvetii possent.   CAES.
*There was no doubt that in the whole of Gaul the Helvetii were
the most powerful.*

Quis dubitet q u i n in virtute divitiae positae sint?   CIC.
Who would doubt that riches consist in virtue ?

Note 1.—A Consecutive ut clause sometimes depends on the phrase
tantum abest followed by a Substantival ut clause, the meaning being so
far from . . . . that . . .

Tantum a b e s t ut nostra miremur, ut nobis non satisfaciat
ipse Demosthenes.   CIC.
*So far am I from admiring my own productions, that Demosthenes
himself does not satisfy me.*

Note 2.—In Consecutive Clauses the Sequence of Tenses sometimes
varies from the general rule.   If it is intended to mark the consequence as
something exceptional, the Primary Perfect in the Clause may follow the
Imperfect or Historic Perfect in the Principal Sentence.

Non adeo virtutum sterile erat saeculum ut non et bona ex-
empla prodiderit.   TAC.
*The age was not so bare of virtues that it has not furnished some
good examples.*

(For Consecutive Clauses with Qui, see **452**.)

2. Final Clauses.

423　　Final Clauses express the aim or purpose of the action of the Principal Sentence. They are formed by **ut**, or, if negative, by **ne, ut ne**, with the Conjunctive :

> Venio ut videam.　　　　　Abii ne viderem.
> *I come that I may see.*　　　*I went away that I might not see.*
>
> Ut jugulent homines surgunt de nocte latrones. Juv.
> *Robbers rise by night that they may kill men.*
>
> Scipio rus abiit ne ad causam dicendam adesset. Cic.
> *Scipio went into the country that he might not be present to defend his cause.*

Ut, with a Final Clause, often corresponds to the Demonstratives **eo, ideo, idcirco, propterea, ob eam rem** :

> Legum idcirco servi sumus ut liberi esse possimus. Cic.
> *We are the bondmen of the law in order that we may be free.*

Note 1.—A Final Clause with **ut** or **ne** is used parenthetically in such phrases as : ut ita dicam, *so to say* ; ne longus sim, *not to be tedious.*

Note 2.—Nedum, *much less (not to say)*, may take a Verb in the Conjunctive :

> Mortalia facta peribunt,
> Nedum sermonum stet honos et gratia vivax. Hor.
> *Mortal deeds will perish, much less can the honour and popularity of words be lasting.*

Note 3.—The purpose of action is expressed in many ways, all equivalent to ut with a Final Clause. *He sent ambassadors to seek peace* may be rendered :

> Legatos misit ut pacem peterent.
> 　　　,,　　,, 　qui pacem peterent.
> 　　　,,　　,, 　ad petendam pacem.
> 　　　,,　　,, 　petendi pacem causā.
> 　　　,,　　,, 　petendae pacis causā.
> 　　　,,　　,, 　petitum pacem.

Note 4.—The Sequence of Tenses in Final Clauses always follows the general rule.

(For Final Clauses with Qui, see 453.)

8. Causal Clauses.

424   **Causal Clauses** assign a reason for the statement made in the Principal Sentence.

425   When an actual reason for a fact is given, **quod, quia, quoniam, quando, quandoquidem, quatenus, siquidem,** are used with the Indicative : *

> Adsunt propterea quod officium sequuntur; tacent quia periculum metuunt. Cic.
> *They are present because they follow duty; they are silent because they fear danger.*

> Vos, Quirites, quoniam jam nox est, in vestra tecta discedite. Liv.
> *Since it is already night, depart, ye Quirites, to your tents.*

> Geramus, dis bene juvantibus, quando ita videtur, bellum. Liv.
> *Let us wage war, the gods helping us, since so it seems good.*

Note.—**Quod, quia, quoniam** correspond to eo, ideo, idcirco, propterea; ideo quia uxor ruri est (Ter.); *for the reason that my wife is in the country.*

426   Cum, *since*, with a Causal Clause takes the Conjunctive;

> Quae cum ita sint, ab Jove pacem ac veniam peto. Cic.
> *Since these things are so, I ask of Jupiter peace and pardon.*

Note 1.—After gratulor, laudo, gaudeo, doleo, **cum**, *for the reason that,* takes the Indicative, if the Verb is in the first person :

> Gratulor tibi cum tantum vales apud Dolabellam. Cic.
> *I congratulate you that you have so much weight with Dolabella.*

Note 2.—**Non quod, non quia** take the Indicative when they refer to the actual cause of a fact; if they refer to a cause thought of, not actual, they take the Conjunctive, and a following clause, with **sed,** gives the true reason :

> Non quia salvos vellet, sed quia perire causa indicta nolebat. Liv.
> *Not because he wished them to be saved, but because he did not wish them to die without trial.*

(For Causal Clauses with Qui, see **454**.)

* Clauses in Oratio Obliqua must be understood to be excepted from this and all following rules for the use of the Indicative.

4. Temporal Clauses.

427   Temporal Clauses define the time when anything has happened, is happening, or will happen.

The Mood of a Temporal Clause is Indicative if its Connexion with the Principal Sentence is one of time only, and if the time of each is independent of the other; but, if the time of the Clause is thought of as depending on the time of the Principal Sentence, the Mood of the Clause is Conjunctive.

428   **Ubi, ut, postquam, simulac, quando, quotiens, cum primum** are generally used with the Indicative:

> Olea ubi matura erit quam primum cogi oportet. CATO.
> *When the olive is (shall be) ripe, it must be gathered in as soon as possible.*

> Ut Hostus cecidit, confestim Romana inclinatur acies. LIV.
> *When Hostus fell, immediately the Roman line gave way.*

> Eo postquam Caesar pervenit, obsides, arma poposcit. CAES.
> *After Caesar had arrived there, he demanded hostages and arms.*

429   **Dum, donec, quoad,** *while, as long as,* take the Indicative:

> Homines dum docent discunt. SEN.
> *Men learn while they teach.*

> Dum haec Veiis agebantur, interim Capitolium in ingenti periculo fuit. LIV.
> *While these things were being done at Veii, the Capitol was meanwhile in dire peril.*

> Cato, quoad vixit, virtutum laude crevit. NEP.
> *Cato increased in the renown of virtue as long as he lived.*

430   **Dum** is used with the Historic Present, the Verb of the Principal Sentence being in a Historic tense:

> Dum haec in colloquio geruntur, Caesari nuntiatum est equites accedere. CAES.
> *While this parley was being carried on, it was announced to Caesar that the cavalry were approaching.*

431 **Dum, donec, quoad,** *until,* and **antequam, priusquam,** *before that,* take the Indicative when the only idea conveyed is that of time :

> Milo in senatu fuit eo die, quoad senatus dimissus est. Cic.
> *On that day Milo was in the Senate until the Senate was dismissed.*

> Priusquam de ceteris rebus respondeo, de amicitia pauca dicam. Cic.
> *Before I answer about other matters, I will say a few things about friendship.*

432 But when the idea of expecting or waiting for something comes in, they take the Conjunctive :

> Exspectate dum consul aut dictator fiat Kaeso. Liv.
> *Wait till Kaeso become consul or dictator.*

433 **Cum,** if it expresses only the time when something happens, is used with the Indicative :

> De te cum quiescunt probant, cum tacent clamant. Cic.
> *Concerning you, when they are quiet they approve, when they are silent they cry aloud.*

> Cum Caesar in Galliam venit, alterius factionis principes erant Haedui, alterius Sequani. Caes.
> *When Caesar came into Gaul, the Haedui were chiefs of one faction, the Sequani of another.*

The addition of the Demonstratives **tum, tunc,** marks that the times of the Principal Sentence and Clause correspond more exactly :

> Lituo Romulus regiones direxit tum cum urbem condidit. Cic.
> *Romulus marked out the districts with a staff at the time when he founded the city.*

> Tum cum in Asia res amiserant, scimus Romae fidem concidisse. Cic.
> *At the time when they had lost their power in Asia, we know that credit sank at Rome.*

434   If the action of the Clause with **cum** takes place while that of the Principal Sentence is continuing, or if it quickly follows it, the Clause sometimes contains the main statement, while the Principal Sentence defines the time (**inverse cum**) :

> Jam ver appetebat c u m Hannibal ex hibernis m o v i t. Liv.
> *Spring was already approaching when Hannibal moved out of his winter quarters.*

> Commodum discesserat Hilarus c u m v e n i t tabellarius. Cic.
> *Hilarus had just departed, when the letter-carrier came.*

Note.—**Cum** with the Indicative sometimes expresses what has long been and still continues :

> Multi anni sunt c u m Fabius in aere meo e s t. Cic.
> *For many years past Fabius has been in my debt.*

435   **Cum** is used in narrative with the Imperfect or Pluperfect Conjunctive, the Verb of the Principal Sentence being in the Perfect or the Historic Present (**historic cum**) :

Note.—It is used with the Imperfect for contemporary time, with the Pluperfect for prior time.

> C u m triginta tyranni oppressas t e n e r e n t Athenas, Thrasybulus his bellum indixit. Nep.
> *When the thirty tyrants were oppressing Athens, Thrasybulus declared war against them.*

> C u m Pausanias de templo e l a t u s e s s e t, confestim animam efflavit. Nep.
> *When Pausanias had been carried down from the temple, he immediately expired.*

> C u m hostes a d e s s e n t, in urbem pro se quisque ex agris d e m i-grant. Liv.
> *On the approach of the enemy, they move, each as he best can, from the country into the city.*

436   *Note.*—In and after the Augustan age the Conjunctive is used in Temporal Clauses for repeated action like the Greek Optative:

> Id fetialis **ubi dixisset**, hastam in fines hostium mittebat. Liv.
> *As soon as a fetial had thus spoken, he used to fling a spear within the enemy's boundaries.*

> Saepe **cum** aliquem **videret** minus bene vestitum, suum amiculum dedit. Nep.
> *Often when he saw someone ill dressed, he gave him his own cloak.*

But **cum** is used down to the time of Cicero and Caesar (inclusive) with the Indicative for repeated action; in reference to present time with the Perfect, in reference to past time with the Pluperfect:

> Verres **cum** rosam **viderat**, tum ver esse arbitrabatur. Cic.
> *Whenever Verres had seen a rose, he considered that it was spring.*

5. Conditional Clauses.

437   **Conditional** Statements consist of a Clause introduced by **si, nisi**, containing the preliminary condition, which is called the Protasis, and a Principal Sentence, containing that which follows from the condition, which is called the Apodosis.

They have two chief forms:

(1) where the Indicative is used in both Protasis and Apodosis;

(2) where the Conjunctive is used in both.

A Primary tense in the Protasis is usually followed by a Primary in the Apodosis, and a Historic by a Historic.

438   (1) The Indicative is used in the si-Clause and in the Principal Sentence when the truth of the one statement depends on the truth of the other; if one is a fact, the other is also a fact:

> **Si vales**, bene est. Cic.
> *If you are in good health, all is well.*

> Parvi sunt foris arma, **nisi est** consilium domi. Cic.
> *Arms are of little avail abroad, unless there is counsel at home.*

> **Si feceris** id quod ostendis, magnam habebo gratiam. Cic.
> *If you shall have done what you offer, I shall be very grateful.*

Siquod erat grande vas, laeti afferebant. Cic.
If there was any large vessel, they gladly produced it.

Si licuit, patris pecuniam recte abstulit filius. Cic.
If it was lawful, the son rightly took his father's money.

Note 1.—A si-Clause with the Indicative is often used with the Imperative:

Si me amas, paullum hic ades. Hor.
If you love me, stand by me here a short time.

Causam investigato, si poteris. Cic.
Search out the cause if you can.

Note 2.—A si-Clause with the Indicative also follows a Conjunctive (Optative use) ;

Moriar, si vera non loquor. Cic.
May I die if I am not speaking the truth.

439 (2) The Conjunctive is used both in the si-Clause and in the Principal Sentence when the condition is imaginary :

(*a*) The Present Conjunctive is used when the statements are thought of as possible, more or less probable :

Sexcenta memorem, si sit otium. Plaut.
I could mention endless things, had I leisure.

Si a corona relictus sim, non queam dicere. Cic.
If I were forsaken by my circle of hearers I should not be able to speak.

(*b*) The Historic Conjunctive is used when the statements are purely imaginary ; when there is no possibility of their becoming actual :

Si foret in terris, rideret Democritus. Hor.
Democritus would be laughing, if he were upon earth.

'Si id scissem, numquam huc tulissem pedem. Ter.
If I had known that, I should never have come hither.

Magis id diceres, si adfuisses. Cic.
You would have said so all the more, had you been present.

440   *Note.*—The Indicative may be used in the Principal Sentence with a si-Clause in the Conjunctive,

(*a*) When the truth of the statement in the Principal Sentence is less closely dependent on the si-Clause :

Te neque debent adjuvare si possint, neque possunt si velint. Cic.

They neither ought to help you if they could, nor can if they would.

(*b*) When the Principal Sentence expresses action begun, but hindered by the condition in the si-Clause :

Numeros memini si verba tenerem. Verg.

I remember the measure if I could recall the words.

(*c*) With the past tenses of Verbs of duty and possibility :

Poterat utrumque praeclare fieri, si esset fides in hominibus consularibus. Cic.

Both might have been done admirably if there had been honour in men of consular rank.

(*d*) With the past tenses of esse, especially in Periphrastic conjugation :

Si unum diem morati essetis, moriendum omnibus fuit. Liv.

If you had delayed a single day, you must all have died.

Et factura fuit, pactus nisi Juppiter esset ... Ov.

And she would have done it, if Jupiter had not agreed ...

441   *Note 1.*—Si is sometimes omitted :

Ait quis, aio; negat, nego. Ter.

If anyone affirms, I affirm; if anyone denies, I deny.

Note 2.—Nisi forte, nisi vero are ironical. Si non throws the emphasis of the negative on a single word :

Si non feceris, ignoscam.

If you have not done it, I will pardon.

Note 3.—Sive ... sive, seu ... seu, *whether ... or, or if,* are used for alternative conditions :

Sive retractabis, sive properabis.

Whether you delay or hasten (it).

442   **Dum, dummodo, modo,** *if only, provided that,* take the Conjunctive :

Oderint dum metuant. Suet.

Let them hate provided they fear.

Modo ne laudarent iracundiam. Cic.

If only they did not praise wrath.

443 *Note* 1.—The following table shows how to convert Conditional Sentences into Oratio Obliqua when the Apodosis becomes an Infinitive Clause, and the Protasis is subordinate to it.

After a Primary Tense.

1. Si peccas (peccasti), doles.	1. si pecces (peccaveris), dolere.
2. Si peccabis, dolebis.	2. { pecces, } doliturum
3. Si peccaveris, dolueris.	3. si { peccaveris, } esse.
4. Si pecces, doleas.	4. { peccaturus sis, }
5. Si peccares, doleres.	5. si peccares, doliturum esse.
6. Si peccavisses, } doluisses.	6. si { peccavisses, } doliturum
7. Si peccares, }	7. { peccares, } fuisse.
8. Si peccavisses, doleres.	8. si peccavisses, doliturum fore.

Aio te,

After a Historic Tense.

Aiebam te,
1. si peccares (peccavisses), dolere.
2. { peccares,
3. si { peccavisses, } doliturum esse.
4. { peccaturus esses, }

The other four forms remain unchanged.

Note 2. Si peccavisses, doluisses is equivalent to si peccavisses, doliturus fuisti ; and this may either be converted, as above, into the Infinitive Clause, or into the Conjunctive :

Aio te, si peccavisses, doliturum fuisse.

Haec talia sunt ut, si peccavisses, doliturus fueris.

6. Concessive Clauses.

444 Concessive Clauses are introduced by etsi, etiamsi, tametsi, quamquam, quamvis, licet.

Note.—A Concessive Clause is so called because it concedes, or allows, an objection to the statement in the Principal Sentence. The rule for mood is the same as in Conditional Clauses.

445 Etsi, etiamsi, tametsi are used (*a*) with the Indicative, (*b*) with the Conjunctive :

(*a*) Etiamsi tacent, satis dicunt. Cic.
Even if they are silent, they say enough.

(*b*) Etiamsi non is esset Caesar qui est, tamen ornandus videretur. Cic.
Even if Caesar were not what he is, yet he would be considered worthy of honour.

446 Quamquam is used with the Indicative :

Quamquam festinas, non est mora longa. Hor.
Although you are in haste, the delay is not long.

447 Quamvis, licet are used with the Conjunctive :

Quamvis non fueris suasor, approbator fuisti. Cic.
Although you did not make the suggestion, you have given your approval.

448 Licet vitium sit ambitio, frequenter tamen causa virtutum est. QUINT.

Granted that ambition be a fault, yet often it is a cause of virtues.

Note 1.—**Quamquam** is used by later writers with the Conjunctive, and quamvis is often found in poets with the Indicative.

Note 2.—**Ut, ne, cum** are occasionally used in a Concessive sense, and take the Conjunctive :

Ut desint vires, tamen est laudanda voluntas. Ov.
Though strength be wanting, yet must the will be praised.

Ne sit summum malum dolor, malum certe est. CIC.
Granted that pain be not the greatest evil, it surely is an evil.

His, cum facere non possent, loqui tamen et scribere honeste et magnifice licebat. CIC.
These, though they could not so act, were yet at liberty to speak and write virtuously and loftily.

Note 3.—Concessive Clauses are sometimes formed without Conjunctions.

Naturam expellas furca, tamen usque recurret. HOR.
Though you drive out Nature with a pitchfork, yet she will always come back.

449 **7. Comparative Clauses.**

In **Comparative** Clauses the action or fact of the Principal Sentence is compared with a supposed condition ; they are formed by **quasi** (quamsi), **tamquam, tamquam si, ut si, velut si, ac si** with the Conjunctive :

Assimulabo quasi nunc exeam. TER.
I will pretend to be just going out.

Tamquam de regno dimicaretur ita concurrerunt. LIV.
They joined battle as if it were a struggle for the kingdom.

Tamquam si claudus sim, cum fusti est ambulandum. PLAUT.
I must walk with a stick as if I were lame.

Ejus negotium sic velim cures, ut si esset res mea. CIC.
I would wish you to care for his business just as if it were my affair.

Note.—The Demonstratives are **ita, sic, perinde, proinde, aeque, similiter.**

III. Adjectival Clauses.

450   The Relative qui in its simple use takes the Indicative :

> Est in Britannia flumen, quod appellatur Tamesis. Caes.
> *There is in Britain a river which is called the Thames.*
>
> Quis fuit horrendos primus qui protulit enses? Ov.
> *Who was (the man) who first invented terrible swords ?*

Note.—This rule applies to Correlatives, qualis, quantus, quot, and to Universals, quisquis, quicumque, &c.

Non sum qualis eram. Hor.	Quidquid erit, tibi erit. Cic.
I am not what I was.	*Whatever there is will be for you.*

451   But the Relative often introduces a Clause Consecutive, Final or Causal, with the Conjunctive, corresponding to the Adverbial Clauses with similar meaning.

452   Qui with the Conjunctive forms a **Consecutive** Clause with the meaning *of such a kind that* :

(*a*) After a Demonstrative :

> Non sum is qui his rebus delecter. Cic.
> *I am not one to delight in these things.*
>
> Ea est Romana gens quae victa quiescere nesciat. Liv.
> *The Roman race is such that it knows not how to rest quiet under defeat.*
>
> Nihil tanti fuit quo venderemus fidem nostram et libertatem. Cic.
> *Nothing was of such value that we should sell for it our faith and freedom.*

(*b*) After Indefinite and Interrogative Pronouns, or Negatives, nemo, nihil, nullus :

> Est aliquid quod non oporteat, etiamsi licet. Cic.
> *There is something which is not fitting, even if it is lawful.*
>
> Quis est cui non possit malum evenire? Cic.
> *Who is there to whom evil may not happen ?*
>
> Nihil est quod tam deceat quam constantia. Cic.
> *Nothing is so becoming as consistency.*

Note.—**Quin** for qui non is similarly used :

Nemo est quin audierit quemadmodum captae sint Syracusae.
Cic.
There is no one who has not heard how Syracuse was taken..

(c) After Impersonal est, *there is,* sunt, *there are* :

Sunt qui duos tantum in sacro monte creatos tribunos esse
dicant. Liv.
*There are who say that only two tribunes were elected on the sacred
mount.*

but est qui, sunt qui take the Indicative if they refer to
Definite Antecedents :

Sunt item quae appellantur alces. Caes.
There are also (some animals) which are called elks.

(d) After Comparatives with quam :

Majora deliquerant quam quibus ignosci posset. Liv.
They had committed greater offences than could be pardoned.

(e) After dignus, indignus :

Dignus est qui imperet. Cic.
He is worthy to govern.

453

Qui with the Conjunctive forms a **Final** Clause, *in order that* :

Clusini legatos Romam, qui auxilium a senatu peterent, misere.
Liv.
The Clusini sent ambassadors to Rome to seek aid from the senate.

Quo with a Comparative introduces a Final Clause, and
takes the Conjunctive :

Solon furere se simulavit, quo tutior ejus vita esset. Cic.
Solon pretended to be mad in order that his life might be the safer.

454

Qui introduces a **Causal** Clause, and usually takes the Conjunctive :

Miseret tui me qui hunc facias inimicum tibi. Ter.
I pity you for making this man your enemy.

Note 1.—Qui causal is sometimes strengthened by quippe, ut, utpote.

Note 2.—Non quo is sometimes used for non quod : non quo quemquam
plus amem, eo feci (Ter.), *I have not done it because I love anyone more.*

Note 3.—Qui with the Indicative forms a Causal Clause as a parenthesis :

Quā es prudentiā, nihil te fugiet. Cic.
Such is your prudence, nothing will escape you.

o

455   The rules for the use of qui with Indicative or Conjunctive apply also to the Relative particles **quo** (*whither*), **qua** (*where, in what way*), **ubi** (*where*), **unde** (*whence*).

> Locus, quo exercitui aditus non erat. Caes.
> *A place whither there was no approach for the army.*
> Colles, unde erat despectus in mare. Caes.
> *The hills, from which there was a view over the sea.*
> Qua ducitis, adsum. Verg.
> *Where you lead, I am present.*
> Ne illi sit cera, ubi facere possit litteras. Plau'
> *Let him have no wax on which to write.*

A clause introduced by a Relative particle may be adverbial, unless the clause distinctly qualifies a noun in the Principal Sentence :

> Antonius quo se verteret non habebat. Cic.
> *Antony had no place whither he could turn.*

456   *Note.*—Qui with the Conjunctive sometimes limits a statement : quod sciam, *so far as I know* ; omnium, quos quidem cognoverim, *of all those at least whom I have known.*

457   *Note.*—The Relative is often used at the beginning of a Principal Sentence to show the connexion with something which has gone before ; quo facto, *this being done* ; quā de causā, *for which reason* ; quod dicis, *as to that which you say.*

ORATIO OBLIQUA.

458   Oratio Obliqua is used in reports, whether short or long, of speeches, letters, &c. Indirect Statement, Command, and Question are often contained in the report of one speech by historians, especially by Caesar, Livy, and Tacitus.

459   In **Indirect Statement** the Principal Verbs are changed from the Indicative to the Infinitive in the same tense :

Direct.	*Indirect.*
Romulus urbem condidit.	Narrant Romulum urbem condidisse.
Romulus founded the city.	*They say that Romulus founded the city.*

460   *Note.*—If the actual words of the speaker or writer are quoted, they are often introduced with **inquit**, *he says,* following the first word :

> Romulus haec precatus, 'hinc,' inquit, 'Romani, Juppiter iterare pugnam jubet.' Liv.
> *When Romulus had thus prayed, 'Hence,' he says, 'Romans, Jupiter commands (you) to renew the battle.'*

461 In **Indirect Commands**, the Conjunctive (usually in the Imperfect, but sometimes in the Present Tense) takes the place of the Imperative of Direct Commands :

Direct.	*Indirect.*
Ite, inquit, create consules ex plebe.	(Hortatus est:) irent crearent consules ex plebe.
Go, he says, and elect consuls from the plebs.	

462 In **Indirect Questions** in the Second Person, the Verbs are in the Conjunctive (usually in the Imperfect or Pluperfect Tense, but sometimes in the Present or Perfect) :

Direct.	*Indirect.*
Quid agis? inquit. Cur non antea pugnam commisisti?	Quid ageret? Cur non antea pugnam commisisset?
What are you about? he says. Why have you not joined battle before?	

463 Indirect Questions in the First or Third Person are generally expressed by the Accusative and Infinitive :

Direct.	*Indirect.*
Cur ego pro hominibus ignavis sanguinem profudi? Num semper hostes ad pugnam cessabunt?	Cur se pro hominibus ignavis sanguinem profudisse? Num semper hostes ad pugnam cessaturos?
Why have I shed my blood for cowards? Will the enemy always be slow to fight?	

464 The Pronouns ego, me, nos, meus, noster of Oratio Recta are converted in Oratio Obliqua into se, suus; tu, te, vos, tuus, vester, are converted into ille, illum, illi, illos, illius, illorum :

Ego te pro hoste habebo; socii quoque nostri amicitiam tuam exuent.	Se illum pro hoste habiturum; socios quoque suos illius amicitiam exuturos.
I shall regard you as an enemy; our allies also will throw off your friendship.	

* Such Questions are really Statements put for rhetorical effect in an Interrogative form. 'Why have I shed my blood for cowards?' means, 'I have shed my blood for cowards—why?' I have shed my blood for cowards to no purpose. 'Will the enemy always be slow to fight?' means, 'The enemy will not always be slow to fight.'

The Reflexive Pronoun, **se suus,** in Compound Sentences is often used to refer, not to the Subject of the Principal Sentence (316), but to the Subject of the Clause in which it stands :

465

Nervios hortatur ne sui liberandi occasionem dimittant. CAES.

He urges the Nervii that they should not lose the opportunity of freeing themselves.

Rex supplicem monuit ut consuleret sibi.

The king warned the suppliant that he should take heed to himself.

Sometimes **ipse** is used for the sake of clear distinction. Caesar asked the soldiers :— ·

466

Quid tandem vererentur aut cur de sua virtute aut de ipsius diligentia desperarent? CAES.

What cause had they to fear, why did they despair either of their own bravery or of his carefulness ?

SUBORDINATE CLAUSES IN ORATIO OBLIQUA.

Substantival Clauses may have Clauses subordinate to them ; if the Verb in such Clauses is Finite, it is generally in the Conjunctive Mood, and the construction is called Suboblique.

This construction is seen in the following examples :

467

Caesar ad me scripsit gratissimum sibi esse quod quieverim. CIC.

Caesar has written to me that it is very pleasing to him that I have remained quiet.

Ais, quoniam sit natura mortalis, immortalem etiam esse oportere. CIC.

You say that, since there is a mortal nature, there must also be an immortal one.

Quotiens patriam videret, totiens se beneficium meum videre dixit. CIC.

He said that, as often as he saw his country, so often did he see my service.

Sapientissimum esse dicunt eum, cui, quod opus sit, ipsi veniat in mentem; proxime accedere illum, qui alterius bene inventis obtemperet. CIC.

They say that the wisest man is he to whose mind whatever is needful occurs : that the next to him is he who turns to account

Note 1.—A Relative Clause in Oratio Obliqua, if added merely by way of explanation, may be in the Indicative :

> Xerxem certiorem feci id agi ut pons, quem in Hellesponto fecerat, dissolveretur. NEP.
>
> *I sent Xerxes word that a plot was being arranged that the bridge (which he had made over the Hellespont) might be broken down.*

The words '*which he had made over the Hellespont*' were not part of the message to Xerxes, but are added by the writer for explanation.

Note 2.—Dum, *while*, is used with the Indicative, even in Oratio Obliqua :

468
> Vident se, dum libertatem sectantur, in servitutem prolapsos.
>
> *They see that, while striving for liberty, they have themselves fallen into slavery.*

A Finite Verb subordinate to a Conjunctive is usually in the Conjunctive :

> Miraris si nemo praestet quem non merearis amorem? HOR.
>
> *Are you surprised if no one shows you the love which you do not deserve ?*

469
> Utinam tunc essem natus quando Romani dona accipere coepissent. SALL.
>
> *Would that I had been born when the Romans began to receive gifts.*

A Clause may be virtually oblique, with the Verb in the Conjunctive (Virtual Oratio Obliqua), when it contains the speaker's statement of another person's words or opinions, for which he does not make himself responsible. If the speaker made the statement his own, as being one of fact, the Verb would be in the Indicative :

> Laudat Africanum Panaetius quod fuerit abstinens. CIC.
>
> *Panaetius praises Africanus because (as he says) he was temperate.*

> Caesar Haeduos frumentum, quod polliciti essent, flagitabat. CAES.
>
> *Caesar demanded of the Haedui the corn which (he reminded them) they had promised.*

> Themistocles noctu ambulabat, quod somnum capere non posset. CIC.
>
> *Themistocles used to walk at night because (as he said) he could not sleep.*

> Alium rogantes regem misere ad Jovem,
> Inutilis quoniam esset qui fuerat datus. PHAEDR.
>
> *They (the frogs) sent envoys to Jupiter to ask for another king,*

470

NARRATIVE IN ORATIO OBLIQUA.

Direct Statement.

(1) Ars earum rerum est quae sciuntur; oratoris autem omnis actio opinionibus, non scientia, continetur; nam et apud eos dicimus qui nesciunt, et ea dicimus quae nescimus ipsi. CIC.

Art belongs to the things which are known; but the whole sphere of an orator is in opinion, not in knowledge; for we both speak in the presence of those who know not, and speak of that which we ourselves know not.

(2) Cum Germanis Haedui semel atque iterum armis contenderunt; magnam calamitatem pulsi acceperunt, omnem nobilitatem, omnem equitatum amiserunt. Sed pejus victoribus Sequanis quam Haeduis victis accidit; propterea quod Ariovistus, rex Germanorum, in eorum finibus consedit, tertiamque partem agri Sequani, qui est optimus totius Galliae, occupavit. Ariovistus barbarus, iracundus, temerarius est, non possunt ejus imperia diutius sustineri.

Indirect Statement.

(Antonius apud Ciceronem docet:)
Artem earum rerum esse
    quae sciantur;
oratoris autem omnem actionem
    opinione, non scientia, contineri;
    quia et apud eos dicat
        qui nesciant:
    et ea dicat
        quae ipse nesciat.
(*Antonius teaches in Cicero:*)
*That art belongs to the things
    which are known;*
*but that the whole sphere of an orator
    is in opinion, not in knowledge;*
*because he both speaks before those
        who know not;*
    *and speaks of that
        which he himself knows not.*
Locutus est pro Haeduis Divitiacus: Cum Germanis Haeduos semel atque iterum armis contendisse; magnam calamitatem pulsos accepisse, omnem nobilitatem, omnem equitatum amisisse. Sed pejus victoribus Sequanis quam Haeduis victis accidisse; propterea quod Ariovistus, rex Germanorum, in eorum finibus consedisset, tertiamque partem agri Sequani, qui esset optimus totius Galliae, occupavisset. Ariovistum esse barbarum, iracundum, temerarium, non posse ejus imperia diutius sustineri.

The Haedui have repeatedly fought with the Germans; they have been defeated and have suffered great misfortune; they have lost all their nobles and all their cavalry. But worse has befallen the conquering Sequani than the conquered Haedui, for Ariovistus, king of the Germans, has settled in their dominions and occupied a third part of their territory, which is the best in all Gaul. Ariovistus is barbarous, passionate and violent; his commands can no longer be endured.

Divitiacus said on behalf of the Haedui: 'That the Haedui had fought repeatedly with the Germans; that, having been defeated, they had suffered great misfortune (and) had lost all their nobles, all their cavalry. But that worse had befallen the conquering Sequani than the conquered Haedui, for Ariovistus, king of the Germans, had settled in their dominions and had occupied a third part of their territory, which was the best in all Gaul. Ariovistus was barbarous, passionate, violent; his commands could no longer be endured.'

(3) Consules scripta ad Caesarem mandata remittunt, quorum haec erat summa:

'In Galliam revertere, Arimino excede, exercitus dimitte; quae si feceris, Pompeius in Hispanias ibit.'

In Galliam reverteretur, Arimino excederet, exercitus dimitteret; quae si fecisset, Pompeium in Hispanias iturum.

The Consuls sent back to Caesar written instructions, of which this was the sum total: 'Return into Gaul, quit Ariminum, and disband your armies; when you have done these things, Pompey will go into Spain.'

(4) Thrasybulus, cum exercitus triginta tyrannorum fugeret, magna voce exclamat:

'Cur me victorem fugitis? Civium hanc mementote aciem, non hostium esse; triginta ego dominis, non civitati, bellum infero.'

Cur se victorem fugiant? Civium illam meminerint aciem, non hostium esse; triginta se dominis, non civitati, bellum inferre.

Thrasybulus, when the army of the thirty tyrants was in flight, cried aloud: 'Why do you fly from me as your conqueror? Remember that this is an army of fellow-citizens, not of foreign enemies; I am waging war on the thirty tyrants, not on the community.'

(5) Oro vos, Veientes (inquit), ne me extorrem egentem, ex tanto modo regno cum liberis adolescentibus ante oculos vestros perire sinatis. Alii peregre in regnum Romam acciti sunt; ego rex, augens bello Romanum imperium, a proximis scelerata conjuratione pulsus sum. Patriam regnumque meum repetere, et persequi ingratos cives volo. Ferte opem, adjuvate; vestras quoque veteres injurias ultum ite, totiens caesas legiones, agrum ademptum.

I entreat you, men of Veii (said Tarquin), not to let me with my young children die before your eyes, banished in destitution from a kingdom lately so great. Others were fetched to Rome from abroad to reign. I, their king, while enlarging by war the Roman empire, was expelled by a wicked conspiracy of my nearest kinsmen. I wish to reclaim my country and my kingdom, and to punish ungrateful citizens. Give me help, assist me: hasten to avenge also your own old wrongs, your legions so often slaughtered, your land taken from you.

Orat Tarquinius Veientes ne se extorrem egentem ex tanto modo regno cum liberis adolescentibus ante oculos suos perire sinerent: alios peregre in regnum Romam accitos; se regem augentem bello Romanum imperium, a proximis scelerata conjuratione pulsum:.. patriam se regnumque suum repetere et persequi ingratos cives velle: ferrent opem, adjuvarent; suas quoque veteres injurias ultum irent, totiens caesas legiones, agrum ademptum. Liv.

PROSODY.

PROSODY treats of the Quantity of Syllables and the Laws of Metre.

I. GENERAL RULES OF QUANTITY.

1. A syllable is short when it contains a short vowel followed by a simple consonant or by another vowel : as păter, dĕus.

2. A syllable is long when it contains a long vowel or diphthong: frātĕr, cāedēs, nēmo.

3. A vowel short by nature becomes long by position when it is followed by two consonants, or by x or z : cānto, sīmplēx, orȳza.

Exception.—A short vowel before a mute followed by a liquid becomes doubtful : lugŭbre, tenĕbrae, trĭplex.

4. A long vowel or diphthong becomes short before another vowel, or before *h* followed by a vowel : prŏavus, trăho, prăĕesse.

But in Greek words the vowel or diphthong keeps its length: āer, Aenēas, Enȳo, Melibŏēus.

Exceptions.—In fīo, Gāius, Pompēi, dīus, diēi, Rhëa (Silvia), the vowel remains long.

> *Note.*—Prăe in compounds is the only Latin word in which a diphthong occurs before a vowel.

5. A syllable is called doubtful when it is found in poetry to be sometimes long, sometimes short : Dĭana, fidĕi, rĕi, and genitives in -ius, as illĭus, except alīus, alterīus.

6. The quantity of a stem syllable is kept, as a rule, in compounds and derivatives : cădo occĭdo, rătus irrĭtus, flūmĕn flūmĭneus.

Exceptions to this rule are numerous, lūceo, lŭcerna.

472 II. RULE FOR MONOSYLLABLES.

Most monosyllables are long : dā, dēs, mē, vēr, sī, sīs, sōl, nōs, tū, vīr, mūs.

Exceptions :

Substantives : cŏr, fĕl, mĕl, ŏs (*bone*), vĭr.

Pronouns : ĭs, ĭd, quă (*any*), quĭs, quĭd, quŏd, quŏt, tŏt.

Verbs : dăt, dĕt, ĭt, scĭt, sĭt, stăt, stĕt, făc, fĕr, ĕs (from sum).

Particles : ăb, ăd, ăn, ăt, bĭs, cĭs, ĕt, ĭn, nĕc, ŏb, pĕr, pŏl, săt, sĕd, sŭb, ŭt, vĕl.

and the enclitics -nĕ, -quĕ, -vĕ.

III. Rules for Final Syllables.

1. A final is short.

473

Exceptions.—Ablatives of decl. 1. mensā, bonā; Vocative of Greek names in **as**, Aeneā; and of some in **es**, Anchisā; Indeclinable Numerals, trigintā; Imperatives of conj. 1. amā (but pută); most Particles in **a**; frustrā, intereā (but ită, quiă, short).

2. E final is short: legĕ, timetĕ, carerĕ.

Exceptions.—Ablatives of declension 5. rē, diē, with the derivatives quarē, hodiē. Cases of many Greek nouns; also famē. Adverbs formed from Adjectives; miserē; also ferē, fermē (but benĕ, malĕ, facilĕ, impunĕ, temĕrĕ, short). Imperatives of conj. 2. monē (but cavĕ is doubtful). Also the Interjection ohē.

3. I final is long: dicī, plebī, dolī.

Exceptions.—Vocatives and Datives of Greek nouns; Chlorĭ, Thyrsidĭ; but Datives sometimes long: Paridī. Particles; sicubĭ, necubĭ, nisĭ, quasĭ. Mihĭ, tibĭ, sibĭ, ubĭ, and ibĭ are doubtful.

4. O final is long: virgō, multō, juvō.

Exceptions.—Duŏ, octŏ, egŏ, modŏ, citŏ, and a few verbs: putŏ, sciŏ, nesciŏ. In the Silver age o was often shortened in Verbs and Nouns.

5. U final is long: cantū, dictū, diū.

6. Finals in c are long: illīc; except nĕc and donĕc.

7. Finals in l, d, t are short: Hannibăl, illŭd, amavĭt.

8. Finals in n are short: Iliŏn, agmĕn.

Exceptions.—Many Greek words: Hymēn, Ammōn.

9. Finals in r are short: calcăr, amabitŭr, Hectŏr.

Exceptions.—Many Greek words: aēr, cratēr; and compounds of pār: dispār, impār.

10. Finals in as are long: terrās, Menalcās.

Exceptions.—Greek nouns of decl. 3. Arcăs (gen. -ădis) and acc. pl. lampadăs; anăs, *a duck*.

11. Finals in ēs are long: nubēs, viderēs.

Exceptions.—Cases of Greek nouns: Arcadĕs, Naĭadĕs. Nominatives of a few substantives and adjectives with dental stems in ĕt, ĭt, or ĭd: segĕs, pedĕs, obsĕs; also penĕs. Compounds of ĕs: adĕs, potĕs.

12. Finals in is are short: dicerĭs, utilĭs, ensĭs.

Exceptions.—Datives and Ablatives in īs, including gratīs, forīs. Accusatives in īs: navīs; some Greek Nouns in īs: Salamīs. Sanguĭs, pulvĭs, are doubtful. 2nd Pers. Sing. Pres. Ind. conj. 4. audīs; compounds of vīs, sīs; also velīs, malīs, nolīs. In 2nd Pers. Sin . Fut. Perf. the ending is doubtful: dixerĭs.

13. Finals in **os** are long: ventōs, custōs, sacerdōs.

> *Exceptions.*—Greek words in ŏs (os): Delŏs, Arcadŏs; also compŏs, impŏs, exŏs.

14. Finals in **us** are short: holŭs, intŭs, amamŭs.

> *Exceptions.*—Nominatives from long stems of decl. 3. are long: virtūs, tellūs, incūs, juventūs; the contracted cases of decl. 4.: artūs, gradūs; and a few Greek words: Didūs, Sapphūs (genitive).

15. The Greek words chely̆s, Tiphy̆s, Eriny̆s have the final syllable short and the vocative ending y̆.

474

IV. On the Laws of Metre.

A Verse (versus, *line*) is composed of a certain number of Feet.

A Foot consists of two or more syllables, of which one has the ictus or principal accent, said to be in **arsis**; the other syllable or syllables are said to be in **thĕsis**.

The principal feet in Latin poetry are the following:

Iambus, one short and one long syllable (˘‐), cărō.

Trochee, one long and one short syllable (‐˘), ārmă.

Dactyl, one long and two short syllables (‐˘˘), lītŏră.

Anapaest, two short and one long syllable (˘˘‐), pătŭlāē.

Spondee, two long syllables (‐‐), fātō.

Tribrach, three short syllables (˘˘˘), tĕmĕrĕ.

The Spondee often takes the place of the Dactyl in Dactylic verse. It may also take the place of the Iambus or Trochee in certain parts of an Iambic or Trochaic verse.

The Tribrach can take the place of the Iambus or the Trochee in any place but the last, but is more rarely used.

> *Note.*—A short syllable in versification constitutes one ' mora,' or ' time.' A long syllable (= two short) constitutes two 'morae,' or ' times.'

The Iambus, Trochee, Tribrach are feet of three ' times;' Dactyl, Anapaest, Spondee, are feet of four ' times.'

A vowel is cut off at the end of a word if there be a vowel at the beginning of the next word: ' Phyllĭd' ăm' ant' ăliās,' for ' Phyllida amo ante alias;' this is called Elision (Synaloepha).

A vowel and **m** are cut off at the end of a word if there be a vowel at the beginning of the next word: ' Ō cūras hŏmĭn'—Ō quant'—est in rēbŭs inane,' for ' hominum,' ' quantum.' This is called Ecthlipsis.

A vowel unelided in such a position is said to be in Hiatus.

Tēr sūnt|cōnā|tĭ īm|pōnĕrĕ|Pēliŏ|Ossam.

475

V. Metre and Rhythm.

A. Metre (metrum, *measure*) is used in two different senses.

    i. It means any system of versification : which may take its name either (1) from the Foot which prevails in it : Dactylic (Iambic, Trochaic, Anapaestic) metre ; or (2) from the subjects of which it treats : Heroic (Elegiac) metre ; or (3) from the musical instrument to which it was sung : Lyric metres ; or (4) from the poet who is said to have invented or chiefly used it : Alcaic metre (from Alcaeus), Sapphic (from Sappho), etc.

    ii. Some part of a Verse is called ' a metre.' In Dactylic and some other verses each foot constitutes ' a metre.' In Iambic, Trochaic, and Anapaestic verses, two feet constitute ' a metre.'

Note.—Hence a verse gains a name from the number of such metres.

A verse with two metres is called Dimeter.

,,	,,	three	,,	,,	Trimeter.
,,	,,	four	,,	,,	Tetrameter.
,,	,,	five	,,	,,	Pentameter.
,,	,,	six	,,	,,	Hexameter.

A verse which has its metres complete is said to be acatalectic (unclipt). If its metres are incomplete, it is catalectic (clipt).

476

B.—Harmonious order of words is called Rhythm. Prose has rhythm as well as verse ; but that of verse is called Poetic Rhythm. The dividing of a verse according to rhythm is called scanning or scansion. The method of scansion may be shown by two Dactylic Hexameters of Vergil :

     1   2   3   4   5   6

(a) Tītўrĕ | tū ‖ pătŭ|lae ‖ rĕcŭ|bāns ‖ sūb | tēgmĭnĕ | fāgī

(b) Fōrmō|sām ‖ rĕsŏ|nārĕ ‖ dŏ|cēs ‖ Amă|rўllĭdă | sīlvās.

    Note.—The numerals and single strokes show the six feet or metres of the Hexameter.

Caesura means the division of a word before the ending of a foot. There are three caesuras in each of the verses (a), (b), marked by a short double stroke. A verse without caesura is unrhythmical and inadmissible. Caesura after a long syllable is called strong, and is most frequent. Caesura after a short syllable is called weak, as that in the third foot of (b) after -nărĕ. (See ' Dactylic Hexameter.') The ending of word and foot together is called Dialysis :—Tityre, tegmine.

VI. Dactylic, Iambic and some Lyric Systems of Verse.

477

A. **Dactylic Hexameter :**

This Metre has six feet. The first four may be Dactyls or Spondees. The fifth must be a Dactyl (rarely a Spondee). The sixth a Spondee or Trochee (the last syllable in a verse being doubtful).

Scheme.

478   1   2   3   4   5   6

$$-\cup\cup \mid -\cup\cup \mid -\cup\cup \mid -\cup\cup \mid -\cup\cup \mid -\cup$$
$$- - \mid - - \mid - - \mid - - \mid \mid - -$$

(See the Examples, *a*, *b*, 476).

Note.—A verse called Hypermeter (a syllable over-measure) is occasionally found, the syllable in excess being elided before the initial vowel of the next line:

Āerĕă cuī grădĭbūs sūrgēbānt līmĭnă nēxāē|que
Āerĕ trābēs . . .

The Caesura by far most common in Dactylic Hexameters is that in the third foot (called Penthemimeral), which is generally strong, as in (*a*) after patulae, but occasionally weak, as in (*b*) after resonare.

Next in importance is that in the fourth foot, called Hephthemimeral, which is sometimes the chief caesura of the verse: as

(*c*) clāmōr|ēs sĭmŭl | hōrrēn|dŏs ‖ ād | sīdĕră | tōllit.

The Trihemimeral Caesura in the second foot often contributes to the rhythm usefully, as after clamores (*c*).

Note.—Hemimeris means 'a half.' Hence 'Trihemimeral' means 'after three half-feet': cla-mor-es; 'Penthemimeral' means 'after five half-feet': hic il-lum vi-di; 'Hephthemimeral' means 'after seven half-feet': quam Juno fertur terris. This notation counts two short syllables as one half-foot: Tītўrĕ tū *pătŭ*-lae *rĕcŭ*-bans.

The Heroic Measure of Epic poets, Vergil, Lucan, &c., consists of Dactylic Hexameters only.

B. **Dactylic Pentameter:**

This Verse consists of two parts, called Penthemimers, which are kept distinct. The first Penthemimer contains two feet (Dactyls or Spondees) and a long syllable. The second contains also two feet (both Dactyls) and a long syllable.

Scheme.

1   2   1   2

479
$$-\cup\cup \mid -\cup\cup \mid - \; \| \; -\cup\cup \mid -\cup\cup \mid -$$
$$- - \mid - - \mid$$

Example.

tū dŏmĭ|nūs tū|vīr ‖ tū mĭhĭ | frătĕr ĕ|rās.

This Verse is not used alone, but follows an Hexameter in the Elegiac Distich:

Dōnĕc ĕrīs fēlīx, mūltōs nŭmĕrābĭs ămīcos,
Tēmpŏră sī fŭĕrīnt nūbĭlă, sōlŭs ĕris.

The chief Elegiac poets are Ovid, Tibullus, and Propertius.

C. **Iambic Trimeter or Senarius:**

This Metre has six feet. Each may be an Iambus:

Sŭĭs | ĕt ī|psă Rō|mă vī|rĭbūs | rŭit.

But a Spondee may stand in the first, third, and fifth foot; and (rarely) a Dactyl or Anapaest in the first. A Tribrach sometimes takes the place of an Iambus, except in the two last feet.

Scheme.

Examples.

lăbūn|tŭr āl|tĭs ‖ ĭn|tĕrīm | rīpīs | ăquae.
Cănĭdī|ă brĕvī|bŭs ‖ īm|plĭcā|tă vī|pĕris.
pŏsĭtōs|quĕ vēr|nās ‖ dī|tĭs ĕx|āmēn | dŏmus.

The usual Caesura is after the first syllable of the third foot. Another less usual, is after the first syllable of the fourth foot; as,

Ĭbē|rĭcīs | pĕrūs|tĕ ‖ fū|nĭbūs | lătus.

The Trimeter may form a distinct measure.

480 *D.* **Iambic Dimeter:**

This Verse leaves out the third and fourth feet of the Trimeter, with which it is used to form an Iambic Distich:

481
pătēr|nă rū|ră bō|bŭs ēx|ērcēt | sŭis,
sŏlū|tŭs ōm|nī fē|nŏre.

Horace uses this Distich oftener in his Epodes than any other measure.

E. Strophic Metres:

The lyric poets Horace and Catullus have used more than twenty metres. But we shall notice here only the Sapphic and Alcaic Stanzas, each of four lines.

> *Note.*—Anacrusis is a short or long syllable, which introduces the scansion of a verse.

Base is a foot of two syllables (Spondee, Iambus or Trochee) which introduces the scansion.

These may be represented in English:

Anacrusis 1   2   3
O | Mari|on's a | bonnie | lass

Base   1   2   3
O my | Mari|on's a | bonnie | lass

A double base means two feet, each of two syllables, introducing the scansion.

1. The Sapphic Stanza:

The Stanza is scientifically scanned in Latin by three verses of this form:

482
Double Base   Dactyl   Trochee   Trochee

$$- \smile - - \parallel - \smile \smile \mid - \smile \mid - \bar{\smile}$$

followed by a verse called Adonius,

Dactyl   Trochee

$$- \smile \smile \mid - \bar{\smile}$$

1. Tērrŭīt gēn|tēs grăvĕ | nē rĕ|dīret
2. Saēcŭlŭm Pўr|rhaē nŏvă | mōnstră | quēstae
3. Ōmnĕ cŭm Prō|tēūs pĕcŭs | ēgĭt | āltos
4.   Vīsĕrĕ | mōntes.

Sappho used two Trochees as the double base; but Latin poets always lengthened the fourth syllable.

The strong Caesura after the fifth syllable is most frequent, but the weak Caesura after the sixth is occasionally used for variety.

        Nōn sĕmēl dīcēmŭs ‖ Ĭō trĭūmphe.

The Adonian verse is so closely united with the third line that Hiatus at the close of this line is unusual, and words are sometimes divided between the two:

        Thrācĭō bācchāntĕ măgīs sŭb ĭnter-
                            lūnĭă vēnto.

Note.—A Hypermeter also occurs (**477**, *note*).

483   Dīssĭdēns plēbī nŭmĕrō bĕātō | rum
                Ēxĭmĭt vīrtūs.

2. The Alcaic Stanza:

Anacr.   Double Base   Dactyl   Troch.
1.
2. $\bar{\smile} \mid - \smile - - \parallel - \smile \smile \mid - \smile \mid \smile$

Anacr.   Troch.   Spond.   Troch.   Troch.
3. $\smile \mid - \bar{\smile} \mid - - \mid - \smile \mid - \smile$

4. $- \smile \smile \mid - \smile \smile \mid - \smile \mid - \smile$

1. Quī | rōrĕ pūrō | Cāstălī | aē lă|vĭt
2. Crī|nēs sŏlūtōs | quī Lўcĭ|aē tĕ|net
3.   Dū|mētă | nātă|lēmquĕ | sīlvam
4.   Dēlĭŭs | ēt Pătă|reus Ă|pōllŏ.

Rules for the Rhythm of the Alcaic Stanza.

(a) *First and Second Lines.*

(1) A short syllable at the beginning is rare.

(2) The fifth syllable generally ends a word ; but an Elision often occurs after it : as

Quō Stӯx ĕt īnvīs|ĭ hōrrĭdă Taēnărĭ.

(3) The fifth and the last syllables are rarely monosyllables.

(b) *Third Line.*

(1) The first syllable is seldom short.

(2) The line rarely begins with a word of four syllables, and only when Elision follows : as

Fūnālĭa ēt vēctēs ĕt ārçus.

never with two dissyllables.

(3) The line should not end with a word of four syllables : rarely with two dissyllables.

(4) No monosyllable should end the line except (rarely) et or in, with an Elision :

Cūm flōrĕ Maēcēnās rŏsārum, et
Īncūdĕ dīffīngās rĕtūsum in

(c) *Fourth Line.*

(1) If the first Dactyl ends a word, the second should end in the middle of a word.

(2) A weak Caesura in the second Dactyl should be avoided, but is sometimes justified by the sense of the passage :

Jūppĭtĕr īpsĕ rŭēns tŭmūltu.
Stēsĭchŏrīqŭe grăvēs Cămēnae.

Note.—Hypermeters occur only twice in Horace :

Sōrs ēxĭtūra, ēt nōs ĭn aēter|num
Ēxĭlĭum īmpŏsĭtūră çӯmbae.
Cūm pācĕ dēlăbēntĭs Etru|scum
Ĭn mărĕ.

But in his third and fourth books he avoids ending a verse with a vowel or m before a verse in the same stanza beginning with a vowel.

APPENDIX I.

DERIVED AND COMPOUNDED WORDS.

SUBSTANTIVES are derived from Verbs, Adjectives and other Substantives. The chief classes of Substantives derived from Verbs are the following :—

From the Verb-Stem:

With Suffix

-a, denoting the agent: scriba, *notary* (scribo); advena, *new comer* (ad-venio); conviva, *guest* (con-vivo).

-or, abstract words denoting action or feeling: amor, *love* (amo); timor, *fear* (timeo); clamor, *outcry* (clamo); terror, *terror* (terreo).

-ium, denoting action or effect: gaudium, *joy* (gaudeo); ingenium, *mind* (ingigno); judicium, *judgment* (judico, for jus-dico); naufragium, *shipwreck* (naufragio, formed from the Stems of navis, *ship*, and frango, *break*).

-ies, denoting a thing formed: acies, *line of battle* (aceo); facies, *face, form* (facio); effigies, *likeness* (effingo); species, *appearance* (specio); series, *order* (sero).

-es: sedes, *seat* (sedeo); nubes, *cloud* (nubo).

io, denoting the thing acted on: regio, *region* (rego); legio, *legion* (lego); opinio, *opinion* (opinor).

-men, denoting the instrument or the thing done: agmen, *column* (ago); tegmen, *covering* (tego); unguen, *ointment* (unguo).

-mentum: documentum, *document* (doceo); instrumentum, *instrument* (instruo).

bulum, -brum, denoting the instrument or object: vocabulum, *name* (voco); venabulum, *hunting-spear* (venor); flabrum, *blast* (flo, Stem fla-).

-culum, -crum: curriculum, *course* (curro); spectaculum, *spectacle* (specto); sepulcrum, *tomb* (sepelio).

-ile, denoting the instrument: sedile, *seat* (sedeo); cubile, *couch* (cubo).

From the Supine Stem:

-tor, -sor, denoting the agent: arator, *ploughman* (aro); auctor, *author* (augeo); victor, *victor* (vinco); auditor, *hearer* (audio); dictator, *dictator* (dicto); sponsor, *surety* (spondeo); cursor, *runner* (curro). A few Nouns in -tor form a feminine in -trix, as victrix.

P

With Suffix

-tus, -sus, denoting action : eventus, *event* (e-venio) ; motus, *motion,* (moveo) ; sonitus, *sound* (sono) ; cursus, *running* (curro) ; plausus, *clapping* (plaudo) ; lusus, *game* (ludo).

-tura, -sura, denoting function or result of action : dictatura, *dictatorship* (dicto) ; cultura, *culture* (colo) ; pictura, *picture* (pingo) ; tonsura, *tonsure* (tondeo) ; caesura, *dividing* (caedo).

-tio, -sio, abstract : actio, *action* (ago) ; cogitatio, *thought* (cogito) ; relatio, *relation* (refero) ; visio, *sight* (video) ; pensio, *payment* (pendo).

Substantives derived from Adjectives :

-ia : memoria, *memory* (memor) ; concordia, *peace* (concors) ; sapientia, *wisdom* (sapiens) ; divitiae, pl., *riches* (dives).

-itia : laetitia, *joyfulness* (laetus) ; amicitia, *friendship* (amicus) ; mollitia, also mollities, *softness* (mollis).

-tas : libertas, *freedom* (liber) ; veritas, *truth* (verus) ; felicitas, *happiness* (felix).

-tudo : fortitudo, *valour* (fortis) ; multitudo, *multitude* (multus).

-monia : acrimonia, *sharpness* (acer) ; sanctimonia, *sanctity* (sanctus) ; parcimonia, *parsimony* (parcus).

Substantives derived from Substantives :

-tor : viator, *traveller* (via) ; janitor, *doorkeeper* (janua) ; balneator, *bath-keeper* (balneum). The feminines janitrix, balneatrix are used.

-atus : senatus, *senate* (senex) ; magistratus, *magistracy* (magister) ; consulatus, *consulship* (consul).

-io, -o : ludio, *player* (ludus) ; pellio, *furrier* (pellis) ; centurio, *captain of a hundred* (centum, centuria) ; praedo, *robber* (praeda).

-arius : aquarius, *water-carrier* (aqua) ; tabularius, *registrary* (tabula). A secondary derivative is tabellarius, *letter-carrier* (tabella).

-arium : granarium, *granary* (granum) ; tabularium, *archives* (tabula).

-etum, -tum : olivetum, *olive-grove* (oliva) ; rosetum, *rose-garden* (rosa) ; arbustum, *shrubbery;* also the later form arboretum (stem arbos-, arbor-) ; salictum, *willow-ground* (salix).

-ina, -inum : textrina, *weaver's shop* (textor) ; pistrinum, *bakehouse* (pistor).

-ulus -olus, -a, -um : anulus, *little ring* (annus) ; gladiolus, *little sword* (gladius) ; formula, *little form* (forma) ; lineola, *little line* (linea) ; scutulum, *little shield* (scutum) ; palliolum, *little cloak* (pallium).

-ellus, -a, -um : agellus, *small field* (ager) ; fabella, *short story* (fabula) ; flagellum, *little whip* (flagrum) ; corolla, *chaplet* (corona).

-culus, -a, um : versiculus, *little verse* (versus) ; matercula, *little mother* (mater) ; reticulum, *little net* (rete).

Adjectives derived from Verbs:

With Suffix ·

-**ax**: audax, *daring* (audeo); rapax, *grasping* (rapio); tenax, *tenacious* (teneo); ferax, *fruitful* (fero).

-**bundus, -cundus**: furibundus, *raging* (furo); moribundus, *dying* (morior); jucundus, *pleasant* (juvo).

-**uus**: continuus, *continuous* (con-tineo); vacuus, *empty* (vacuo); assiduus, *persevering* (assideo).

-**ulus**: tremulus, *trembling* (tremo); querulus, *complaining* (queror); credulus, *trustful* (credo).

-**idus, -idis**: calidus, *hot* (caleo); pavidus, *timid* (paveo); viridis, *green* (vireo).

-**ilis**: utilis, *useful* (utor); facilis, *easy* (facio); docilis, *teachable* (doceo).

-**bilis**: penetrabilis, *penetrable* (penetro); flebilis, *lamentable* (fleo); but sometimes active; penetrabile frigus, *penetrating cold.*

-**ivus**, joined to the Supine Stem: captivus, *captive* (capio); nativus, *native* (nascor); fugitivus, *fugitive* (fugio).

Adjectives derived from Nouns:

-**ius**: regius, *royal* (rex); plebeius, *plebeian* (plebs); egregius, *out of the common* (grex).

-**icus**: bellicus, *warlike* (bellum); barbaricus, *barbarous* (barbarus); Gallicus, *Gaulish*; civicus, *civic* (civis).

-**ticus**: rusticus, *belonging to the country* (rus); domesticus, *domestic* (domus).

-**anus, -ianus**: humanus, *human* (homo); urbanus, *urban* (urbs); Romanus, *Roman* (Roma); Africanus, *African*; praetorianus, *praetorian* (praetor).

-**nus**: fraternus, *fraternal* (frater); aeternus, *eternal* (aetas); externus, *external* (exter); alternus, *alternate* (alter).

-**inus**: marinus, *marine* (mare); Latinus, *Latin*; palatinus, *belonging to the palace* (palatium).

-**estis**: caelestis, *heavenly* (caelum); agrestis, *rural* (ager).

-**ensis**: forensis, *belonging to the forum*; castrensis, *belonging to the camp* (castra).

-**alis, -aris**: naturalis, *natural* (natura); generalis, *general* (genus); regalis, *kingly* (rex); vulgaris, *common* (vulgus); salutaris, *healthful* (salus). (See 20.)

-**osus**: formosus, *beautiful* (forma); gloriosus, *glorious* (gloria).

-**lentus**: fraudulentus, *deceitful* (fraus); turbulentus, *noisy* (turba).

-**bris, -cris**: funebris, *funereal* (funus); mediocris, *middling* (medius).

-**eus**: aureus, *golden* (aurum); ferreus, *iron* (ferrum).

-**ulus**: parvulus (parvus).

-**ellus**: misellus (miser).

With Suffix

    -tus : modestus, *moderate* (modus) ; robustus, *strong* (robur) ; vetustus, *aged* (vetus).

    -tinus : crastinus, *of to-morrow* (cras) ; diutinus, *lasting* (diu).

DERIVED VERBS.

Verbs derived from Nouns.

A-Stems	curo, *take care* (cura) ; onero, *burden* (onus) ; paco, *pacify* (pax). **Deponents**: moror, *delay* (mora) ; dignor, *deem worthy* (dignus) ; miseror, *pity* (miser).
E-Stems	floreo, *bloom* (flos) ; luceo, *shine* (lux) ; flaveo, *am yellow* (flavus).
U-Stems	metuo, *fear* (metus) ; minuo, *diminish* (minus).
I-Stems	finio, *limit* (finis) ; servio, *am a slave* (servus) ; largior, *bestow* (largus).

VERBS COMPOUNDED WITH PREPOSITIONS.

a, ab, abs-	a-verto, *turn away* ; ab-sum, *am absent* ; abs-terreo, *frighten away.*
ad	ad-eo, *go to* ; ad-spicio, *look at* ; accipio, *accept* ; affero, *carry to* ; alloquor, *address* ; appono, *place near* ; arripio, *seize* ; assentior, *agree* ; attraho, *attract.*
ambi	amb-io, *go around.*
con	con-traho, *contract* ; compono, *compose* ; committo, *commit* ; colligo, *collect* ; corripio, *seize violently* ; confido, *rely on.*
de	de-cedo, *depart* ; decipio, *deceive* ; descendo, *come down.*
e, ex	e-duco, *lead forth* ; e-loquor, *utter* ; e-voco, *evoke* ; effundo, *pour out* ; ex-eo, *go forth* ; ex-pello, *expel.*
in	in-fero, *bring into* ; impero, *command* ; immineo, *overhang* ; illigo, *bind on* ; irrigo, *water* ; induro, *make hard.*
inter	inter-sum, *am among* ; interrogo, *question* ; intellego, *understand.*
ob	ob-tineo, *maintain*; offero, *offer*; oppono, *oppose*; occurro, *meet, occur.*
per	per-mitto, *let go, permit* ; pereo, *perish* ; pelluceo, *shine through, am transparent* ; perterreo, *frighten greatly.*
post	post-pono, *put after.*
prae	prae-cedo, *go before* ; praefero, *prefer* ; praesto, *excel.*
praeter:	praeter-eo, *pass by.*
pro, prod-:	prod-eo, *go or come forth* ; pro-cedo, *proceed* ; pro-pono, *propose* ; promo, *produce.*
red-, re-:	red-eo, *return* ; re-cordor, *remember* ; re-fero, *refer* ; restituo, *restore.*
sed-, se-:	sed-eo, *sit* ; se-cerno, se-paro, *separate* ; se-cludo, *shut up, seclude.*
sub	sub-do, *subdue* ; sub-mergo, *submerge* ; suc-curro, *succour* ; suf-fero, *suffer* ; sug-gero, *suggest* ; sup-plico, *supplicate* ; sur-ripio, *steal* ; suspicio, *look up at, suspect.*
trans, tra-:	trans-mitto, *transmit* ; trans-porto, *transport* ; traduco, *lead across* ; trajicio, *throw across.*

A few Verbs are compounded with Adverbs, as :

benedico, *commend* (bene dico) ; benefacio, *benefit* (bene facio)
maledico, *speak ill (of)* (male dico) ; malefacio, *do evil (to)* (male facio).
satisfacio, *satisfy* (satis facio) ; satisdo, *give bail* (satis do).

The following are a few specimens of compound words :

Noun and Verb.

auceps, *birdcatcher* (avis avi-, capio).
agricola, *husbandman* (ager agro-, colo).
fidicen, *lute-player* ⎰fides fidi- ⎱
tibicen, *flute-player* ⎱tibia tibia- ⎰cano
tubicen, *trumpeter* ⎰tuba tuba- ⎱
artifex, *artisan* (ars arti-, facio).
Lucifer, *morning star* (lux luc-, fero) ; frugifer, -a, -um, *fruit-bearing*
(frux frug-, fero).
Grajŭgĕna, *Greek* (Graius Graio-, gigno).
armiger, *armour-bearer* (arma armo-, gero).
jusjurandum, *oath* (jus-, juro).
senatusconsultum, *decree of the senate* (senatus senatu-, consultum
consulto-, from consulo).

Two Substantives, or Substantive and Adjective.

paterfamilias, *father of a family* (pater, familias, an old genitive).
respublica, *state, republic* (res, publicus).
bipes, *two-footed* (bis, pes).
tridens, *three-pronged, trident* (tres, dens).

APPENDIX II.

ROMAN MONEY, WEIGHTS, MEASURES, AND TIME.

MONEY.

a. The As (Libra), or pound of 12 ounces (unciae), was thus divided :

Uncia	=1 oz. or $\frac{1}{12}$ of the As.			Septunx	=	7 oz. or $\frac{7}{12}$ of the As.		
Sextans	=2	,,	$\frac{1}{6}$	,,	Bes	= 8	,,	$\frac{2}{3}$	,,
Quadrans	=3	,,	$\frac{1}{4}$	,,	Dodrans	= 9	,,	$\frac{3}{4}$	,,
Triens	=4	,,	$\frac{1}{3}$	,,	Dextans	=10	,,	$\frac{5}{6}$	,,
Quincunx	=5	,,	$\frac{5}{12}$	,,	Deunx	=11	,,	$\frac{11}{12}$	,,
Semissis	=6	,,	$\frac{1}{2}$	,,					

b. Unciae usurae = $\frac{1}{12}$ per cent. per month = 1 per cent. per annum.

Sextantes	= $\frac{1}{6}$	,,	,,	= 2	,,	,,
etc.		etc.		etc.	

Asses usurae = 1 per cent. per month = 12 per cent. per annum.

Asses usurae were also called centesimae : binae centesimae = 2 per cent. per month = 24 per cent., probably. Unciarium fenus was 1 uncia yearly per as = $8\frac{1}{3}$ per cent. per annum for the year of 10 months.

c Heres ex asse . . . means heir to the whole estate.

Heres ex semisse, or . $\left.\begin{array}{c} \bullet \\ \bullet \end{array}\right\}$,, heir to $\frac{1}{2}$ of the estate.
Heres ex dimidia parte .
   etc.   etc.

d. The Sestertius (Nummus), or Sesterce, was a silver coin equal to more than 2 asses, being $\frac{1}{4}$ of the Denarius (coin of 10 asses). Its symbol is HS (for IIS., duo et semis, $2\frac{1}{2}$ asses).

The Sestertium (= 1,000 sestertii) was not a coin, but a sum, and is only used in the Plural number.

Sestertia, in the Plural (also represented by HS.) joined with the Cardinal or Distributive Numbers, denotes so many 1,000 sestertii.

The Numeral Adverbs, joined with (or understanding) sestertii (Gen. Sing.), sestertium, or HS., denote so many 100,000 sestertii :

Thus HS.X = Sestertii decem, 10 sesterces.

HS.$\overline{\text{X}}$ = Sestertia decem, 10,000 sesterces.

$\overline{\text{HS.X}}$ = Sestertium deciens, 1,000,000 sesterces

e. Fractions might also be expressed by the Ordinals as Denominators and the Cardinals for Numerators (above 1). Thus, $\frac{1}{2}$ is *dimidia pars*; $\frac{1}{3}$ *tertia pars*, etc.; $\frac{1}{6}$ *sexta* or *dimidia tertia* ($\frac{1}{2} \times \frac{1}{3}$); $\frac{1}{8}$ *octava pars* or *dimidia quarta* ($\frac{1}{2} \times \frac{1}{4}$), etc. So $\frac{1}{21}$ was *tertia septima* ($\frac{1}{3} \times \frac{1}{7}$). Again, $\frac{2}{3}$ is either *duae tertiae*, or *duae partes*, or *dimidia et sexta* ($\frac{1}{2} + \frac{1}{6} = \frac{2}{3}$). And $\frac{3}{4}$ is *tres quartae*, or *tres partes*, or *dimidia et quarta* ($\frac{1}{2} + \frac{1}{4} = \frac{3}{4}$).

WEIGHT.

The unit or 'as' of weight was the 'libra,' or Roman pound (the supposed weight which a man could support on his hand horizontally extended). It was divided duodecimally, the 'uncia' (*ounce*) being its 12th part; the 'scripulum' (*scruple*) the 24th part of an uncia. Some authorities rate the libra at 5·044 English grains nearly.

LENGTH.

The unit or 'as' of length was 'pes' (*foot*), also divided duodecimally, the 'uncia' (*inch*) being its 12th part.

'Cubitus' (*cubit*) was $1\frac{1}{2}$ foot. 'Ulna' (*ell*) was variously measured, sometimes = cubit. Land was measured out by the 'decempeda' (rod of 10 feet). In roads the unit was 'passus,' a pace or double step (5 feet). Mille passus (5,000 feet) were the Roman mile; $\frac{1}{8}$ of which was called 'stadium' (*furlong*). The exact measure of the 'pes' is a difficult point. High authorities make it less than the English foot by $\frac{3}{10}$ of an inch.

SURFACE.

The 'as' of surface was 'jugerum' (the Roman acre), about $\frac{5}{8}$ of an English acre. 'Scripulum,' or 'decempeda quadrata' (ten square feet) was its most important subdivision.

CAPACITY.

1. Liquid measure.

The '·as' was 'sextarius' (less than a pint), divided into 12 'cyathi,' one of which (its 'uncia') was not quite half an ordinary wine-glass. 24 sextarii were 1 'urna,' and 2 urnae were an 'amphora,' a vessel of 10 cubic Roman feet.

2. Dry measure.

Here too the 'as' was 'sextarius' and the 'cyathus' its 'uncia; 16 sextarii made the 'modius,' which approached 2 gallons English ($\frac{1}{4}$ bushel).

TIME.—THE ROMAN CALENDAR.

Every Roman month had three chief days: Kalendae (Calends), Nonae (Nones), Idus (Ides). The Calends were always the 1st day of the month; the Nones were usually on the 5th; the Ides on the 13th; but in four months the Nones were on the 7th, the Ides on the 15th.

March, May, July, October; these are they
Make Nones the 7th, Ides the 15th day.

These three days, the Calends, Nones, and Ides, were taken as points, from which the other days were counted backwards. That is, the Romans did not say, such and such a day *after*, etc., but such and such a day *before* the Calends, or Nones, or Ides. They reckoned inclusively, counting in the days at both ends; therefore the rules are: (1) For days before the Calends subtract the day of the month from the number of days in the month increased by two. (2) For days before the Nones or Ides subtract from the day on which they fall, increased by one.

Examples.—May 31, Pridie Kalendas Junias.
     „   30, Ante diem tertium (a.d. III.) Kal. Jun.
     „   11, „   „   quintum (a.d. V.) Id. Mai.
     „   2, „   „   sextum (a.d. VI.) Non. Mai.

English Month.	MARTIUS, MAIUS, JULIUS, OCTOBER, 31 Days.	JANUARIUS, AUGUSTUS, DECEMBER, 31 Days.	APRILIS, JUNIUS, SEPTEMBER, NOVEMBER, 30 Days.	FEBRUARIUS, 28 Days — in every fourth Year 29.
1	Kalendis	Kalendis	Kalendis	Kalendis
2	a.d. VI.	a.d. IV.	a.d. IV.	a.d. IV.
3	a.d. V.	a.d. III.	a.d. III.	a.d. III.
4	a.d. IV.	Pridie	Pridie	Pridie
5	a.d. III.	Nonis	Nonis	Nonis
6	Pridie	a.d. VIII.	a.d. VIII.	a.d. VIII.
7	Nonis	a.d. VII.	a.d. VII.	a.d. VII.
8	a.d. VIII.	a.d. VI.	a.d. VI.	a.d. VI.
9	a.d. VII.	a.d. V.	a.d. V.	a.d. V.
10	a.d. VI.	a.d. IV.	a.d. IV.	a.d. IV.
11	a.d. V.	a.d. III.	a.d. III.	a.d. III.
12	a.d. IV.	Pridie	Pridie	Pridie
13	a.d. III.	Idibus	Idibus	Idibus
14	Pridie	a.d. XIX.	a.d. XVIII.	a.d. XVI.
15	Idibus	a.d. XVIII.	a.d. XVII.	a.d. XV.
16	a.d. XVII.	a.d. XVII.	a.d. XVI.	a.d. XIV.
17	a.d. XVI.	a.d. XVI.	a.d. XV.	a.d. XIII.
18	a.d. XV.	a.d. XV.	a.d. XIV.	a.d. XII.
19	a.d. XIV.	a.d. XIV.	a.d. XIII.	a.d. XI.
20	a.d. XIII.	a.d. XIII.	a.d. XII.	a.d. X.
21	a.d. XII.	a.d. XII.	a.d. XI.	a.d. IX.
22	a.d. XI.	a.d. XI.	a.d. X.	a.d. VIII.
23	a.d. X.	a.d. X.	a.d. IX.	a.d. VII.
24	a.d. IX.	a.d. IX.	a.d. VIII.	a.d. VI.
25	a.d. VIII.	a.d. VIII.	a.d. VII.	a.d. V.
26	a.d. VII.	a.d. VII.	a.d. VI.	a.d. IV.
27	a.d. VI.	a.d. VI.	a.d. V.	a.d. III.
28	a.d. V.	a.d. V.	a.d. IV.	Pridie.
29	a.d. IV.	a.d. IV.	a.d. III.	
30	a.d. III.	a.d. III.	Pridie	
31	Pridie	Pridie		

[In Leap-year, Feb. 24th (a.d. VI. Kal. Mart.) was twice reckoned,— hence this day was called DIES BISSEXTUS, and leap-year itself ANNUS BISSEXTUS.]

Note 1.—Ante diem tertium (a.d. III.) Kal. Jun., means 'on the third day before the Kalends of June,' or ' before the Kalends of June by three days.' Diem tertium, being placed between ante and Kalendas, is attracted to the Accusative Case. This mode of expression became so purely idiomatic that it was used with Prepositions: ante diem tertium, ante diem sextum, &c.

Note 2.—The names of the months are adjectives used in agreement with mensis, m. expressed or understood, Januarius, Aprilis, September, &c. The old names of July and August were Quintilis, Sextilis, but later they were called Julius and Augustus after the two Caesars.

ABBREVIATIONS.

(1) Praenomina.

A. Aulus	M. Marcus	S. (Sex.) Sextus
C. Gaius	M'. Manius	Ser. Servius
C. Gnaeus	Mam. Mamercus	Sp. Spurius
D. Decimus	P. Publius	T. Titus
K. Kaeso	Q. Quintus	Ti. (Tib.) Tiberius
L. Lucius		

Note.—A Roman of distinction had at least three names: the Praenomen, individual name; the Nomen, name showing the Gens or clan; and the Cognomen, surname showing the Familia or family. Thus, Lucius Junius Brutus expressed Lucius of the Gens Junia and Familia Brutorum. To these were sometimes added one or more Agnomina, titles either of honour (as Africanus, Macedonicus, Magnus, etc.), or expressing that a person had been adopted from another Gens: as Aemilianus, applied to the younger Scipio Africanus, who was the son of L. Paulus Aemilius, but adopted by a Scipio. The full name of the emperor Augustus (originally an Octavius) after he had been adopted by his uncle's will and adorned by the Senate with a title of honour, was Gaius Julius Caesar Octavianus Augustus.

(2) Varia.

A. D. Ante diem	F. Filius	P. M. Pontifex Maximus
A. U. C. Anno urbis conditae	HS. Sestertius, Sestertium	P. R. Populus Romanus
Aed. Aedilis	Id. Idus	Pl. Plebis
Cal. (Kal.) Calendae	Imp. Imperator	Proc. Proconsul
Cos. Consul	L. Libra	S. Senatus
Coss. Consules	LL. Dupondius	S. P. Q. R. Senatus Populusque Romanus
D. Divus	Non. Nonae	S. C. Senatusconsultum
Des. Designatus	O. M. Optimus Maximus	S. D. P. Salutem dicit plurimam
Eq. Rom. Eques Romanus	P. C. Patres (et) Conscripti	Tr. Tribunus

APPENDIX III.

FIGURES OF SPEECH;

OR PECULIAR FORMS FOUND IN SYNTAX AND IN RHETORIC.

FIGURES OF SYNTAX.

Ellipsis (*omission*).—Words are left out which can be supplied from the sense. Thus are used:

(1) An Adjective without its Substantive: Gelida, calida (aqua); dextra, sinistra (manus).

(2) A Genitive without the word on which it depends: Caecilia Metelli (filia), Faustus Sullae (filius).

(3) A Verb without its Object: obire (mortem); movere (castra).

(4) A Sentence without its Verb: Suus cuique mos. Quid multa? (dicam).

Pleonasmus (*redundance*).—Use of needless words: Sic ore locuta est. VERG.

Zeugma.—Connexion of a Verb or Adjective with two words or clauses to both of which it does not equally belong; therefore Zeugma is a sort of Ellipsis: Ex spoliis et torquem et cognomen induit; *put on the necklace and assumed the surname.* Agreement with one only of two or more Subjects is also called Zeugma.

Syllepsis.—Connexion of a Verb or Adjective with a Composite Subject.

Synēsis.—Agreement with meaning not with form:

1 Gender. Capita conjurationis virgis caesi sunt. LIV. Capita, though Neuter in form, is Masculine in meaning, therefore caesi.

2. Number. A Collective Noun or a Phrase implying more than one, though Singular in form, may take a Plural Verb: Cetera classis ...fugerunt. LIV. Optimus quisque jussis paruere. TAC.

Attraction.—Words are drawn by the influence of others to take irregular constructions: (1) attraction of Copulative Verb (**196**); (2) attraction of Relative and of Adjective to Relative Clause (**332**). Attraction of Case happens after Copulative Verbs, especially the Dative (**224**), and especially with licet esse: Vobis licet esse beatis. HOR. Licuit esse otioso Themistocli. CIC.

Asyndĕton.—Omission of Conjunctions : Abiit, excessit, evasit, erupit. Cıc.

Polysyndĕton.—Redundance of Conjunctions : Una Eurusque Notusque ruunt creberque procellis Africus. Verg.

Hendiădys.—Use of two Substantives coupled by a Conjunction for a Substantive and Adjective : Pateris libamus et auro (for pateris aureis). Verg.

Hyperbăton.—Alteration of natural order of words : Per te deos oro (for per deos te oro). The four following figures belong to Hyperbaton :

(1) **Anacolūthon.**—Passing from one construction to another before the former is completed : Si, ut Graeci dicunt, omnes aut Graios esse aut barbaros, vereor ne Romulus barbarorum rex fuerit. Cıc.

(2) **Hysteron-proteron.**—When, of two things, that which naturally comes first is placed last : Moriamur et in media arma ruamus. Verg.

(3) **Anastrophe.**—Placing a Preposition after its Case : quos inter for inter quos. Hor.

(4) **Parenthesis.**—Interpolation of one sentence within another : At tu (nam divum servat tutela poetas), praemoneo, vati parce, puella, sacro. Tibull.

Tmesis.—Separation of the parts of a compound word : Quae me cumque vocant terrae. Verg. (for quaecumque).

Enallăge.—Use of one word for another :

(1) One Part of Speech for another : aliud cras (alius dies crastinus).

(2) One Case for another : Matutine pater, seu Jane libentius audis. Hor. (for Janus.)

(3) One Number for another : nos for ego; miles for milites.

Hypallăge.—Interchange of Cases : Dare classibus Austros. Verg. (for dare classes Austris.) Also attraction of Adjectives to Substantives to which they do not properly belong : Fontium gelidae perennitates. Cıc. (for fontium gelidorum perennitates.)

FIGURES OF RHETORIC.

Metaphŏra.—One expression put for another which has some resemblance to it in a different kind, generally a concrete for an abstract ; portus for refugium ; sentina (*dregs*) reipublicae for turpissimi cives ; exulto for gaudeo. A strong metaphor is often qualified by quasi, tamquam, quidam, or ut ita dicam : In una philosophia quasi tabernaculum vitae suae allocarunt. Cıc. Scopas, ut ita dicam, mihi videntur dissolvere. Cıc.

Metonymia.—A related word conveying the same idea is put for another. Mars for bellum; cedant arma togae (Cɪᴄ.) for cedat bellum paci; juventus for juvenes; Graecia for Graeci; aurum for vasa aurea.

Synecdŏche.—The part stands for the whole: Caput for homo; tectum for domus; carina for navis.

Allegoria.—A chain of metaphors:

> Claudite jam rivos, pueri, sat prata biberunt. Vᴇʀɢ.
> *Cease to sing, shepherds, recreation enough has been taken.*

Hyperbŏle.—Exaggeration.

Litŏtes.—Less is said than is meant: Non laudo for culpo.

Ironĭa.—One thing is said while the contrary is meant, but so that the real meaning may be understood: Egregiam vero laudem et spolia ampla refertis tuque puerque tuus. Vᴇʀɢ. (*ignoble praise* and *paltry spoils*).

Climax.—A high point of effect led up to gradually: Quod libet iis, licet; quod licet, possunt; quod possunt, audent. Cɪᴄ.

Polyptŏton.—Cases of the same Noun are brought together: Jam clipeus clipeis, umbone repellitur umbo; ense minax ensis, pede pes et cuspide cuspis. Sᴛᴀᴛ.

Paronomasia.—A play upon the sound of words: Tibi parata sunt verba, huic verbera. Tᴇʀ.

Antithĕsis.—Contrast of opposites: Urbis amatorem Fuscum salvere jubemus ruris amatores. Hᴏʀ.

Oxymŏron.—Union of seeming contraries: Temporis angusti mansit concordia discors. Lᴜᴄᴀɴ.

Periphrăsis.—Description of a simple fact by various attending circumstances. Instead of 'Now night is approaching,' Vergil says Et jam summa procul villarum culmina fumant, majoresque cadunt altis de montibus umbrae. See the beautiful periphrases of old age and death in Ecclesiastes, ch. xii.

Simile.—Illustration of a statement by an apt comparison, as: Per urbes Hannibal Italas ceu flamma per taedas vel Eurus per Siculas equitavit undas. Hᴏʀ.

Apostrŏphe.—An appeal to some person or thing: Quid non mortalia pectora cogis, auri sacra fames? Vᴇʀɢ.

Aposiopēsis.—The conclusion of a thought is suppressed: Quos ego ... sed motos praestat componere fluctus. Vᴇʀɢ.

Prosopopoeia.—Personification. An abstract idea, as faith, hope, youth, memory, fortune, is addressed or spoken of as a person: Te Spes et alho rara Fides colit velata panno. Hᴏʀ.

APPENDIX IV.

MEMORIAL LINES ON THE GENDER OF LATIN SUBSTANTIVES.

I. General Rules.
The Gender of a Latin Noun
by meaning, form, or use is shown.

1. A Man, Month, Mountain, River, Wind.
and People Masculine we find:
Rōmŭlŭs, Octōber, Pindus, Pădŭs, Eurŭs, Ăchīvī.

2. A Woman, Island, Country, Tree,
and City, Feminine we see:
Pēnĕlŏpē, Cȳprus, Germāniă, laurŭs, Ăthēnae.

3. To Nouns that cannot be declined
The Neuter Gender is assigned:
Examples fās and nĕfās give
And the Verb-Noun Infinitive:
Est summum nĕfās fallĕrĕ:
Deceit is gross impiety.

Common are: săcerdōs, dux,	*priest (priestess), leader*
vātēs, părens ĕt conjux,	*seer, parent, wife (husband)*
cīvĭs, cŏmēs, custōs, vindex,	*citizen, companion, guard, avenger*
ădŭlescens, infans, index,	*youth (maid), infant, informer*
jūdex, testĭs, artĭfex	*judge, witness, artist*
praesŭl, exsŭl, ŏpĭfex,	*director, exile, worker*
hērēs, mīlĕs, incŏlă,	*heir (heiress), soldier, inhabitant*
auctŏr, augŭr, advĕnă,	*author, augur, new-comer*
hostĭs, obsĕs, praesĕs, ālĕs,	*enemy, hostage, president, bird*
pātruēlĭs ĕt sătellēs,	*cousin, attendant*
munĭceps et interprēs,	*burgess, interpreter*
jŭvĕnĭs ĕt antistēs,	*young person, overseer*
aurīgă, princeps : add to these	*charioteer, chief*
bōs, dammă, talpă, serpens, sūs,	*ox (cow), deer, mole, serpent, swine*
cămēlŭs, cănĭs, tīgrĭs, perdix,	
grūs.	*camel, dog, tiger, partridge, crane*

(For exceptions see p. 15.)

II. Special Rules for the Declensions.

Decl. 1 (**A-Stems**).

Rule.—Feminine in First ă, ĕ,
     Masculine ās, ēs will be.

Exc.   Nouns denoting Males in ă
     are by meaning Mascula :
     and Masculine is found to be
     Hădriă, *the Adriatic Sea.*

Decl. 2 (**O-Stems**).

Rule.—O-nouns in ŭs and ĕr become
     Masculine, but Neuter um.

Exc.   Feminine are found in *us,*
     alvŭs, Arctŭs, carbăsŭs,   *paunch, Great Bear, linen*
     cŏlŭs, hŭmŭs, pampĭnŭs,   *distaff, ground, vine-leaf*
     vannŭs : also trees, as pĭrŭs ;   *winnowing-fan, pear-tree*
     with some jewels, as sapphīrus ;   *sapphire*
     Neuter pĕlăgŭs and vīrŭs.   *sea, poison*
     Vulgŭs Neuter commonly,   *common people*
     rarely Masculine we see.

Decl. 3 (**Consonant and I-Stems**).

Rule 1.—Third-Nouns Masculine prefer
     endings *o, or, os,* and *er;*
     add to which the ending *es,*
     if its Cases have increase.

Exc. (a)   Feminine exceptions show
     Substantives in *dō* and *gō.*
     But lĭgō, ordō, praedō, cardō,   *spade, order, pirate, hinge*
     Masculine, and Common margō.   *margin*

(b)   Abstract Nouns in *ĭo* call
     Fēmĭnĭnă, one and all :
     Masculine will only be
     things that you may touch or see,
     (as curcŭlĭō, vespertĭlio,   *weevil, bat*
     pŭgiō, scīpio, and pāpĭliō)   *dagger, staff, butterfly*
     with the Nouns that number show,
     such as ternio, sēnio.   3, 6

(c)   Echō Feminine we name :   *echo*
     cărō (carnĭs) is the same.   *flesh*

(d) Aequŏr, marmŏr, cŏr decline   *sea, marble, heart*
     Neuter; arbŏr Feminine.   *tree*

(e) Of the Substantives in *os*,
     Feminine are cōs and dōs;   *whetstone, dowry*
     while, of Latin Nouns, alone
     Neuter are ŏs (ossĭs), *bone*
     and ōs (ōrĭs), *mouth* : a few
     Greek in ŏs are Neuter too,

(f) Many Neuters end in *ĕr*,
     sīlĕr, ăcĕr, verbĕr, vēr,   *withy, maple, stripe, spring*
     tūbĕr, ūbĕr, and cădāvĕr,   *hump, udder, carcase*
     pīpĕr, ĭtĕr, and păpāvĕr.   *pepper, journey, poppy*

(g) Feminine are compēs, tĕgĕs,   *fetter, mat*
     mercēs, mergĕs, quĭēs, sĕgĕs,   *fee, sheaf, rest, corn*
     though their Cases have increase :
     with the Neuters reckon aes.   *copper*

Rule 2.—T h i r d-N o u n s Feminine we class
     ending *is*, *x*, *aus*, and *as*,
     s to consonant appended,
     es in flexion unextended.

Exc. (a) Many Nouns in *ĭs* we find
     to the Masculine assigned :
     amnĭs, axĭs, caulĭs, collĭs,   *river, axle, stalk, hill*
     clūnĭs, crīnĭs, fascĭs, follĭs,   *hind-leg, hair, bundle, bellows*
     fustĭs, ignĭs, orbĭs, ensĭs,   *bludgeon, fire, orb, sword*
     pānĭs, piscĭs, postĭs, mensĭs,   *bread, fish, post, month*
     torrĭs, unguĭs, and cănālĭs,   *stake, nail, canal*
     vectĭs, vermĭs, and nātālĭs,   *lever, worm, birthday*
     sanguĭs, pulvĭs, cŭcŭmĭs,   *blood, dust, cucumber*
     lăpĭs, cassēs, Mānēs, glīs.   *stone, nets, ghosts, dormouse*

(b) Chiefly Masculine we find,
     sometimes Feminine declined,
     callĭs, sentĭs, fūnĭs, fīnĭs,   *path, thorn, rope, end*
     and in poets torquĭs, cĭnĭs.   *necklace, cinder*

(c) Masculine are most in *ex* :
     Feminine are forfex, lex,   *shears, law*
     nex, sŭpellex : Common, pūmex,   *death, furniture, pumice*
     imbrex, ŏbex, sĭlex, rŭmex.   *tile, bolt, flint, sorrel*

As mĕlŏs, *melody*, ĕpŏs, *epic poem.*

(*d*) Add to Masculines in *ix*,
     fórnix, phoenix, and cǎlix.   *arch, —, cup*

(*e*) Masculine are ădămās,   *adamant*
     ĕlĕphās, mās, gīgās, ās :   *elephant, male, giant, as*
     vǎs (vădĭs) Masculine is known,   *surety*
     vās (vāsĭs) is a Neuter Noun.   *vessel*

(*f*) Masculine are fons and mons,   *fountain, mountain*
     chǎlybs, hydrops, gryps, and pons, *iron, dropsy, griffin, bridge*
     rŭdens, torrens, dens, and cliens, *cable, torrent, tooth, client*
     fractions of the ās, as triens.   *four ounces*
     Add to Masculines trĭdens,   *trident*
     ŏriens, and occĭdens,   *east, west*
     bĭdens (*fork*) : but bĭdens (*sheep*),
     with the Feminines we keep.

(*g*) Masculine are found in *ēs*
     verrēs and ăcīnăcēs.   *boar, scimetar*

Rule 3.—Third-Nouns Neuter end *ŭ, ĕ,*
     ar, ur, us, c, l, n, and *t.*

Exc. (*a*) Masculine are found in *ur*
     furfŭr, turtŭr, vultŭr, fūr.   *bran, turtle-dove, vulture, thief*

    (*b*) Feminine in *ūs* a few
     keep, as virtūs, the long *ū* :   *virtue*
     servĭtūs, jŭventūs, sǎlūs,   *slavery, youth, safety*
     sĕnectūs, tellūs, incūs, pǎlūs. *old-age, earth, anvil, marsh*

    (*c*) Also pĕcŭs (pĕcŭdĭs)   *beast*
     Feminine in Gender is.

    (*d*) Masculine appear in *us*
     lĕpŭs (lĕpŏrĭs) and mūs.   *hare, mouse*

    (*e*) Masculines in *l* are mūgĭl, *mullet*
     consŭl, sǎl, and sōl, with pŭgĭl, *consul, salt, sun, boxer*

    (*f*) Masculine are rēn and splēn, *kidney, spleen*
     pectēn, delphīn, attăgēn.   *comb, dolphin, grouse*

    (*g*) Feminine are found in *ōn*
     Gorgōn, sindōn, halcўōn.   *Gorgon, muslin, king-fisher*

    Decl. 4·(**U-Stems**).

Rule.—Masculines end in *us* : a few
     are Neuter nouns, that end in *u.*

Exc. Women and trees are Feminine,
with ăcŭs, dŏmŭs, and mănŭs,   *needle, house, hand,*
trĭbŭs, Īdūs, portĭcŭs.   *tribe, the Ides, porch*

Decl. 5 (E-Stems).

Rule.—Feminine are Fifth in *ēs*,
Except meridiēs and diēs.   *noon, day*

Exc. Diēs in the Singular
Common we define :
But its Plural cases are
always Masculine.

List of Prepositions.

With Accusative :

Antĕ, ăpŭd, ăd, adversŭs,
Circum, circā, cĭtrā, cĭs,
Contrā, intĕr, ergā, extrā,
Infrā, intrā, juxtā, ŏb,
Pĕnĕs, pōnĕ, post, and praetĕr,

Prŏpĕ, proptĕr, pĕr, sĕcundum,
Suprā, versŭs, ultrā, trans;
Add sŭpĕr, subtĕr, sŭb and ĭn,
When '*motion*' 'tis, not '*state*,'
they mean.

With Ablative :

A, ăb, absquĕ, cōram, dē,
Pălam, clam, cum, ex, and ē,
Sĭnĕ, tĕnŭs, prō, and prae :

Add sŭpĕr, subtĕr, sŭb and ĭn,
When '*state*,' not '*motion*,' 'tis they
mean.

NOUNS NOT INCREASING IN GENITIVE SINGULAR WHICH HAVE GENITIVE PLURAL IN -um.

Consonant Stems.
um in Plural Genitive
pater, mater, frater give,
With accipiter and canis,
senex too and iuvenis.

I Stems.
In the Plural Genitive
vates (*bard*) does vatum give :
And generally agree with this
panis, apis, volucris.

NOUNS INCREASING IN GENITIVE SINGULAR, WHICH HAVE GENITIVE PLURAL IN -ium.

Consonant Stems.
ium in Plural Genitive
os (ossis) and as (assis) give,
mas, mus, dos, and cos and lis,
nox and nix, and sol and glis.

I Stems.
In the Plural Genitive
frons (frontis) does frontium give,
so frons (frondis), stirps, arx, and dens,
mons, urbs, ars, bidens and parens.

Q

INDEX I.

SUBJECTS.

[*The reference is to Sections.*]